Toward a Free Housing Market

Toward a Free Housing Market

By Daniel Jay Baum

In collaboration with Karen Orloff Kaplan

University of Miami Press
Coral Gables, Florida

For my children,
Aaron and Miriam

Contents

Acknowledgments

This book would not have been completed without the help and co-operation of many people, chief among them Mrs. Karen Orloff Kaplan. Mrs. Kaplan is supervisor of Adult Medical-Surgical Social Service at the Tufts-New England Medical Center Hospitals. She holds a B.A. from Goucher College and an M.S.W. from Ohio State University. Formerly an instructor in Psychiatric Social Work at the University of Cincinnati College of Medicine, she is now a clinical instructor in Medicine, Tufts University School of Medicine, Boston, Massachusetts.

Foreword

Where a person lives and the kind of housing he occupies are key factors in determining the quality of life he will achieve. The school the child attends and the quality of education he receives are to a great extent determined by the neighborhood he lives in. For the worker, the attainment of a good job at a comfortable wage depends in large part on where he lives in relation to job information and job opportunities. For the poor, their ability to rise from poverty and become full and productive members of the community is influenced strongly by whether they are housed in isolation from the rest of the community or are full participants in community life. Above all, housing is of paramount importance in determining whether alienation among racial and economic groups will continue to be a festering sore on the American scene or whether this disastrous trend will be reversed.

For black Americans, choice of housing and neighborhood has been severely circumscribed for generations regardless of income. In most American cities, black families have been restricted to the least attractive parts of town, to the neighborhoods where housing is most likely to be old, deteriorating, and overcrowded. The neighborhood schools are often among the oldest in the city with inferior facilities and poorly qualified teachers. Those who must work are frequently isolated by both distance and poor transportation from the mainstream of job opportunities, especially from opportunities in new or expanding industries. Community facilities and services are all too often grossly inadequate to the needs of the neighborhood.

The federal government has been an active agent in the promotion of housing segregation. At first, its posture was as guardian of physical separation of the races—encouraging, requiring, even practicing itself the art of segregation. More recently, its posture has been one of acquiescence and acceptance of local policies.

In a 1967 survey of subdivisions in which mortgages had been insured by the Federal Housing Administration since 1962, FHA found that only about three percent of the housing units had been sold to Negroes. In some major metropolitan areas, participation by black Americans in FHA insured subdivision housing was even lower. In the Saint Louis metropolitan area, where the United States Commission on Civil Rights recently conducted a public hearing, the number of FHA insured subdivision units sold to black families between 1962 and 1967 was only 56, or less than one percent of the total units sold.

The federal government also has accepted actions by local communities that promote racial segregation and has continued to extend the benefits of its programs to these communities. There are numerous examples throughout the country of the exercise of local government authority used to keep out all but those who are white and affluent. Many of these examples, such as zoning laws, minimum lot size requirements, and building codes, are seemingly neutral on racial matters, yet they have the same exclusionary effect as overt discrimination.

Urban renewal, the federally supported effort to remove blighted conditions from our communities, also has often been used to remove Negro residents not only to another location but to another political jurisdiction altogether. In its hearing in Saint Louis, the Commission on Civil Rights was told of several instances where local urban renewal agencies in the suburbs, with the knowledge and acquiescence of federal officials, proposed public housing in the city of Saint Louis as a principal relocation source for displaced families.

During the past two years, major steps have been taken to eliminate the practice of overt discrimination as a perpetrator of housing segregation, most notably the Civil Rights Act of 1968 making fair housing the law of the land, and the decision of the Supreme Court, in *Jones* v. *Mayer and Company,* that practices of racial discrimination in the housing market are illegal, whether the discrimination is by private or public action, and whatever the kind of housing involved. As a nation, we have begun to address ourselves to the problems of overt discrimination in the housing market although we have by no means eliminated them.

Other major problems remain, however. These are the more intractable problems of social and economic injustice, rooted often in a history of past discrimination and reflected today in our social, political, and economic institutions.

These problems are less responsive to the impact of law although law can provide valuable tools with which to attack them. The programs provided by the Economic Opportunity Act, the Elementary and Secondary Education Act, and, most important for housing, the Housing and Urban Development Act of 1958, are important resources. None of these can work, however, without a firm national commitment that we can and will solve the problems they address.

If justice is to become a reality for black Americans, it is essential that we attack with a great sense of urgency both the problems of direct and overt discrimination in housing today and the problem of economics. We shall have achieved our goal only when black Americans move as freely in schools, in jobs, and in housing as does the white majority.

Dr. Daniel J. Baum, in collaboration with Mrs. Karen Orloff Kaplan, has described in the work that follows one community's efforts to reach this goal. While the Indianapolis experiment was only in part directed at the discrimination factor in the housing market, it involves most of the elements likely to be confronted by similar efforts elsewhere: public officials, some eager to test out new ideas but others timid about upsetting the established way of doing business; representatives of private industry, a few interested in finding new outlets for their services but others concerned that another's gain may be their loss; and individual citizens, concerned but sometimes sparing of their time and all too frequently discouraged by the slow pace of change. While conditions and opportunities will vary from one locality to another, Dr. Baum's report should provide helpful insights both for designers of national policy and for those who wish to bring about change at the community level.

Reverend Theodore M. Hesburgh, C.S.C.
President, University of Notre Dame

Introduction

Many goals of the civil rights revolution seem unattainable. Protests resulting in legislative reform and an aggressive federal Supreme Court providing a solid constitutional foundation for liberal interpretations of pace-setting statues have accomplished little. Never before have government, business, and religion combined to press for implementation of rights for black citizens, but the black community remains segregated. Why the black community is still segregated is a pertinent question in our country today.

A partial answer to the question is offered in this book. There is no attempt to resolve all of the complex objectives of the civil rights revolution. A single problem—the achievement of the operative right to open housing—was studied. Answers, workable solutions, were sought in real life.

On the historic scale of civil rights values, open housing was a proper subject. Municipal ordinances, state statutes, and even a current federal law coupled with impressive high court rulings made open housing a theoretical right held by the citizenry. One after another, religious and civil rights organizations have joined to make the legal right effective through such organizations as the National Committee Against Discrimination in Housing. On its own big business, the representatives of the major auto companies have attempted the same end.

Yet these efforts brought minimal results. Even in communities where the climate for open housing appeared favorable, segregation seemed obvious from a glance at any racial density map or a drive through the inner city. Open housing marches in Chicago, Cleveland, Louisville, and Minneapolis protested "paper rights." The business-oriented *Wall Street Journal* said the many open housing laws "have proved about as useful as a sieve would be for bailing out a sinking rowboat."[1]

Examples were plentiful. In New York City as late as August of 1967, two black sisters, one a welfare supervisor and the other a registered nurse, were living among packing boxes after trying for nearly three years to buy a house in an all white neighborhood in Brooklyn. The legal processes designed to help them were encumbered and slow. In 1964, they presented the asking price of $38,490 for a house. The owner told the sisters the house had been sold but then offered to let them have it for $42,500. Following complaint, a New York court found the "belated offer" excessive and discriminatory. The city's Commission on Human Rights was ordered to "promptly proceed" with efforts to effect the sale. The court order came seventeen months after the sisters first tried to buy the home. Sixteen months after the court order, one of the sisters said, "We are no nearer to realizing our hopes of having a nice home than we were almost three years ago. . . . What is happening to me in my efforts to secure a home will be held up to others of my race as an example of what trusting in and abiding by our laws can or cannot do. . . . My sister and I are articulate, the kind of people who halfway know where to go to get things done, and look how far we've gotten out of the ghetto in three years. . . . How, then, can the man in the street, who doesn't know where to turn, and cannot afford legal advice, be expected to think the Government is in his corner?"[2]

Eight days after the story of the Brooklyn sisters appeared in *The New York Times, The Cleveland Plain Dealer* published a similar article. In Columbus, Ohio, a black air force captain and his family met a "solid wall of resistance" while house hunting on the city's northside. The captain, transferred from Eglin Air Force Base in Florida for advanced studies at Ohio State University, sought a home in the $22,000 to $28,000 range near the university. A real estate agent told them that the northside listings were held exclusively "by the white realtors, and these realtors are bound by a strict code of 'ethics' not to introduce a non-white family into an all-white neighborhood."[3]

There are some persons who still have confidence in the system and its capacity for change. They have tried to touch the conscience of the people using methods of petition and picket and nonviolent refusal to accept the status quo. Their leader was Dr. Martin Luther King, Jr., who led marches pressing for open housing in such cities as Chicago and Louisville. Joined by white supporters, he asked for more legislation at the local and federal levels. Dr. King knew the "sieve-like" nature of open housing laws but he seemed to possess an optimistic faith that people ultimately would be just. Perhaps he felt that legislation is but a means of expression, the codification of the people's will. Dr. King's faith seemed to be shared only by some.[4] The *Louisville Courier-Journal* editorially struck at the city's board of aldermen for following the "same old pattern of evasion" in not passing enforceable open housing legislation. According to one of the protest leaders, the city's mayor had promised a "real open housing law," but the board proposed an ordinance with no enforcement provisions when the mayor was out of the city. "Why are local officials playing charades with such a serious and explosive issue? What do they hope to gain except time? And, if that is their object, for what purpose? Why couldn't Louisville do what Lexington had already done?"[5]

Milwaukee was another example of open housing long frustrated. There the open housing leader was a white Catholic priest, the Reverend James A. Groppi. Before moving across the "Mason-Dixon" line to the adjoining all black ghetto, Father Groppi spent four years in the all white, Polish-American southside. On August 29, 1967, after the Common Council four times voted down an open housing ordinance by a vote of eighteen to one, Father Groppi led marchers from the northside into the southside. A mob of 3,000 white persons chanting "kill, kill, kill" stoned the marchers, and an arsonsist later destroyed their headquarters, the Milwaukee Youth Council of the National Association for the Advancement of Colored People. Forty-five persons were arrested, and twenty-two, including eleven policemen, were injured.[6]

Milwaukee Mayor Henry Maier reacted. A ban was placed on further demonstrations—only to be lifted on September 3. Maier said, "I appeal to the overwhelming majority of Milwaukeeans who hate violence not to be a part of it by becoming part of a mob. While the mob may think it is opposing Father Groppi it is helping him in his desire to injure Milwaukee's good name."[7] Priests in the all white southside complained that the demonstrators led by Father Groppi were needlessly provocative. Their response to a march planned for September 11 was to caution their parishioners to stay away from the protesters if they disapproved of them.[8]

The September 11 march took place with more than 2,000 participants including national civil rights leaders. They crossed to the southside over the Sixteenth Street viaduct, locally referred to as the longest bridge in the world "because it separates Africa from Poland." "Because of the crowd and the high volume of the marchers' singing and chanting, it was hard for marchers to hear the taunts and jeers hurled at them." They viewed their march as an integrated demonstration for "justice." In contrast to the black separatist appeals of H. Rap Brown and Stokeley Carmichael, white support was solicited.[9] The march was a prelude to legislative effort. A few days later an open housing ordinance was introduced again to the Common Council only to meet the renewed opposition of the mayor who argued that passing the ordinance would produce a white exodus to the suburbs and thereby damage the city's tax base.[10]

This time the mayor's argument might have found less support in the white community. Opinion surveys of southside residents since the disturbances began indicated a softening attitude toward open housing. The view of most of the city's aldermen was not the norm. Even a *New York Times* spot check in the Polish Koscuiszko Park neighborhood showed a sizable minority for an open housing law. Some said the proposed ordinance was "right." Some said a law would get "this commotion over" or that "it won't really make any difference because Negroes don't want to move down here anyway."[11]

Father Groppi's "constructive tension" was effective. Statistics told part of the story in terms of those arrested and injured and of property damaged. Tension was growing in the community, and strife was hurting the city financially. In addition to the cost of additional city police patrols, there was a daily loss in sales by retail businesses. To Father Groppi the price of "constructive tension" was necessary if the community was to reexamine itself. He seemed to hope for public consensus made manifest through law. The same day the open housing ordinance was presented to the Milwaukee Common Council for the fifth time, newspapers reported the strife in Hartford, Connecticut. A civil rights march through downtown Hartford had erupted into violence. The protesters were demanding more stringent enforcement of the state's open housing law.[12]

Answers, relief, had to be forthcoming or the lessons of history would again be repeated. Violence could take the place of nonviolence. If government could not respond to the citizenry it would weaken itself and limit its own effectiveness. There had been bitter Detroit riots in

1942 and 1943 when the black slogan was "We Want Homes, Not Riots." White pickets had attempted to keep blacks from entering a federal housing project, the Sojourner Truth Homes—named after a free black of the Civil War. Even then overcrowding had angered the black community. When the riots came to an end, however, there was no relief. Restrictive covenants continued to confine the black. Neighborhood improvement associations continued to provide a base for solidarity in the all white areas. "Given the size of the Negro population, its growing proportion to the whole in a northern city and the lack of available housing, a crisis may be viewed as inevitable. The improvement associations of Detroit made clear that they would not budge from a policy of full segregation in housing." [13]

After more than twenty years how much has been learned? What of the more massive 1967 social-racial disorder in Detroit? The assassination of Dr. King in 1968 prompted further ruptures, and, it must be added, curatives. Congress enacted a federal open-housing law. Whether the law measures up to its promise will be determined by the willingness of the people to comply with the law.

Where do the people stand? The Supreme Court and Congress have spoken. More than twenty states and as many cities earlier had added their voices. At this point, hasn't a consensus developed? The answer is clouded. "Has there ever before been such a determined mobilization of governmental power concentrated on a single domestic problem? One would surmise from it that there is an overwhelming national approval for the cause of integration . . . and yet time after time, voters have said the opposite. So far, the most revealing referenda have been on the housing question, each one of which—in Berkeley, Tacoma, Seattle, Detroit, Akron, and statewide in California—has shown voters favoring retention of the privilege of discriminatory sale of homes." [14]

There are groups who do not consider open housing to be the immediate *summum bonum* of the civil rights movement. They believe equality should be sought by encouraging black cohesion and black population concentration since such coalescence would bring political power that would provide a base for developing economic power. These groups would build ghetto institutions, not destroy them. Senator Philip A. Hart stated that this is "bound to have a tremendous appeal to the man who is trying to build a better life for his family and is worried right now—at this hour—about the foul-smelling air shaft and the gang down on the corner." [15]

For those who would center their efforts for black improvement solely on the ghetto, a sociological base was laid with the publication of "The Case Against Urban Desegregation."[16] The authors, Francis Fox Piven and Richard A. Cloward, faculty members of Columbia University's School of Social Work, attempted to provide a factual and scientific foundation for the proposition that pursuit of an integrated society makes inadequate the supply of low-income housing. They supported the development of ghetto organizations run by blacks and wanted to put an end to the idea that integration is a basic good. "It is not only the feasibility of integration that is open to question, it is also far from clear that integration is always desirable. Liberals are inclined to take a 'melting pot' view of American communities and to stress the enriching qualities of heterogeneous living; however, the history of ethnic groups in American society belies this view. There have always been ethnic institutions and these, as has been widely observed, have served important functions in the advancement of different groups."[17]

The two professors argued that certain facts should be faced. Racism has doomed the most determined efforts to end segregated housing and thus ease the blight of the deteriorating ghetto. "Indeed, residential segregation is increasing rapidly."[18] Assuming a continued white suburban exodus and a sustained higher black birthrate, within the next two decades many central cities are apt to become predominantly black. For example, to bring about a fifty-fifty white-black population balance in Washington, D.C., beginning with a population that today is sixty-three percent black, "twelve thousand non-white families would have to be dispersed to suburban areas and four thousand white families induced to return to the District of Columbia *every year* until 2,000."[19]

According to Piven and Cloward any "success" that is achieved comes to the middle-class black, not the poor. Even the more affluent blacks can anticipate little since most housing opportunities remain under the control of the private real estate market where patterns of sale mirror racism. Demographic studies indicate money is not the determining factor; "residential segregation prevails regardless of the relative economic status of the White and Negro resident."[20] Where government attempts to effect a change by housing subsidies, no better results are obtained. Public housing in suburbia tends to be accepted only when white tenants predominate. "In the city of Newark, N.J., the racial balance in [public housing] projects is regularly graded from over 90 percent Negro for projects located in central ghetto ward to over 90 percent white in outlying 'country club' projects. Coincidentally, Newark has been able to obtain much more public support for public housing and to build more units per capita than most other cities."[21] Piven and Cloward contend that neither rent supplements nor heightened individual mobility through job training and education will bring any meaningful variation to the pattern of segregation.

Against this background of attempted integration, the urban theoreticians have planned for the city as a whole. Slums have been cleared in the name of urban renewal to retrieve the middle class and improve the city tax base. Highways have been constructed. Where have the inner-city residents gone? In the three decades since it was initiated, the federal public housing program has produced 600,000 low-income dwelling units. The federal highway and urban renewal programs in less than half that time demolished nearly 700,000 units, most of which were low rental.[22] The inner-city blacks have been pushed deeper into the ghetto.[23]

The planners are destroying the ghetto to rebuild the city. Some have termed urban renewal black removal. Face reality, the two Columbia University professors plead. There is no place other than the ghetto for the black at this time. There alone "ethnic identity, solidarity and power must be forged through a series of organized communal experiences in a variety of institutional areas."[24] Naturally there was reaction to the thesis of the two professors. Clarence Funnye, formerly New York chairman of the Congress on Racial Equality (CORE), and later director of Idea Plan Associates of New York, said there was nothing new in the professors' ideas.[25] Funnye and his associate, Ronald Shiffman, wrote in response to the article, "such acquiescence in the face of racial discrimination, in the name of survival, is not new. Booker T. Washington proudly proclaimed that 'in all things that are purely social, we can be as separate as the fingers,' in exchange for economic advancement promised by white missionary benefactors. And now, almost 100 years later, other missionary benefactors urge that Negroes defer their manhood for yet another generation, in the interest of strategy."[26]

Whitney Young, the executive director of the National Urban League, responded with an article entitled "The Case for Urban Integration."[27] Young said that frustration and resultant anger over goals expected and not yet achieved should not feed the flames of separatism. "Are not the goals of the separatist essentially the same as those of the back-lasher? The white suburbanite who says, 'I don't want Negroes living here,' and the separatist who says, 'All right, I won't move to your nice neighborhood; I'll try to make my own a bit more livable,' are in substantial agreement."[28] Both accept separation, Young argues; some areas shall be white, others black with the corresponding constraint on black opportunities. According to Young, the rationale behind the common end differs. The white seeks exclusion of the black from the mainstream of society. The black grabs at self-segregation as a means to strengthen the black community, for with strength comes the power to negotiate with whites on an equal basis "and thus achieve integration."[29]

"It will not work," said Young. "All that comes from segregation is more segregation. The problems faced by Negroes today stem from segregation. Whether imposed from outside or sought from within, segregation leads to disadvantage in competing for the rewards of society."[30]

Like the former New York CORE director, Young pressed in his article for a dual front: build the ghetto institutions and at the same time strive for an integrated society. Realistically, Young left unsaid how organizations with limited resources in money and manpower would drive on two fronts. In July 1967, when Young's article was published, both goals seemed to have equal priority for the Urban League.[31] Nationally, however, the assassination of Dr. Martin Luther King, Jr., brought modification and a shifting in priorities.

In May 1968, meetings with local Urban League directors were held in New York. There the new priorities were discussed in terms of local application, but the message was firm. Building the ghetto institutions was to be the first order of business for the Urban League.

Neither Young nor Funnye challenged the fact that urban renewal has had the effect of thrusting blacks and poor whites deeper into ghettos. Nor was there any firm defense indicating that the process of integration had kept pace with dislocation resulting from government activity. The open society was slow in evolving. Some, like the two Columbia professors, thought that it would be better to restrain city development, urban renewal, and highway construction until decent housing could be found for those dislocated.

There are still others who deny the value of integration. "We reject the goal of assimilation into middle-class America because the values of that class are, in themselves, anti-humanist, and because that class as a social force perpetuates racism."[32] Beyond this there is the positive value of preserving and enhancing an Afro-American culture that may even provide a base for a new nationalism. Delegates attending a Black Nationalist Convention expressed these ideas in their declaration of independence from the United States on March 30, 1968, in Detroit. Some fifty delegates indicated a desire to renounce their United States citizenship to become part of a new black government that would encompass Mississippi, Alabama, Georgia, South Carolina, and Louisiana. Milton Henry, a convention organizer who is a Yale Law School graduate and a leader of the Malcolm X Society, stated that "life is meaningless for black people in these United States."[33]

At one end of the spectrum are those blacks who would contract out of American society. Next to them and a part of "Black Power" are those who would prefer the establishment of a black community within the United States but free of white influence. "The ultimate values and goals are not domination or exploitation of other groups but rather an effective share in the total power of the society."[34] In describing how Black Power will be obtained, CORE in its 1967 convention also gave an indication of the term's meaning. To CORE, Black Power is:

1. an increase in political power;
2. an increase in economic power;
3. an improved self-image for the black man;
4. the development of young militant leadership;
5. the enforcement of federal statutes against police brutality;
6. development of a black consumer group.[35]

Unity, the kind of unity that springs from geographic proximity, is a necessary factor in the development of any of the six points. For many of the ideologies, strengthening the ghetto is a categorical imperative. Out of the hell of the ghetto may emerge a cultural heaven, but there is no doubt that it is the ghetto that may provide the most essential source for power. A supermarket with black ownership, control, and employees and selling "soul food," needs black consumers nearby. A black bank making capital funds available to the development of other black enterprises should be located in an area where it can draw black depositors.[36] If the black population is dispersed, vital elements of Black Power disintegrate. Stokeley Carmichael's message leaves no room for doubt:[37]

The concept of black power rests on a fundamental premise: *Before a group can enter the open society, it must first close ranks.* By this we mean that group solidarity is necessary before a group can operate effectively from a bargaining position of strength in a pluralistic society. Traditionally, each new ethnic group in this society has found the route to social and political viability through the organization of its own institutions with which to represent its needs within the larger society. Studies in voting behavior specifically, and political behavior generally, have made it clear that politically the American pot has not melted. Italians vote for Rubino over O'Brien; Irish for Murphy over Goldberg, etc. This phenomenon may seem distasteful to some, but it has been and remains today a central fact of the American political system.

The extent to which black Americans can and do "trace their roots" to Africa, to that extent will they be able to be more effective on the political scene.

To the blacks who would leave the ghetto, Carmichael gives a warning: Mainstream America means dissociation from the black race, its culture, community, and heritage. For the black, mainstream America does not mean assimilation; it means living the life of a marginal man in a "make-believe" world. "As with the black African who had to become a 'Frenchman' in order to be accepted, so to be an American, the black must strive to become 'white.' "[38]

It may well be that neither the white majority nor the black majority favors open housing. It also may be true that the best interest of individual blacks would be served by a willingness on their part to live in and develop the ghettos of America. Nevertheless, there are laws and a Constitution designed to afford an individual the right to choose where he will live. From the majorities, acceptance of the laws can be anticipated, for the people, like the government, are bound to the restraint of law, and courts have been established to help them comply with the mandate of law. A former solicitor general put the matter this way: "It is the capacity to command free assent that makes law a substitute for power. The force of legitimacy—and conversely the habit of voluntary compliance—is the foundation of the law's civilizing and liberalizing influence."[39] Acceptance, however, does not mean that the people will embrace the law or restrain themselves from avoiding the thrust of the law. The task is to face the people with the law, not in the abstract, but as it affects them specifically. Then the durability of law may be tested. In "The Democratic Resolution," Edmond Cahn wrote, "It is here and now that a man posesses his full freedom of thought, the vine of his belief, and the fig tree of his conscience; in enjoying them he is completely secure, and government exists to serve as his safeguard. No creed, dogma, or orthodoxy can be imposed to constrict the free play of his intelligence."[40]

Open housing laws have been enacted. The people can be called upon to respect these laws and not hinder their enforcement. Little has been achieved, however, and open housing remains a hollow term, perhaps because there was no effective machinery for applying the law. Neither the institutions nor the procedures existed for carrying out statute. Neither had yet encompassed the specific human targets that the law was to touch and the times and occasions when it would affect them. Neither had been formed from the perspective of the law consumers.

Some believe that developing machinery for the implementation of law is the peculiar function of the bar and, more significantly, of the law school. The president of the American Bar Association on May 1, 1968, wrote of the recent American Assembly on Law and the Changing Society to "Members of the ABA Official Family." The brief final report of the assembly said that lawyers "have special skills—as advocates, planners, negotiators and organizers—needed in achieving the objectives of social justice. They must help provide leadership in both the public and private sectors."[41]

Who were the persons being asked to comply with the law of open housing? Many had assumed that in the sale of occupied residential housing there was only the individual homeowner. It was to the individual homeowner that the real estate boards had directed their attention with notices such as: "This is a FORCED HOUSING ordinance that would deprive you of a basic individual freedom—the right to dispose of your private property as you choose."[42] The individual, however, only constitutes a portion of the housing market. He can expect tension to confront him, moreover, if he sells in a hostile environment.

In Indianapolis some concerned persons began to ask how the legal right could be made real. They approached the problem with certain major assumptions. Since the words "open housing" are emotionally charged for both the white and black communities, vocabulary void of emotion was needed. Further, any approach had to leave the individual homeowner free. He had to feel that not only was his emotional castle defended but that no action would threaten his neighborhood to the exclusion of others. In this context the black man was to know that homes throughout the city could be his. He was not in the name of civil rights to be segregated out for the purpose of integration. He was to be treated as a buyer looking for a home of his choice in an area of his choosing at a price that was fair and within reach.

Not all homes that were for sale could be made available since the individual homeowner was to be left alone. An inventory of other than individually owned homes was sought.

First, however, it seemed necessary to find a group of buyers, black and white, who were simply in need of housing without primary emphasis being placed on open housing. All urban areas have such a group in the inner-city families displaced by government projects such as highway construction and urban renewal. Those displaced often are black, but they also are white and sometimes elderly, forced by fixed income to remain behind as their friends move to suburbia. As a group, they are people for whom much of the community has a measure of sympathy. It is not their fault that they have been displaced but that of government.

The same government that funds a large portion of highway construction and urban renewal also happens to be a large owner of residential property throughout urban America. Every year the Federal Housing Administration, which underwrites much suburban residential development, is compelled to honor its insurance commitments to lenders on mortgages in default. Every year in more than a dozen urban areas that may happen to coincide with black population concentrates, FHA takes title to approximately 40,000 units. The houses are then generally placed in repair that makes each as good as, if not better than, comparable housing in the neighborhood. Each home is sold at a fair market price and financing is made available at low rates through an agency of the federal government, the Federal National Mortgage Association (now the Government National Mortgage Association).

To the Indianapolis group it seemed that some of the housing needs of the displaced could be met by the repossessed FHA houses, and in the process a step be taken toward achieving a free housing market. Frequently government has responded to the displaced with public housing, a concept that is costly not only in human life but also in the property that is constructed and excluded from the tax rolls.

Measured over three years, 1967-1969, the Federal Housing Administration took title to nearly 90,000 individual housing units. How many of these could have been afforded by the inner-city displaced? How many might have proved attractive enough to induce a family to greater economic productivity in the hope of home ownership? How much larger would the community tax base have become with a new infusion of homeowners? Must it be assumed that all inner-city residents, especially all inner-city blacks, are destined for public housing?

Acting on an Indianapolis proposal, the Federal Housing Authority provided a national format to test this possibility of matching needs of the displaced to FHA houses. After January 4, 1968, under agency regulations FHA acquired property was to be made available on a preferential basis to those displaced as a result of government action. The preference was limited. It went only to the right to make the first bid on the acquired property following repair and before public sale. The time preference was narrow; only ten days were allowed. No preference was granted in price, required credit rating, or income needed for purchase.

In Indianapolis alone a community group was established to complement the FHA program. This group, the "Committee on Special Housing," received support from private and governmental civil rights organizations, but the work on the opportunity provided by FHA was done in the name of the committee.

The experience of Indianapolis is of value to other cities. The basic problems seem the same. Highways and urban renewal are displacing thousands. Indianapolis is a city of 750,000 people, nearly a quarter of whom are black and confined to the inner city. It is a city that is typically midwestern, politically conservative, and slow to accept federal assistance and acknowledge the problems of an urban society. It is the capital of a state once dominated by the Ku-Klux Klan. If the committee's project could be made acceptable to both races in Indianapolis, surely it would have some application in urban areas with a more liberal political orientation.

If utilized, the 400 FHA homes acquired annually in Indianapolis might begin to free the housing market. Their sale left the individual owners free to make individual decisions as to what they would do in the disposition of their own homes. As individuals they might not feel entirely able to ignore the institutional sector of the residential real estate market. A private homeowner might control the sale of his own residence, but he should not be able to control FHA disposal of the property next door. If an all white area became integrated through an FHA sale, would the individual homeowners panic and sell, knowing that the same thing might happen in any other neighborhood? Would those homeowners who sold in the ordinary course of events refuse to accept a high bid from a black if one already lived in the neighborhood?

A successful program involving FHA property could open the way for similar efforts in their own self interest by other institutional owners of residential property. Another federal agency acquires property as does FHA, though on a lesser scale. Throughout the nation the Veterans Administration (VA) insures and then through default takes back thousands of units annually. In Indianapolis, for example, 300 units are repossessed and sold each year by VA. The price range is slightly higher than that of FHA. For returning veterans from Vietnam, so many of whom are black, couldn't these properties be made available on a meaningful preferential basis rather than being offered through distribution channels dominated by white real estate brokers? As in the FHA program the preference need only be in terms of time, not price or credit rating.

Corporations often buy the homes of executives transferred to another community when the employee is unable to market the home soon enough at a reasonable price. The corporation does not want a large inventory of residences. It wants to rid itself of the property as soon as it is possible to recapture its expenditure. If another group could find willing buyers for these corporate properties, which range in price from $20,000 to $50,000, wouldn't it be in the interest of the corporation to sell? Couldn't corporations join together and create a pool of property to be made available to employees transferred into an area?

Corporate transfer policy is often essential to corporate effectiveness. William H. Whyte, Jr., in the now classic, *The Organization Man,* noted that "When the recruit joins up he does not do so because he *wants* to move a lot, and it is often in spite of it; but moving, he knows, has become part of the bargain, and unsettling as transfer might be, even more unsettling are the implications of not being asked to transfer."[43] Now more than ten years later, the process of movement has accelerated.

Transferred black executives sometimes face unexpected discrimination. *Fortune* magazine states:

Half believing that their incomes and educations will make them welcome in white neighborhoods, middle-class Negroes are hurt and infuriated at the rebuffs. . . . For all its discontent, the Negro middle-class is basically oriented toward the larger society of both blacks and whites—not toward a separatist black nationalism. Its discontent, indeed, is in large part frustration with the failure of the white community to allow Negroes full participation. Thus the Negro middle-class, which constitutes white society's best potential link with the increasingly violence-prone masses in the slums, is still generally ready to play a constructive role. Will it remain so? . . . For a moment, the question can only be posed—not answered.[44]

Why should a corporation hiring or transferring a black executive feel obliged to call the Urban League and ask for assistance in finding housing when that same corporation can turn to its own inventory?

In Indianapolis it was estimated that nearly 200 parcels of corporate property were sold each year. In one year one company accounted for eighty units. If this amount of corporate property was sold in Indianapolis, more heavily industrialized communities where the same corporations do business should also have a substantial number of residences available.

The Indianapolis group saw the potential for freeing the housing market. Indianapolis became a laboratory and the FHA program the focus of the experiment. First, a statement leading toward the promulgation of the FHA program was prepared. Next came an effort to determine the relationship and relevance of the FHA program to what should have been complementary efforts by civil rights groups. The group found little harmony between that sought in the Indianapolis action program and that articulated by some of the more responsible civil rights groups.

Before undertaking the Indianapolis project, a measure was taken of local and state enforcement of open housing law and the success of relevant governmental agencies. The group tried to determine the potential supply of buyers, those displaced by government action. If they numbered in the thousands and if many of them could afford the housing available through FHA, then through appropriate relocation agencies it might be possible to take large strides in freeing the housing market. The facts obtained indicated that 400 FHA homes should have been taken promptly.

The operations of the Committee on Special Housing are described in detail. Of the thousands who might have viewed the 400 homes and made offers to purchase, there are clear statistics of the number reached by the committee, the methods used to reach them, and the involvement of private and governmental groups in assisting and in using the FHA inventory as a source. Also, there is a detailed description of those who came and were served by the committee in the first seven months of operation from January 4, 1968. Who were they? What were their needs? What did they buy and where? How did they compare as credit risks with others seeking conventional FHA financing? Once moved, how did the displaced accept their new neighborhood? How did the black families moving into all white areas think they were received.

Answers to these and many other questions were found and categorized under the supervision of Karen Orloff Kaplan, M.S.W., the committee's chief social work consultant. The questionnaires used are set forth as appendices in the hope that others might find them of value. Other data were compiled with the cooperation of Allen Dale, Indiana insuring director for FHA; Harold Hatcher, executive director of the Indiana Civil Rights Commission at the time this project was undertaken; and Mrs. Howard F. Gustafson, deputy director of the Indianapolis Urban League.

The last chapter's evaluation of the project questions whether it achieved the end anticipated. It is enough to say that a beginning was made. More, much more, can be done. There are other institutional holdings that might be opened without substantial fear. There is a basis for corporate involvement. People have moved under the FHA program, and they are living in peace in homes of their choice purchased at fair prices. Other Indiana cities, Gary and Fort Wayne, in their own way are making use of the committee's approach.

In conclusion it should be clear that no total answer is intended nor offered in these pages. This approach to the housing problem has been tested though, and for some it has been of value.

1

The Need for and the
Beginning of the Committee

Cool weather in Indianapolis during the summers of 1966, 1967, and 1968 may have kept the city from experiencing a major racial upheaval. Certainly the factors involved in disruptions were present then. Tension could be seen on the faces of blacks and whites throughout the city. Even suburbanites experienced tension when they suddenly and unexpectedly found themselves faced with problems they thought they had escaped.

In 1967 a senior partner with an established law firm spoke of black real estate agents trying to panic his neighborhood. There were telephone calls: "Sell now before it's too late. The one black in the neighborhood will soon be joined by others." White real estate agents stimulated the panic by terming the neighborhood "unsettled" and thus not fit for white buyers.

The attorney sought to preserve his neighborhood; he began his search for an answer by helping to organize and shape a neighborhood association. He didn't mind the neighborhood being mixed racially, but he hoped the mix would occur as the white mix had occurred over the years. Originally the homes in the area had been occupied almost entirely by white Anglo-Saxon Protestants, but the area gradually had become fairly representative of the total white community. The first Catholic and Jewish families to enter the neighborhood had met some resistance and antagonism, but no one became panic-stricken. For sale signs did not pop up on neighboring yards. In time the original settlers found that the "foreigners" were very much like them. They mowed their lawns, planted flowers, painted their homes, bathed their children, and chained their dogs. They generally behaved as decently as those who had left—better than some.

The attorney hoped the newly formed neighborhood association would be able to control the infusion of blacks into the neighborhood as the infusion of "outsiders" had been controlled by economics a generation ago. There had been no arbitrary quota system. No one suggested that the neighborhood be limited to three Catholic and two Jewish families. As a family's income increased to the point where it could afford a home in the suburbs, it bought those homes that came on the market normally.

The attorney did not know what percentage of the black families in Indianapolis had reached the economic level that would enable them to move into his neighborhood, but he did know that there had to be quite a few. If these families were the ones to move into the neighborhood, perhaps the change could be accomplished with as little disturbance as had accompanied the change a generation earlier. Neighbors would learn that these families also mowed their lawns, planted flowers and shrubberies, painted their homes, bathed their children, and chained their dogs. Economics could now determine the balance of the neighborhood as it had before.

The neighborhood association went to work. Neighbors met and exchanged views. They agreed it would be fine to maintain stability of ownership and they promised to hold the neighborhood intact.[1]

These efforts failed. Homes were placed for sale through real estate agents who refused to show them to white customers. Prices dropped. The four black families in the three block area increased to twelve. The neighborhood association reacted by trying to educate and motivate white real estate brokers. More than twenty-five real estate firms were invited to a weekend tour of the neighborhood to hear their plea for economic stability in the sale of homes. Only six firms bothered to respond.

Although the battle for neighborhood stability was lost, the attorney stayed. This small neighborhood, consisting of homes owned mainly by professional or business people—mostly university graduates—had significance. Here was a limited challenge—open housing—that an element of the white community could understand. If those who felt a vested interest in a stable neighborhood could not bring minimal change, what hope was there for more dramatic movement in the inner city? Why did there have to be loss? Was the blame to be placed on the shoulders of the real estate brokers? The attorney had viewed the broker as the most effective method of marketing houses. Buyers turn to the professional salesmen; consequently brokers hold the power to control the flow and direction of home buyers.

Could a legal mechanism be found to redirect the real estate brokers and end discriminatory selling practices? An individual needs the services of a broker. If a broker were prohibited from yielding to the seller's pressure, real or imagined, to discriminate in the sale of the house, a reassessment would occur on economic grounds.

The sources of seller pressure, according to brokers, were the exclusive listing and multiple listing associations. A significant portion of residential real estate placed for sale by white owners went to Realtors, members of the Indianapolis Real Estate Board. Realtors obtained exclusive listings for as long as sixty or ninety days. The seller under the terms of the listing promised to use only the services of the designated Realtor. For a limited period the Realtor tried to market the home himself and take the full commission, but he knew that many listings in themselves were of limited value; his livelihood depended on turnover. Property had to be sold if commissions were to be earned. Realtors hoping to do much "white" business paid a substantial membership fee to belong to one or more of four area multiple listing associations. There the exclusive listing had to be submitted after a short time following its receipt for distribution to the multiple members. Any member then had the right to present an offer for sale, a buyer bid, and to share the commission with the exclusive broker if the bid were accepted by the seller.

The multiple groups met regularly. Their members were known to one another. They had a vested interest in the areas where they did business, they were concerned with the status quo. Owners may come and go, but the established area real estate firm remains. The multiple associations were self-enforcing entities. The free flow of information among a few allowed them to freeze others out and take action against any member who broke their unwritten law. A member selling to a black in an all white area might expect the news to be made known among his colleagues and discussed by area residents.

If the patent combination of the multiple listing groups within the white-dominated real estate boards could be broken, a way might be opened for a free housing market. If each listing were opened to any broker, white or black, the web of conspiracy would be destroyed.

Members of multiple listing groups could no longer hide behind the action of the board and, more important, members could not control the actions of other members through economic sanctions. A white broker no longer would need fear retaliation if he sold property in a white area to a black because if he did not sell the home, then another agent, a licensed black broker, would sell it.

The exercise of such power already was being tested under both state and federal laws relating to restraints against trade. In 1966 a New Jersey court found a common law restraint, in essence a group boycott, in a real estate board rule that property on multiple listings may not be sold by a nonmember. The New Jersey Superior Court recognized the benefits of multiple listing services in terms of exposure of properties to large numbers of potential buyers. But the barriers of exclusion of multiple listing membership where applications can be rejected, a $1,000 initiation fee, and a one-year waiting period, made what might have been a good competitive device bad.[2]

The *Wall Street Journal* wrote of intense government antitrust activity in 1966. Based on its interviews, the paper said the theory for action was, "If real estate agents agree among themselves to steer Negro buyers away from white neighborhoods, this restrains trade by limiting the market open to Negro buyers and by depriving white property owners of would-be Negro buyers; also, if agents conspire to keep Negro or white brokers who favor integration off local realty boards, this deprives these brokers of a share of the boards' cooperative pooling of house listings and lessens competition."[3]

Yet, by 1968 the power had not been broken. Law had but minimum effect. There were inherent limitations in any study project designed to find the facts necessary for attack. The hard proof of conspiracy rests in individual actions, often the subtle deeds and words of the people. An effective means for probing the existence of conspiracy is to record that which transpires between broker and buyer. But this is time-consuming and often futile. Though individual cases might be proved, there was no necessary assurance that widespread compliance by the industry would follow.

Objectively what could be done in the present? The attorney's concern had spread. A number of professional persons were studying the challenge of open housing in Indianapolis. They wondered what mechanisms existed or could be created to bring change. They knew the answers could not be found in office speculation alone; facts had to be found and understood. As an informal committee, they began gathering information.

In the northwestern sector of the city, people were interviewed whose homes were being taken by eminent domain for a beltway that would connect the downtown area to the suburbs. This area was inhabited almost exclusively by blacks who held professional, skilled, or semi-skilled jobs. Their homes were handsome and moderately priced. They liked their homes, their schools, their churches, their neighbors; they showed no strong desire to live next to a white family. In their individualized existence, color was not a relevant concern; family and friends were.

They were angry, but it had nothing to do with integration. Their community faced the levelling blade of the bulldozer.[4] Seven hundred and fifty families—3,000 individuals—stood in the path of the access highway that was to cut through their neighborhood.[5] The highway, moreover, was to be elevated, requiring more land than a depressed highway and walling the area with concrete and steel while limiting the access to the homes left standing. Government offered no relief. Only a temporary stay in demolition and evictions was granted during the general elections along with a vague promise to reconsider the highway design—perhaps it could be depressed rather than elevated.[6]

The homeowners began seeking a way out. They looked for other housing. They shunned the help of city and state government. Relocation offices handed uninspected rental listings to these sophisticated homeowners. The city promised more and better public housing to people who had long been independent and proud taxpayers on incomes eliminating them from any consideration of public housing. What a frustrating dichotomy: the law could take the home in which the black man lived but the law could not provide the black man with another home he might want.

They moved where they could, and as they moved the racial lines shifted. The so-called ghetto area expanded from its inner-city core. Adjacent white areas were penetrated. Some toppled. The line of restriction retrenched; it did not break.

In at least one instance where the racial line shifted the Indiana Civil Rights Commission entered the picture. Blacks had lived next to whites for several years in Forest Manor, an area comparable to the northwest but somewhat newer and located in the northeast. Now highway displacement threatened a dramatic increase in the number of black purchasers. After all, in real estate parlance, this was an "open" neighborhood.[7] The Civil Rights Commission attempted to divert an almost irrestible force. Homeowners were urged not to panic. A neighborhood association was formed and a voluntary quota system, lawful under the Indiana open housing law, was proposed.[8] Meetings were held with real estate firms. The Civil Rights Commission urged them to cooperate. Some did. To reach those who refused, mortgage bankers were asked to agree not to finance sales from whites to blacks in the area. Without mortgage financing, of course, there could be no sale.

Forest Manor is a changing area. Whites are moving out, and blacks are moving in. Despite the frustration of not being able to live where they want to live and the temporary price inflation, the blacks in Forest Manor are relatively well off compared to those in the inner city who lack the means to find comparable housing.

A black Baptist minister, the Reverend Mozelle Sanders, who supports himself in no small part by operating a restaurant near the core of the inner city, was able to speak of those who could not find adequate housing. Interviewed at his business, the Keyless Restaurant, in the summer of 1967, he stated, "I live in the northwest, but I work here. My restaurant and church are here. If you want to see dislocation, let me show you."

The state university, not the highway department, was the primary "mover" among the minister's congregation. Building expansion uprooted scores of families. "One day a family is here. The next day they're gone, and nobody knows where. They've lived in these run-down homes for a long time. If they own them, all they can get from the university is a few thousand dollars at best. We know that many have moved across the river to Houghville. Now, you just know that there will be trouble there."

Houghville is a small, close-knit, largely Slavic neighborhood composed primarily of low-cost housing. On one side, blacks had begun to buy homes, and on the other side the city was building a public housing project whose tenants would be mostly black. Politicians admitted that arson was twice suspected as the cause of fires at the project. In this heavily Democratic area, a black administrative assistant to a Democratic congressman in the presence of the congressman and county chairman of the Democratic party was denied service at a cafe near the project.

A tiny spark could ignite Houghville. Many not only expected but eagerly anticipated violence. Their homes, poor as they were, had been taken. There was no place for them to go. Pressure was mounting and new housing had to be found if an explosion was to be avoided.

Asked about the open housing law in the city and in the state, the Reverend Sanders answered, "Like hell there is. I don't care what's on the books. Black people can't buy homes in white neighborhoods. And if they could, how many do you think could afford to? Let me tell you something. There's a pretty fancy restaurant in town. They don't have to tell me they don't want black people. They charge prices that I can't pay. So I don't go."

The words of statute held little meaning for Reverend Sanders. There was a problem, and it was not being resolved successfully. To the minister it seemed rather clear that the law did not bring freedom. Quite the contrary. The law brought restriction. No restatement of public policy, no law school lecture would alter his decision on that point. To some the problem could be put in terms of a gap between law and its fulfillment, but as far as the black families of Indianapolis and obedience to open housing provisions were concerned, there had been promises without performance.

Was there a way to fulfill any part of the housing need in Indianapolis? The government that had destroyed many inner-city residences in the name of urban renewal also owned many homes throughout the city. There were FHA owned properties in almost every neighborhood except the inner city. More than 400 houses priced from $8,500 to $18,000 were available on favorable financing terms with as little as $300–$500 down payment needed, through an agency of the federal government, the Federal National Mortgage Association (FNMA). After FHA houses were rehabilitated they were offered for public sale through bids submitted by real estate brokers.

The Federal Housing Administration had been made a part of the Department of Housing and Urban Development. This was presided over by the nation's first black cabinet level secretary and a white commissioner who publicly stated that they wanted integration in the suburbs and that FHA would actively aid in the process. This was the official policy and there was a sense of urgency about it.

The potential for opening the housing market seemed to exist, but the fact remained that FHA had been selling its acquired property through brokers over a period of several years on an open basis, and there had been no break in racial barriers. The black community had not taken advantage of the government property. Since the white broker was dealing on a volume basis and would get only a five percent commission if his bid were drawn in the lotteries held, he was not about to solicit black customers. He would take whoever walked through the door. The black brokers, although they publicly complained of "artificial" marketing restraints imposed upon them, stayed in their own areas.

Whatever the past record of the FHA-acquired property sales, here was an opportunity. The property available was within the price range of many in the black community. For homes of less than $15,000, FHA required only a three percent down payment, and a mortgage could be obtained from FNMA for twenty to thirty years at a favorable interest rate fixed from time to time by Congress, HUD, and FHA.[9] A couple with two children, an adequate credit rating, and a gross income of about $6,000 annually could afford a $10,000 to $12,000 FHA house. If the government could formulate a workable plan that would allow for implementation of its announced policy, much could be accomplished and much more could be anticipated.

A plan was evolved. The approach would be to FHA. VA properties and property acquired and sold by corporations in the Indianapolis market would not be involved in the initial effort. These latter properties obviously formed a part of the city's housing inventory and eventually perhaps could be brought into the program. For a beginning, though, the plan would involve only FHA property and the city of Indianapolis. At its root the plan was to afford freedom of choice. Blacks and whites should have the right to move as they want. If blacks desire an all black neighborhood that choice should be theirs. If whites prefer a neighborhood that, at the time, is all white, that also should not be condemned by government. What should be held open to all is the opportunity to make a choice, free from restrictive marketing practices.

The limitations of this position should be understood. It does not touch upon public policy favoring desegregation or integration. It neither accepts nor rejects the proposition of some social psychologists that discrimination or segregation causes psychological harm to either the victim or the perpetrator. Such considerations are not, as such, relevant unless they aid in bringing about individual free choice.[10]

An expression was devised to express the project goal—a free housing market. It was hoped that the term might touch a responsive chord in both the black and white communities. It was freedom now that the black community said it wanted. It was the right to say yes or no. It was free enterprise that the conservative element of the white community wanted restored. The envisioned program was one designed to allow more people the opportunity to become homeowners, to have what some might consider a greater stake in the community.

Around the concept of a free housing market, a program was shaped that might be applied in any urban setting. Indianapolis, a city with a population of 750,000, had available on an annual basis at least 400 FHA acquired properties. The FHA could withstand local hostility if any should develop. Four hundred units is not a large number, but if this inventory were available it would constitute new housing for the black community that would cost neither government nor industry a single dollar. If this housing were used, the filter effect would be significant. As black families moved into hitherto unavailable areas, the market would react. The real estate industry could "afford" to make property in those neighborhoods available to blacks. The container pressure of the ghetto would be reduced or eliminated. With all neighborhoods open, there would be no places in which to escape. A kind of natural population dispersion could take place. The crude device of panic selling by real estate agents could be controlled. If the techniques for establishing a free housing market could be maintained, they would follow housing development whatever its course.

The time came to translate theory into practice. There could be no better beginning than an approach to the FHA. The local scene, however, seemed to give little cause for optimism. The director of the Indiana office of FHA was not a career employee; he owed his office to the political patronage of two United States senators. He was not an officer bound by rigid agency rules. It was not known what could be expected of him in terms of implementing national policy. He had not risen through administrative ranks. He had no intimate knowledge of the function and procedures of FHA. One lawyer in Indianapolis said of him, "Hell, he's only been there three months. He won't know the answers to specific legal regulations. All he can do is talk some broad policy."

The FHA director in Indiana, Allen Dale, is in his mid-forties, a veteran of World War II, an active Democrat, and an administrative specialist with a broad background in communications as an author, lecturer, editor, radio and television newscaster, and wire service reporter. He is a native of Pennsylvania, coming from a family that helped build the houses, businesses, and industry in his hometown, a family that traces its lineage to General William Braddock. But he's a tough-minded pragmatist who is more concerned with today's problems than with yesterday's family favors from King George II; and he has spent twenty years of his life in Indiana as both an observer and a participant in state and city affairs.

It was true that he didn't know the answers to specific legal questions, but he knew where to find the answers and, even more important, he knew how to give life and meaning to regulations.

Dale accepted the proposal for use of FHA properties. Preferential status in the purchase of FHA acquired property should be given to those displaced by government action such as highway construction. His only comment was, "It makes good sense." He called in his deputy director and the head of his property management section. He outlined the proposal and asked, "Can I put this into effect by administrative decree or must I get approval from Washington?" The answer was unequivocal; approval had to come from Washington. The head of property management took a negative position from the outset, "Why would you want to submit such a proposal? We have an open housing policy and we have an excellent relationship with the real estate people. Why stir up trouble? Besides we have a good program for moving property quickly. This new program will require new procedures and take time to sell homes."

Dale rejected the arguments of the civil servant head of property management as irrelevant to the intended thrust of FHA programs and procedures as spelled out to him by FHA Commissioner Philip N. Brownstein. "Everyone I talked to at FHA expressed the same deep concern I felt for the conditions of the cities. The proposal is really a modest suggestion, but it does go to the heart of part of the problem. I can't imagine it will run into any serious objection."

Dale then drafted a concise memorandum setting forth the proposal: Families displaced as a result of government action such as state highway construction and urban renewal would be given the first chance to buy FHA repossessed property. Priority would come only in terms of option, not price. The repossessed property would continue to be sold at a figure that FHA thought proper. The memorandum was mailed to Washington after a phone call asking that it be given expeditious treatment. Dale was assured that it would get such treatment and that he could expect an answer within two weeks.

Assuming a favorable reply, Dale began to consider the details that would give the proposal life. He established contacts and meetings with real estate brokers dealing in FHA property to explain the program. Two weeks passed, then three, then six. The director called Washington. The response was surprising. A Washington official acknowledged receipt of the memorandum. He said careful consideration had been given to the suggestion for revising down payment criteria for FHA properties, but the proposal seemed to be without merit.

"But," said Dale incredulously, "I didn't mention down payments. I asked for preferential treatment for dislocated families."

Dale was asked to send another memorandum.

Another memorandum was prepared. To avoid possible misinterpretation, the proposal was repeated several times. It could not be misunderstood. The answer that came at the end of September said, in essence, that FHA had an established procedure for disposing of acquired houses that made such property available to all on an equal basis, and the failure of any group to take advantage of this availability was the fault of the group to act or of the field office to communicate but not the fault of the regulation itself.

About the same time, the director and all other FHA field office directors and their chief underwriters were summoned to Washington for a high-level meeting. There they were told that the theme of the meeting was a "Sense of Urgency," which each of them was to develop in administering the affairs of their offices. They were told that FHA was appalled by a confidential survey showing a minimal amount of black occupancy of federally-insured housing. Bluntly, FHA employees from seventy-six cities were ordered to provide housing for minority groups in the white suburbs or risk unpleasant consequences, including the loss of their jobs. FHA Deputy Assistant Secretary Philip J. Maloney said to the closed meeting, "You have been measured and found wanting. . . . manifest your loyalty and zeal for these causes. . . . If you can't give this much to your positions of leadership in the department, I suggest that, in good conscience, you should step aside for men who can provide leadership in these areas. . . . These are critical times for FHA. . . . We either produce, as we have before, or we are an agency with little future."[11]

Maloney referred to the criticism FHA had been receiving from private groups and the Congress for failing to implement an executive order of 1962 relating to discrimination in housing. That order, among other things, permits the FHA to withdraw federal mortgage insurance from those housing developers who discriminate in their sales because of race. While Washington officials have professed their commitment to the executive order many times, the power to carry out that order rests with the officers in the FHA's seventy-six local insuring offices, the directors and underwriters who, while subject to check from Washington, generally determine the recipients of FHA insurance. "Their vigor or inertia," said the *New York Times,* "also determines the success or failure of any civil rights enforcement program."[12]

Since the executive order of 1962 until November 1967, there were 410,574 FHA insured homes sold by developers. The new survey indicated that of these only 35,000 had gone to minorities, a broadly defined category that when broken down made the indictment much more devastating. Only 13,832, about three percent of the total, went to blacks; 12,765, to Spanish-Americans; 8,784, to Orientals; and 687 to American Indians. Maloney reminded his audience that blacks make up eleven percent of the nation's total population and a much larger percentage in many urban areas such as the District of Columbia where he was speaking.

The facts were beyond dispute. "Virtually no minority family housing has been provided through FHA," said Maloney.[13] On the face of it, the message to insuring directors and underwriters also was beyond dispute. Only two days before Maloney spoke, FHA Commissioner Brownstein, formerly assistant secretary for mortgage credit before President Kennedy appointed him as agency head in 1961, stated publicly that attention had to be given an entire city, the core area as well as suburbia. Not only must all have the opportunity to buy, but FHA had to stimulate rehabilitation of the inner city by overcoming its reluctance to insure homes located therein.

The Indiana FHA director took the speakers seriously. He asked for reconsideration of the proposal relating to FHA acquired property. He produced a newspaper report endorsing a similar but broader proposal by the chairman of the President's Commission on Urban Problems, former Senator Paul H. Douglas, who had suggested that some of the people in the city slums should be moved into existing FHA acquired property. Instead of selling the property, the chairman asked, why not turn it over to a public housing agency?[14] Reconsideration was promised. Dale was told to write another memorandum and within a few weeks a decision would be forthcoming—this was said by the Washington officials who had stressed a sense of urgency and demanded results.

Summer was over and a chill was in the air, but the promised early answer did not come. To inquiries the Indiana FHA director could only report, "I'm sorry. I called. They're giving it serious consideration. We should hear from them soon." November passed. By the second week in December, an additional course of action was pursued. A number of the community's more prominent citizens were called individually and asked to lend their name to a Committee on Special Housing. They were told of the project and, specifically, of the proposal before FHA. The name, Committee on Special Housing, was selected to fit the unemotional, objective concept of a free housing market. The name meant nothing; it evoked no emotional response. The name, like the activity of the committee, was intended to afford a conflict-free means for attaining an emotionally charged goal. Open housing, after all, had long been a source of actual and symbolic black frustration. With that frustration necessarily comes anger. The committee, as it was conceived, would not be a target for that anger. It would not be identified as a civil rights organization, although it was concerned with a free housing market.

Next, congressmen and senators from Indiana were contacted. They were apprized of the committee's work. They asked when the plan would be implemented. A committee member replied, "We will move just as soon as Washington decides that it means what it says, just as soon as the sense of urgency is transformed into reality." The legislators began to make inquiries and seek answers. The FHA responded. The proposal was accepted and new regulations would be in effect by Christmas. Accepting the agency's word, the committee geared itself for action.

Meetings were held. Invitations went to individuals from a number of organizations asking them to lend their services to the committee. Spurred by the active enthusiasm of committee members, the volunteers appeared. There were representatives of the Church Federation, black and white ministers, school social workers, government employees, and, of course, representatives of the Community Action Against Poverty (CAAP) program. While their membership in the varied organizations could not be ignored, the volunteers were asked to participate in committee work only as individuals, free and apart from the inhibitions of policy attendant upon their organizational affiliations. Until the program was proven, until it was demonstrated to be workable, the utmost flexibility was needed. That flexibility rested in large measure on the committee's freedom from the emotional bonds and the policy bonds inherent in affiliation with already established agencies.

From the meetings a plan emerged. An inner-city church, the Fletcher Place Methodist Church, would be made available for persons to apply for housing. There was every reason to believe that the minister would be released by his bishop to spend considerable time on the project. There were, moreover, at least fifteen volunteers, all with social work training, ready to work with applicants. But would there be a sufficient number of applicants displaced as a result of government action? The reply was that the people were there.

The committee had learned not to rely on general promises. So, a month earlier on November 16, in an effort to get actual lists of potential applicants, a meeting was held with a key CAAP staff member, Miss Charlotte Koontz. (The Community Action Against Poverty was the Indianapolis group participating in the war against poverty and funded by the federal Office for Economic Opportunity.) One of her employees, working in the two relocation offices operated by CAAP, had been serving as a volunteer to the committee. The committee had asked for lists of those being displaced and able to qualify under the proposed FHA acquired property program. "Before we turn any list over," said Miss Koontz, "I want to be sure you can render meaningful assistance. We've had enough talk in this city. The time has come for action. We can get the people. There are enough of them being displaced."

Miss Koontz wanted to run a test case. She wanted to see whether a person she selected would be rejected on credit grounds. She chose a young, unmarried black woman who had one child and was expecting another. The applicant had been in her job for a little more than a year. "She had poor credit before, but has rehabilitated herself." An appointment was scheduled with the FHA Counseling Service. Within an hour, the committee received a call from the FHA director, "Were you serious about this applicant? She couldn't qualify under any circumstances." The committee checked. CAAP had sent as their test a woman who had just filed for bankruptcy and was hopelessly in debt.

When asked for an explanation, Miss Koontz said, "We wanted to see whether you were serious. We'll cooperate." Her offer was accepted although her reasoning was difficult to comprehend.

An organization had been shaped to handle the program; assurance had been given that the people were there to be served. The Committee on Special Housing was ready by Christmas, but the FHA was not. There was no word from Washington. The proposed regulations had been drafted and were being subjected to intensive review. What the proposed regulations contained could not be discovered. Why was there additional delay? "Well, you know government. Our administrative structure is rather complex. We move slowly," said an FHA staff member in Washington.

Finally, on January 4 the regulations were promulgated in the form of FHA Property Disposition Letter Number 129.[15] The committee was invited to call Washington and speak with the men responsible for the regulations that made achieving stated policy nearly impossible. "We really rushed this through," said William Cameron, head of FHA's property management. "We didn't have time for written comment. I called or visited about eight of our field officers, including Tampa, Florida. Frankly, the insuring directors didn't think the proposed program will do very much; but they offered no objection, so we're going to give it a try."

The regulations stated that preferential treatment was to be granted on the issuance to applicants of proper certificates by the dislocating agency. Recognizing that several agencies could be involved and multiple bids submitted on a given piece of property, the regulations permitted the locating agencies, which so often vie with each other, to establish a system of priorities. Real estate brokers for all practical purposes could not be used. According to Cameron, at the last minute Commissioner Brownstein added the rule that commissions could not be paid in the sale of properties under the preferred program. The results were devasting. Only relocation officers, government employees with nine-to-five jobs, could show FHA acquired properties to applicants who were available primarily in the evenings or on weekends. Since brokers had been ruled out, the regulations very logically provided that all forms were to be completed by the individual or the displacing agency. The burden of paper work alone would have made the most eager of relocation officers turn aside. To make an offer on an FHA acquired property one had to complete the complex Form 2900 of assets and liabilities, the credit check request, the employment verification form, the bank deposit verification form, and the certificate of eligibility as a displaced person.

The final requirement that must have caused old-line FHA employees to chuckle at the paper tiger program was the extent of preferential treatment. No person was permitted to inspect any acquired property until it had been rehabilitated. Following repair, however, those who qualified as displaced persons, in the presence of a relocation officer, were given ten days to view properties and make an offer to purchase. At the end of that time, if no offer to purchase had been received, the properties were placed on the public market for sale through brokers. Ten days were granted to people who, in all likelihood, never had shopped for a home before—and certainly had never looked beyond the ghetto.

What the FHA granted with one hand, it appeared to take away with the other. Neither the committee nor the director had recommended the elimination of the real estate broker. Both had hoped for broker involvement subject to appropriate checks. The FHA, an agency with an ostensible social matrix, had seen a way for saving some commissions. In the confines of Washington—a place that a HUD senior staffer said seems "terribly removed from the country despite the fires of rioters in the capital"—FHA's action made good paper logic. The regulations did not evidence understanding of the needs of the inner city where residents do not consider themselves the beneficiaries of agency largesse, where they are not apt to rush to take advantage of agency programs.

The Indiana FHA director did not relent. The regulations would be made effective, but the prospects seemed dismal. The minister who was to work for the Committee on Special Housing, freed by his bishop to do so, no longer attended meetings or returned phone calls. Without stated reason, he and his church faded away. There were volunteers but only on a part-time basis. The director of relocation for Indianapolis also made promises. "I want to help. The program is good but I'm awfully busy." None denied the need for new housing. All professed the worth of the FHA program but none seemed ready to put forth the necessary effort.

Miss Koontz of CAAP was called in desperation. After conferences with her superior she said, "Beginning tomorrow I'm going to give the committee, on a half time basis, one of our best people. He's a fellow about twenty-two years old, bright, dedicated, a former seminary student. He seems like a slow starter, but once he catches on, nothing can stop him." This promise was backed by a letter from Miss Koontz to her executive director seeking confirmation of this plan on a permanent basis and asking him to commit the agency to support the program. Following a plan designed by the committee, the man from CAAP was asked to report as scheduled. He was to be given half of a vacant office next to the FHA Counseling Service. A large map was posted in his office on which each FHA property was noted by a number sticker. Pictures of each home had been taken by volunteers. (The costs of which the committee bore, for there was no funding.) The telephone began to ring. The first potential customers were slated for interviews by the FHA receptionist. FHA counselors shared the other portion of the office set aside for the CAAP worker. They were ready to render assistance for any applicant just as they offered to do for the public at large. In this way the battle of the forms could be overcome.

Arrangements were completed; the Indiana FHA director and the committee's executive director waited together on a Monday morning for the CAAP worker who was to be the vital link needed for success. Slight attention was paid when fifteen minutes passed beyond the appointed hour for the arrival of the CAAP representative. There was a feeling of only mild uneasiness when thirty minutes passed. At the end of an hour the waiting room was checked again. Sitting there, without having told the receptionist for whom he was waiting, was an emaciated young man wearing a rumpled sport shirt and open sandals. He was to be the communications link with a dark-suited, pipe-smoking FHA staff not totally dedicated to the program. It took three days to convert the CAAP worker to a suit, and about two weeks to induce him to talk.

The FHA director was patient; his staff held their tongues; and two counselors drilled the CAAP worker in the ways of bureaucracy, in the forms that had to be completed. The first, second, and third buyers kept their appointments, looked at homes, and bought. It was perhaps ironic, or, as events later developed, most fitting, that the first buyer was white, a native of Indianapolis, and an elderly man whose home had been taken by the highway. After inspecting an FHA home, the white buyer said, "I like it." "Why?" the committee relocation worker asked. "I like it because it's a nice neighborhood. There aren't any blacks around." The committee was reminded that a free housing market, not forced integration, stood as its single purpose. People should be given the opportunity to move as they wished. Yet the second buyer also was white, and he selected a home close to his employment in an all white area. The third buyer was black, and he chose a home in an all black area.

What would the future bring? What conclusions, if any, could be drawn from those few purchases already made? Was the committee doing its job properly? Was it making the opportunity to buy demonstrable to black and white alike?

At the very time when these difficult questions were being asked, suggestions for finding answers came from two quarters.

A committee volunteer suggested contacting a research sociologist who was identified with many of the community open housing groups and asking him to shape questionnaires that would permit an impartial analysis of committee activity. His participation, moreover, could bring added skills to the organizational effort. No alternative was to be overlooked; the committee structure was to be kept loose, capable of accommodating new workers and techniques.

On a routine field inspection, two of FHA Commissioner Brownstein's top assistants, one black and one white, visited Indianapolis. In the course of their inquiries they asked about the committee, and its executive director was given the opportunity to explain. Both FHA officials said that the committee had done "a fine job." The black official added. "Please send me whatever material you have. I'd like to study it further. Perhaps you and the director would be willing to come to Washington to discuss this project with others." He seemed to hold out an implied promise of increased manpower, of greater federal involvement.

A memorandum clearly marked "Confidential" setting forth, *inter alia,* possible plans for the future was sent by the committee to the personal attention of the FHA assistant to the commissioner. Without his permission and without his knowledge, the memorandum was copied and widely distributed within the agency. The head of field operations, an old-line FHA employee, apparently evidenced a particular concern about the work of the committee. Allen Dale was summoned to Washington; he was told to take the next available plane. Within twenty-four hours from the time of summons, without either of the two visiting assistants to the commissioner being present, Dale felt the fury of a bureaucracy disturbed. He was told that the committee had no right to the use of free government office space. It did not matter that the space was unused; the government paid the rent. Furthermore, what would real estate brokers say? After all, they were eliminated from the preferred program. Wouldn't they think that the committee was the object of too much favoritism? FHA had to keep good relations with brokers.

The Indiana director had not been informed of a secret. On February 26, a point close in time to the Washington meeting, the same assistant commissioner for field operations addressed the Albuquerque Board of Realtors, the independent real estate brokers and the mortgage lenders of that city. He began his remarks by stating, "As you know, FHA is committed to a close partnership among industry groups, including mortgagees, builders, developers, and real estate brokers. . . . Experience has proved over a period of better than thirty-three years that this is the most effective and efficient way that FHA can work to help serve the housing needs of the American people. . . . So, I would like to repeat my earlier point: We are not going into competition with real estate brokers, either as salesmen of housing, or as counselors of persons seeking housing."[16]

Yet, the committee had not eliminated the real estate broker in the sale of FHA property under the preferred program. It was the FHA itself that benefited from the nonpayment of commissions. It was the FHA that offered a program and at the same time attempted to withdraw its benefits. On his return from Washington, Dale said to the committee's executive director, "I have been instructed to order the committee to remove its worker from our office. I am not permitted to say any more than this." The memorandum and letter that the executive director had forwarded as requested to the assistant to the FHA commissioner was never answered. The Committee was given no opportunity to speak.

What accounted for such agency ambivalence? In a barrage of formal pronouncements Commissioner Brownstein from 1965 to 1967 stressed the need for total city development. No emphasis was placed on private industry as such.

On November 8, 1965, Commissioner Brownstein wrote all insuring office directors, "Directors should at all times be aware of the characteristics and changing patterns of all residential areas within their jurisdiction. They should be alert to situations in which values can be stabilized and property upgraded by an infusion of capital into older residential sections and should help to bring this about by seeing that such areas are not denied the benefits of mortgage insurance."[17]

The drive toward stabilization and equal opportunity in housing was made abundantly clear in a jointly signed letter from Commissioner Brownstein and William J. Driver, administrator of Veterans Affairs, Veterans Administration, on October 23, 1967. The letter was addressed to "all participants in the Federal Housing Administration Mortgage Insurance Programs or the Veterans Administration Home Loan Program." Noting that since the issuance of the 1962 executive order "some complaints" of violation had been received, the letter stated in part:

> As a participant in the FHA's mortgage insurance programs or the VA's GI Home Loan Guaranty or Direct Loan Program, you are aware of the fact that in connection with requests for subdivision and site approval and for appraisal of properties to be constructed and sold to homebuyers with FHA or GI financing, we require a certification that the properties to be sold and/or constructed will be offered for sale to all eligible homebuyers regardless of their race, color, creed, or national origin. As you know, we require this certification pursuant to the provisions of Executive Order 11063, dated November 20, 1962, which seeks to promote equality of opportunity in the sale of housing. FHA's requirements appear in 24 CFR 200.300-200.355. VA's requirements appear in VA Regulation 4363 (38 CFR 36.4363).

> What is required is equal opportunity to purchase and to obtain title and possession regardless of the race, color, creed, or national origin of the homebuyer. Insofar as the Federal Housing Administration and the Veterans Administration are concerned, the equal opportunity concept contemplates a total absence of construction delays and delays in submitting loan packages to lenders because of the prospective homebuyer's race, color, creed, or national origin.

> A builder who requests a FHA commitment or a VA Master Certificate of Reasonable Value and certifies that he will not decline to sell to a prospective homebuyer because of his race, color, creed, or national origin should understand that he is certifying that all homebuyers, regardless of their race, color, creed, or national origin, will be afforded equal opportunity to purchase the properties covered by the commitment or the

Master Certificate of Reasonable Value. If investigation estab-
lishes that in fact discriminatory tactics or procedures have been
employed because of the race, color, creed, or national origin of
the prospective homebuyer, appropriate sanctions will be imposed promptly. This may include suspension of the principals
concerned from future participation in the FHA and GI programs
on the basis that the facts establish a "declination to sell" or that
they constitute an unfair marketing practice.

What became reasonably clear was the gap between word and deed
that reflected a deeper division, an agency that bordered on being
institutionally schizoid. Since 1935, the primary thrust of FHA had
been to forward middle-income home ownership; more than $84 billion
in mortgage insurance had been issued by 1968; in no small measure
suburbia could not have been created without the active support of
FHA and its insuring policies. The inner city was taboo; it was high risk;
mortgages were relatively unsafe in terms of low-income residential
housing.[18] Indeed, to secure the blessings of suburbia, FHA, which
seemed to become the private preserve of the home building and
satellite real estate industry, had inserted in its appraisal manual the
need to maintain racial homogeneity.[19]

In 1967, the FHA was made part of the new cabinet-level office, the
Department of Housing and Urban Development. The old-line FHA was
to assume new goals and direction.

Although FHA was made a part of HUD, "construction lobbies—
notably the National Association of Homebuilders, a group of
forty-seven thousand developers and contractors—in alliance with
friends in Congress forced a continuance of the FHA as a separate, if
not wholly autonomous agency within HUD."[20] Curiously, the
amendment stipulating an assistant secretaryship for private mortgage
financing was filed by Senator Abraham Ribicoff (Democrat from
Connecticut), who later became a severe critic of HUD's failings in
central cities. Within HUD, FHA assumed a dominant position. Of
HUD's 14,395 employees, FHA accounted for more than half, a total
of 8,395. Of the FHA staff, 3,225 are in the field, removed from tight
central control but dichotomously under rigid regulations.

It has been difficult to instill and maintain a sense of mission in the
FHA, particularly when Congress itself has imposed barriers to
fulfillment. By December 1967, FHA handled 73,000 applications for
housing. Of these, said *The Reporter,* "More than 62,000 were of the

single-family, picket fence variety that has characterized FHA efforts since 1935."[21] A minute portion, like those sold through developers, went to minority groups, and the ambivalence was heightened by the sometimes unclear language of the secretary of HUD who said before the National Association of Real Estate Boards on November 15, 1967, that during the past three years "there are 1.6 million more American families who have become homeowners because there is a Federal Housing Administration. . . . Today FHA's energies are undiminished in helping middle-income Americans with housing finance." Here was praise of the past without thought of the future. Given the need to aid those thrusting toward the middle class, and the import of a free housing market "a boast by the HUD secretary about suburban achievements could only be matched by the Postmaster General bragging about junk mail."[22] The contradictory approach of the FHA to the preferred program promulgated by the Indianapolis group was understandable; it merely reflected the agency's past. The amazing point is that the program was ever accepted.

Forced to leave FHA offices in Indianapolis, not only did new quarters have to be found but also a new worker. The CAAP volunteer had been drafted, and his agency was in shambles with a director soon to leave and a budget that had not been approved though the year had ended. Perhaps the research sociologist so active in varied housing groups would lend assistance. But the sociologist wanted nothing to do with the program. It represented an area of potential conflict between HUD and FHA; he wanted no part of any such battle. Even more important to him there was no screening and follow-up program for potential black buyers "to make sure they would be acclimated to new, white neighborhoods." There was no one to train them in home ownership. There were no steps taken to insure tranquility and adjustment on the part of whites after the blacks moved in. There had been no effort made to discuss, refine, and clear the program with the city's many interested social service agencies that could be so necessary in providing back-up services. The sociologist said, "The committee has done a dangerous thing. It is opening the community to the possibility of an explosion. It is tampering with human lives."

The committee and the Indiana FHA director were determined, however, that the program would continue. Freedom of choice meant risk. The committee was not going to build a fence around buyers. They would know the costs of home ownership. They would have professional guidance available but they would decide their own future. The committee adhered to its single goal—the establishment of a free housing market. Yet in view of the objections made questions had to be asked. What is the position of those organizations concerned with the rights of minority groups, particularly black persons, as applied to housing? What, concretely, are the relative housing needs of such persons in Indianapolis? What are others doing to meet these needs?

In seeking answers the committee felt it had passed a beginning point. It had something to talk to other organizations about. It had a guiding principle for its operation, namely, a free housing market. It served white and black families in terms of a community recognized problem, government displacement because of such events as highway construction and urban renewal. It was not as such a civil rights group. Most important, the committee had an ongoing supply of homes in quantity; FHA repossessed property located throughout the community was available for purchase directly from an agency of the federal government at fair prices and with good financing. Now the question seemed to be whether this type of program would bring national support from groups concerned with open housing.

2

Civil Rights Groups and the Committee

National Scene

Officers of the Indiana Civil Liberties Union introduced the committee's program to Alan Reitman, deputy director of the American Civil Liberties Union (ACLU). A meeting was arranged in New York City with the National Committee Against Discrimination in Housing (NCDH) to discuss implementation of the Indiana plan. "Yes," said Mr. Reitman, "at this stage the Indiana program does seem to offer something a little different that may be of value."

The New York meeting seemed to present a grand opportunity. Though the NCDH executive director could not be present, the associate director, Jack E. Wood, a person of ability and in a position to make decisions, would be there. The Committee on Special Housing knew that the NCDH had forty-seven national affiliates, including such diverse groups as the AFL-CIO, the NAACP, and the ACLU. The affiliates were further tied to the NCDH by personal links. In the 1967 hearings on a federal fair housing bill, for example, NCDH board chairman Algernon D. Black spoke for the ACLU. Robert L. Carter, general counsel of the NAACP, also served as vice-chairman of the NCDH executive committee. William Oliver, head of the United Automobile Workers fair practices unit, held a major office in the NCDH.[1]

From this involvement came still further involvement. Private groups and governmental units turned to the NCDH when expert help was needed. "The Ford Foundation sends most of their housing project requests here for our comment," said one NCDH official. "Nothing really happens in housing without our being consulted." There was more than puffing in the words. In a single issue of its regular glossy newspaper, *Trends in Housing,* there appeared two supporting stories.[2] Operating under an extremely tight budget with limited staff, the President's Committee on Equal Opportunity in Housing saw fit to grant NCDH a $20,000 contract "... to finance preparation and distribution of information and publications of practical value to the fair housing movement."[3] At the same point in time, two NCDH professional staffers were among the 1,000 persons who attended the August 1967 emergency convocation of the Urban Coalition in Washington, D.C., where they aided in drafting a housing objective. The coalition called upon the nation "to take bold and immediate action" to provide "a decent home and a suitable living environment for every American family," a goal that *Trends* noted was first set in the nation's 1949 housing law—"with guarantees of equal access to all housing, new and existing."[4]

Here was an organization that might provide deeper insight to aid those working in Indiana. Before going to the New York meeting, however, a representative of the Committee on Special Housing called upon a former professional staff member of the president's committee. What was his view of NCDH? Was it a meaningful force in fact? What was the quality of its staff? What help could the project reasonably expect? The answer was, "Expect nothing, for they have nothing to give. They talk a good talk, but that is all. There are good staff members, and they are sharp; but for your project, I would expect nothing. It doesn't offer a grand design. It's a little too simple."

The former staff member was thanked. His remarks dampened some earlier enthusiasm regarding the trip to New York, but his opinion was not going to interfere with objective discussion. These were the views of only one man, and they might have reflected possible chagrin with the president's committee that he had just left.[5]

The offices of the NCDH were not auspicious. In their second floor walk-up a black receptionist called a white girl who brought two Indianapolis visitors to a pleasant, rather stout lady who had what appeared to be a strong southern accent and was the director of information and publications for NCDH. She said, "Mr. Wood will not be present at the meeting. Governor Rockefeller needed him for a conference; but do tell us about your project while we eat our sandwiches." So she, Reitman, and a black official from FHA ate while the Indiana representatives talked. It was a futile session. The position of the director of information seemed to be that it is the standard of equality here and now that the NCDH wants, not fragmented, hidden programs that do not loudly proclaim the proposition that "fair housing exists." She implied that there was nothing really new in the FHA program, and the proposed corporate program was of the same quality. "Why, didn't you hear of the Urban Coalition? Corporations are intimately involved in furthering open housing."

The NCDH is committed to a grand strategy that it calls "thinking big," but it professes a fundamental concern with grass roots action. It is an organization, funded in part by other national organizations, with headquarters in a megapolis. One of its founders in 1950 and later a prime target of its criticism was Dr. Robert Weaver, secretary of HUD. The NCDH is not modest in its statement of policy carried in each issue by *Trends,* "The National Committee is a non-profit public interest organization working to achieve conditions under which every American family secures a decent home in an integrated living environment."[6] The Indiana plan had made the fatal mistake of not offering integration but rather a free housing market.

There is question as to whether the NCDH recognizes any limitations or even contradictions in its stated goal. It speaks in terms of "an adequate and expanding supply of new housing for low and moderate-income families widely dispersed throughout metropolitan areas."[7] Discussion, "thinking big," analyses of existing programs, and the promotion of new ventures are part of the NCDH approach. It responded to the need for local, positive approaches by describing the establishment of Metropolitan Fair Housing Centers patterned along lines similar to the Denver Plan that couples use of a large, professional staff with the self-interest involvement of the community power structure, that is, the real estate industry, the large employers, the poor, and the news media.[8]

In many ways the Denver Plan parallels the Indianapolis program, particularly in its efforts to work within the community by involving pertinent groups in activities designed to eventually take over the committee's function and keep a free housing market operable in the area. Apart from size and financial backing, a notable difference between the programs is Indianapolis' relatively stronger emphasis on direct approach to the real estate business.[9]

The NCDH also has widely discussed, in literature and in the conference held with the committee representatives, the Open City

Plan, a plan that in theory and practice is a contrast to the Denver program. In New York City where the Open City Plan is operative, no large amount of time is spent involving the real estate industry, bankers, and other representatives of the business community. The crux of Open City is "assertion of the right to move."[10] Together whites and blacks seek housing through direct confrontation with the seller or renter of property.

Much NCDH time is spent viewing and commenting upon the federal government, its laws, Congress, administrative agencies, and the courts. The message of the NCDH is that new legislation may help. As an organization it endorsed a federal fair housing law and even argued in the courts that the Thirteenth and Fourteenth Amendments to the Constitution provide a basis for federal intervention.[11] But why not enforce existing law whether it is in the form of statute, regulation, or court order? Even new laws must be enforced.[12] This was not being done. There was official disregard for law, and it emanated from the Department of Housing and Urban Development. "From its central office to its regional and local offices [HUD] is replete with officials who are out of sympathy with the nondiscriminatory policy and objectives of the Administration and who are unwilling to implement the responsibilities imposed upon them by Executive Order 11063 and Title VI of the Civil Rights Act of 1964."[13]

From the NCDH, the final answer was simple, "Fire them."[14] Here was a response that was in measured step with the new militancy. Here, too, was a response that blended well with the NCDH objective of housing integration everywhere and now, not later. Here was a strident position that the NCDH could afford in its second floor walk-up, isolated in a megapolis, responsible only to a conglomerate grouping of national organizations removed to some extent from the people. NCDH's principal value appears to be that of a conduit of dialogue hopefully leading to a miracle drug for city illnesses rather than as an organizational warehouse of answers for individual ailments.

In an NCDH conference report of April 13 and 14, 1967, Senator Hart spoke candidly of open housing as it might be considered by some. "So many central city Negroes regard fair housing opportunities the way they look at the European travel ads in glossy magazines—nice to think about, but far too remote a possibility to relate to seriously."[15] From the vantage point of Indianapolis, there seemed merit to the senator's comment. The Committee on Special Housing early had an applicant who described her "dream home." It was one that she felt could never be hers. But the committee found among the FHA inventory a home that satisfied the applicant's every criteria and a home that she could afford. It happened to be in an all white area. Walking through the home, stunned, the Negro applicant turned to the committee worker and said quietly, "This is my dream home. It is everything I wanted, but I can't take it. I'm frightened, not of the white neighbors, just frightened."

Individual stories dramatized for the Committee on Special Housing, the measure of truth in the statement of Senator Hart. A large, spacious, and relatively expensive FHA home was available in an all white middle-income area contiguous with the ghetto. In every respect, save one, it satisfied the needs of a displaced Negro purchaser. He would not buy though his need was great. "It's a great home, but I don't want it. I know what will happen to this neighborhood in a few years. It's going to be all black, and I don't want my kids growing up in that kind of a neighborhood." Was this a man who had rejected the black community? What had he become in his desire to be "safe in a secure neighborhood," as he put it?

For others, there was fear in how they would be received in a white neighborhood. Without qualification they would state: "We don't mind living in a white neighborhood." Then they would add, "So long as half of the people are Negro." Why did half have to be Negro? Why couldn't most of the neighborhood be white? Said one thirty-five year old Negro wife and mother, "I wouldn't be comfortable. I'd feel that I'd have to keep up with everyone. My home would have to be the best on the block. Everything would always have to be tidy and clean, otherwise the neighbors might say something. And, I wouldn't be sure how my kids would be treated. No, I'd be more comfortable among my own people."[16]

Those urging black communities under black control within the United States feel history favors their cause. There are ghetto walls built on racism every bit as thick and lasting as the most durable mortar and brick. If there are black people foolish enough to scale the walls, that is their choice once they are warned, say the black power advocates. Within the walls, however, organizations and their staffs will fuse as one, controlled by and in the interests of blacks. Whites may play a supportive organizational role but no more.[17]

Gone are the "color-blind" days of the Student Non-Violent

Coordinating Committee (SNCC) and CORE. Reference to multiracial composition has been removed from CORE's constitution.[18] Some have urged the additional step of expelling its white members.[19] Stokeley Carmichael has written for SNCC, "Many [volunteers] have come seeing 'no difference in color': they have come 'color-blind.' The black organizations do not need this kind of idealism which borders on paternalism. White people working in SNCC homes understood this. There are white lawyers who defend black civil rights workers in court and white activists who support indigenous black movements across the country. Their function is not to lead or to set policy or to attempt to define black people to black people. Their role is supportive."[20] Add this to the words of CORE leader James Farmer:[21]

> No organization was so aggressively color-blind [as the Congress on Racial Equality], so ideologically committed to the utter irrelevance of race. . . . If only the races could get to know each other—living, working, playing in each other's sight—what purpose would there be to note a man's race? We told uplifting stories to each other and to the world.

> . . . yet today these sentiments seem to me to be somewhat out of touch with the real lives and the real needs of the Negro community—and inappropriate, even, to the real task of our movement.

The call for black power was not lost on the hitherto integration-oriented Urban League and even the late Dr. King. The significance of black power was felt at the August 1967 convention of the Southern Christian Leadership Conference. Large placards decked the walls. On them was inscribed "black is beautiful and it is so beautiful to be black."[22] For the Urban League, pledged to ghetto programs on a priority basis, Young earlier made clear that while dedicated to bringing the black into mainstream America, his organization's policies and programs "relate to other civil rights groups in a positive manner" and "if we obviously differ we will not work together."[23]

For those national organizations with predominantly black members, open housing did not stand high on the schedule of goals. Indeed, there was strong logic that dictated a counter policy, the preservation of the ghetto. Open housing found its adherents in predominantly white organizations such as the NCDH, or in men like Father Groppi of

Milwaukee who may have understood the price the white community would pay for failing to open.[24] But even from these groups, the Committee on Special Housing could expect little help. Total answers seemed needed from organizational proponents, and those concerned with the committee were interested only in a free housing market that might not affect the life of the ghetto. The organizations were program oriented. Those concerned with the committee focused mainly upon individual problems of a very specific nature.

Local Situation

What, it was asked, is the measure of national civil rights organizational strength applied locally? The answer, in part, rests in examining the direction of Indianapolis black leadership. What was found solved nothing. When the city council held an evening meeting in May 1968 in a black inner-city high school to hear grievances, only six citizens were present. Two months earlier when another inner-city neighborhood meeting was held to discuss needed housing improvements, only thirty of several hundred residents were present. Among them was Charles (Snooky) Hendricks, chairman of the Radical Action Project. Garbed in African hat and coat, Hendricks asked where the money for improvement was coming from and who would receive it. Then he added, "We want the white man to start accepting us for what we are."[25] He said no more.

In Indianapolis, anyway, black power has not become centralized. Only the old-line ward heeler could command anything approaching power. Such is the story of the late Joseph M. Howard, lawyer and onetime municipal court judge. He "was the prime local example of the white boss in a black ward. Wizened, red-faced and terse, he carried in his pockets the keys to Democratic patronage jobs, to escape hatches in the police courts and to the right numbers on the backs of voting machines. . . . He could deliver about 3,000 votes in the 12th Ward for a primary and 5,000 to 8,000 in a wider area for a general election, Democrats say."[26]

Today in Indianapolis no one can "deliver" the black vote. This the Democratic county chairman readily admits. "You need an issue. You can't deliver unless you get them out of the house to the polls."[27] But who is there to articulate the manifold needs of the black community? In Indianapolis, the political party heads often look to two men, Dr. Frank P. Lloyd, research director at one of the city's largest hospitals, and state Senator Patrick E. Chavis, Jr., a lawyer who still maintains his office in the heart of the black community. When Doctor Lloyd was asked if black leadership exists, his answer was, "There is no real leadership of the Negro community generally as yet, though there is a beginning." This was his answer despite the fact that CORE, SNCC, NAACP, SCLC, Urban League, and the Black Muslims are represented in Indianapolis.[28]

The lack of central leadership does not deny the existence of points of power. Hendricks might have seemed a lonely figure at the neighborhood meeting, but he is an associate at the College Room, a place frequented by young blacks, and to them his words have meaning. Doctor Lloyd does not confine his activities to the hospital or the white community. He is active in supporting several business ventures directed toward blacks. Recently he and others acquired an FM station that had only marginal success in classical music format. Renamed WTLC (With Tender Loving Care), the station holds an enormous black audience. A black public relations executive at the start of the committee's program said, "If you want to attract young blacks, get material to WTLC. They reach the market."

Many black inner-city ministers individually hold influence over their congregations. Although several of these ministers frequently carry other full-time jobs to support themselves, they have taken on an added load of forming a Baptist Alliance. They have not hesitated to address themselves to all relevant issues, including housing, schools, welfare, and police relations. Their ineffectiveness comes not from the lack of dollars but in their staying power. The problems are so numerous that they seem unable to set a table of priorities. When the issue is specific, however, and their action well timed, the inner-city Baptist ministers have demonstrated effectiveness. In May 1968, after a series of alleged incidents of police brutality, they forced a meeting with the thirty-five-year-old Republican mayor of Indianapolis and his young chief of police. The conference, marked by religious singing, was worthwhile. Henceforth police brutality charges would be subject to prompt public hearing and a kind of review by the Indianapolis Human Rights Commission. One minister said, "This is the first time we ever left this place [the City-County Building] with anything."

The Baptist Alliance was not alone when the ministers marched. Their efforts were heralded to the black community by the widely-read black newspaper, the *Indianapolis Recorder;* and, in the moment of crisis, they accepted help from the local Urban League headed by Sam Jones, an articulate, well-educated black born in Mississippi and determined to have the black achieve full citizenship in an open society. Before going to the mayor's office, "Brother Sam" was called to sit on the podium with the ministers to formulate issues and demands.[29]

The black leadership in Indianapolis, such as it was in 1968, had not fused. It had not been centralized. It was difficult even to say that the existing power points reached all or most of the black community and if they did, that significant influence could be exerted. There was no grand design emanating from a single organization and accepted by the black mass. There were, however, people and organizations greatly concerned by the multiplying problems of the ghetto. They could see the problems as they assumed reality, and they sought practical, pragmatic answers. They asked for help in finding decent homes if those existing had to be destroyed. They asked for training and jobs for the unemployed, good schools, and police protection instead of police persecution.

To the Committee on Special Housing one black response, typical of most, was, "I could care less whether I live in a white neighborhood. Just show me a home I can afford and if it's one that I like, I'll buy it." One Baptist minister after another repeated that message. The committee's executive director answered, "Here are the homes. Here are more than a hundred FHA homes in areas where there are good schools and good police protection. Here are homes at fair prices and good financing. Do you want them? Would your congregants and friends want them?"

The answer was that if the facts were as stated and there was no deception or trickery the houses would be wanted. Not once was the cry of self-segregation raised. Not once was the need for integration stressed. No note of fear was sounded if a black family moved into a white neighborhood. There was only amazement that homes actually were available.

On a cold winter day in a small church with a coal-burning furnace, Allen Dale and a committee representative were permitted to speak to the Baptist Alliance. The meeting began with spontaneous group singing and prayers. Then Dale and the representative spoke to the ministers. They spoke only of being able to help. The group was told to bring the displaced families, see the homes that were available, and decide for themselves whether there was help "here and now, not in the future."

The group's response was "amen." As Dale and the committee representative left, eight ministers of the forty present brought names of potential buyers scrawled on paper. Some asked if the committee could help them too. Every person listed was contacted and shown homes within forty-eight hours.

In a sense the way to the Baptist Alliance was paved by the *Recorder.* Although the *Recorder,* a weekly Indianapolis newspaper, was called "irresponsible" by some "responsible" organizations, it gave substantial coverage to the committee's programs. Mrs. Pat W. Stewart, one of the *Recorder*'s key reporters, investigated the committee's work. In an eight-week period, six front-page stories were printed. Skeptical at first, the newspaper later endorsed the committee's activity.

On January 20, 1968, the *Recorder*'s front-page headline was "Plan Offers Repossessed FHA Homes to Displaced Local Persons."[30] The lead paragraph of the story, which included pictures of FHA homes, read: "Through a unique undertaking of the Committee on Special Housing, open housing could become a reality in Indianapolis and residents who heretofore thought it was impossible for them to purchase a home may find they are able to reach the homeowner status. The committee represents a large segment of the community and membership is open to all interested citizens . . . [the committee] stated that integration is not of paramount interest [but] acknowledges that it will come about since the majority of the homes involved are in white neighborhoods and the major portion of displaced persons are Negroes. The Committee points out that the main concern is that people can go wherever they want to through this purely economic approach."[31]

The story gave full details on the kinds of homes held by FHA, including location, size and price range, and financing terms. The article concluded by giving the FHA phone number and the name of the person to call. The story and others like it brought results. In about four weeks, six families had selected homes. Long delayed organizational inquiry began. Although the FHA director had informed all qualified groups personally of the acquired property program at its inception, only several weeks later was there reaction. In the same week the CAAP worker gave notice of his impending induction into the army, the Urban League, whose staff carefully reads the *Recorder,* and the Indiana Civil Rights Commission individually visited the FHA offices.

First came the Urban League delegation, led by its associate director, Mrs. Nellie Gustafson, known and respected by the white community, white herself, and anxious to operate within a total community matrix to the greatest extent possible.[32] With her were two elderly but lively white ladies. They had "come to learn," not from Allen Dale but from James Brown, the head of the FHA Counseling Service, a black who had worked closely with the committee. Brown telephoned a committee member, "You may want to sit in on this meeting. This group may be helpful."

Many months before, the committee had two meetings with Urban League representatives to explain the program. They were polite, even receptive; the program might tie into the Urban League's Fair Listing Service, a referral service scheduled to be announced. There was nothing to be gained, however, until the Urban League established its Fair Listing Service. No more was heard until Brown's call came.

"Well," said Mrs. Gustafson, as the committee representative entered the FHA office, "I see your little project is started." The reality of the committee's work and its relationship with the FHA was made clear to the visitors. A program existed; properties were displayed on a map for all to see; the CAAP volunteer was visible; and calls were being received. Before leaving Mrs. Gustafson said, "The Urban League is in a position to cooperate with FHA and the committee. As requests come in under our Fair Listing Service, we will refer them where relevant either to FHA or the committee." To help stimulate the flow of applicants, Mrs. Gustafson promised to introduce the committee to a prominent black minister who, because of highway construction, had moved his church from the ghetto to suburban northwest Indianapolis.[33] He might have names of congregants or their friends still locked in the inner city. Arrangments were made to meet two days later. The minister acted; from his pulpit and in the church bulletin he spoke of the committee. As a result there were promptly about ten new applicants.

Next came the Indiana Civil Rights Commission, represented by its executive director, Harold Hatcher, and two of his professional staff, Orville Gardner and Mrs. Julia Fangmeier, who held the title of consultants. Hatcher's reaction to the reality of the committee's program was, to say the least, positive. From this lean, quiet man came the kind of help most needed. Speaking in a slow drawl, he said, "I think this program is one to which the Commission could give support. The interest of the Commission is integration. It's our function, in part, to help Negroes move into white areas and to encourage their acceptance. For the first time, the property exists to achieve these ends." Gardner was assigned to work with the committee on a full-time basis; Mrs. Fangmeir, part-time.

Fortune seemed to grace the Committee on Special Housing. Mature, seasoned professionals were to constitute the committee's staff as the CAAP volunteer left. The Urban League increased its offer of help. It made available office space and a telephone line answered at all times: "Hello. This is the Committee on Special Housing." Both the Urban League and the Civil Rights Commission agreed that even with such support, the committee still was to function as an independent entity. As organizations, they were only committee affiliates. Hatcher responded by assigning on a full-time basis an administrative assistant to answer the phone, establish a file system, and draw maps to show committee activity.

Responsible organizations were becoming deeply and actively involved in committee work. Provision was being made against violence, but not at the loss of individual freedom of choice. Applicants were shown homes and they were told the cost of buying and maintaining homes, but the choice was theirs, not that of the committee. This the Civil Rights Commission and the Urban League accepted; if a black wanted to live in a black neighborhood, so be it. The committee would show all homes that met the applicant's price range as determined by the FHA Counseling Service.

Once a black family selected a home in a white neighborhood, however, the Civil Rights Commission, through the very person who effected the sale, either Gardner or Mrs. Fangmeier, would attempt to smooth the way toward neighborhood acceptance. On moving day, they would be present. Neighbors would be visited in advance and given brief biographies of the newcomers. Two to three weeks after a family moved in, volunteers would conduct follow-up interviews to determine whether special problems had been encountered and, whether the committee could be of further service. If there were difficulties, the Urban League with its social service contacts would be called in.

In anticipation of difficulties, the committee met with Griffin Crump, executive director of the Indianapolis Human Rights Commission. He, too, wanted to help, but just didn't have available staff for use as committee workers. Nevertheless, Crump marked on a map those areas of the city considered to be of violence and high violence potential. He asked for the names of those blacks moving into white blocks so that increased police patrol might be ordered by the city's special public relations unit. "I don't know whether we can leave this to regular police patrol," he said.[34]

The committee only felt warned, not hindered by the large danger zones drawn by Crump. Black families did choose homes within the danger areas.[35] Regular, backup procedures were instituted. There was no violence nor significant incident during the first seven months of the committee's operations. Provision had been made to lessen the possibility of violence. Help came locally, not from national groups whose approach bore slight relevance to the reaction of those in the inner city affected by the need for homes.

For the committee, the immediate task was the need to demonstrate the validity of the FHA acquired property program. Then, maybe, an approach to VA and its inventory and perhaps even an avenue to the corporations would open.

The FHA acquired property program was national in its operation; it was embodied in formal regulations available and meaningful to most American urban areas. The Committee on Special Housing had devised a simple mechanism for implementing the FHA program, which, if successful, might provide a means for establishing a free housing market. Despite the potential for broad application, neither the FHA program nor the committee mechanism seemed worth study by those groups concerned with open housing, at least to the extent that the National Committee Against Discrimination in Housing is representative of them.

3
The FHA Counseling Service

A necessary part of the committee's operations was its close relationship with the then newly established FHA Counseling Service. Operative at the time in fifteen cities including Indianapolis, the service was designed to aid any individual in finding housing. Toward this end listings of homes for sale or rent were accepted from licensed real estate agents only. Every listing accepted had to be on a nondiscriminatory basis. The Counseling Service was to determine what the family could afford. Then in the light of that family's stated preference it was to show them available listings within their credit reach. Interviews were to be arranged, one at a time, between the listing broker and the interested applicant.

It was clear, however, that the service was not to impinge upon the real estate broker. Indeed, so carefully did FHA adhere to this position that before the committee program, it did not even make its own acquired listings available to those seeking counseling. The rationale seemed to be that the acquired properties were legally open to all, and, as a matter of policy, brokers were to submit bids on behalf of buyers. Any intervention by FHA might encumber this agency-broker relationship. The assistant commissioner in charge of field operations said, "The counseling service is intended to augment the existing fine counseling services provided by real estate brokers. . . . I can't emphasize too strongly the point that the housing counseling service is designed to work with real estate brokers, not to bring government into competition with them, or to preempt the very valuable service they perform for families who are seeking to buy a home."

The committee's efforts were designed to permit consumers of housing to reach decisions in the context of a free housing market. As consumers they were to be offered reasonable alternatives either in the purchase or rental of property. They were to be given the necessary information to know fully the costs of housing and what they could afford in the light of their income. The FHA Counseling Service seemed a proper mechanism for effecting these goals. The service knew more about FHA acquired property and financing than the committee. The same service could show committee applicants other than FHA acquired homes; it would let applicants survey those private listings of properties for sale or rent.

In carrying out its functions the service could provide a means for integrating the FHA acquired property program and its thrust toward a free housing market into the existing socioeconomic community matrix. Those dislocated as a result of government action were to be treated in all respects as consumers of housing. They were to be placed in the mainstream with other purchasers of housing, free to make choices, limited only by desire and income capacity. The FHA acquired property enlarged their range of selection and assured availability of homes throughout the community.

The FHA counselor was in a position not only to deal with applicants brought to him by the committee, but also to forward new applicants to the committee from those of the general public who were within and had an interest in the displaced persons' program. Working in tandem with a view simply to aid individuals in finding housing of their choice, the committee and FHA, it was thought, could make maximum use of the limited private listings available to the Counseling Service as well as the FHA acquired property.

To open the housing market, to make it free, the committee worked on the assumption that neither great numbers of buyers nor great numbers of sellers were required. If, for example, some blacks exercised their right to move throughout the community and entered several all white areas—and if the white community knew that what had occurred was not a sporadic effort but the result of an institutionalized program—then necessity would force restrictive selling and rental practices to change, for no area of the city could be marked safe.

The committee concentrated on its limited acquired property program. It was hoped the FHA Counseling Service would ultimately absorb the operations of the committee, which, after all, was merely seeking to make visible and real the right of people to live where they choose. Once that right was brought into actuality and once the people exercised that right, there would be no need for a committee. Through its listing service, and its own acquired property, coupled with credit counseling, FHA could do the job of institutionalizing the steps taken by the committee. A steady, though not necessarily heavy, inflow of people who could match themselves to property sprinkled throughout the urban area was needed.

Whether the Counseling Service could perform the tasks the committee thought useful depended upon the answers given to a number of questions. What role did the Federal Housing Administration assign to the Counseling Service? How much flexibility was there in the light of the Washington-imposed limitations of the new program? How did the Counseling Service enact its role? What did those served by the counselors think of their experience?

The FHA assistant commissioner in charge of field operations did not ordain the Counseling Service as a vehicle for establishing a free housing market. Despite the words and the press releases, if the measure of its desire is to be found in its commitment, it is rather difficult to determine just what Washington did want. The Counseling Service did not have a single full-time employee. Although discussion with those involved in this aspect of the FHA program clearly highlighted the necessity for using qualified personnel on a full-time basis, no job classification had been drafted either before or six months after the first Counseling Service was established. No property listing was accepted unless it came through a licensed real estate agent.

Despite these limitations the Indiana FHA director was determined to make the Counseling Service vital. A well-educated black civil servant was selected to head the unit. A former VA employee in his thirties, the counselor was told the service was his to make or break. He was given a kind of open draft by the director. Assisting him was a highly skilled mortgage credit employee. Both had other duties. Both were given the challenge to make the Counseling Service a path to the future.

The FHA director had forgotten what an old-line employee had earlier warned him—Weavers and Brownsteins come and go, but the professional staff stays on. In the final analysis, it alone shapes agency policy and action. Who knew how long the ambitious, energetic director would stay? His job was a political appointment. What would be the fate of a staff too closely identified with a director who was leaving? What would be the chance for promotion?

If there were sharp lines of authority, if there were only that sacred job description, then an ambitious counselor could be imaginative and aggressive. He could blame his deeds on what was written, on formally stated orders.

The odds were against the FHA counselor before he started. He had a difficult game to play. He had to satisfy his superior, the director, and not unduly disturb key staff figures. A person of integrity, he had to be honest with himself in the course of his dealings. He had to ask himself what safely could be done and still achieve something of value.

The listings given by a few Realtors and some Realtists often were inferior. An Indiana Civil Rights Commission survey in March of 1968 indicated that seventy-five to eighty percent of the homes listed with the service were in black or changing areas, but there were a few in all white neighborhoods. Through a bona fide applicant sent to FHA the committee became aware of one such listing in the exclusive Brendonwood area. The home was priced at $49,000. An appraisal by a qualified Realtor gave the home a value of not more than $40,000.

Still, the service might have impact. It did have some listings. It was in a position to educate and through cooperation with brokers to smooth the way for expeditious action in behalf of applicants. On October 13, 1967, the day after the service was established in Indianapolis, Mrs. Hill and her four children were forced to leave their home, which had been destroyed by fire. Two hours after the destruction Mrs. Hill called FHA and within an hour she was being interviewed by a counselor. Hurried credit and employment checks were made. Through a black broker a home was found and the deal was closed. That evening Mrs. Hill was in her new home. Even the assistant FHA commissioner noted this as an achievement.[1]

The committee recognized the value of the Counseling Service. It discovered, however, that no in-depth studies had been contemplated to compile data with which to evaluate the service's functions. All the service sought was a one-line postcard from the broker with whom an appointment had been made for an applicant. With the assistance of a research sociologist, Dr. James Hawkins, a full questionnaire was devised for computer analysis.[2] If service applicants gave permission at the time of their interview with the FHA counselors, the committee planned to visit them later and talk with them about the role of the service, how they regarded the action of the brokers, and how they felt about the Counseling Service. The Indiana FHA director indicated a desire to cooperate and learn. The assistant FHA commissioner in Washington, D.C., insisted on the postcard only.

Not everything was lost. The committee had applicants of its own who seemed to fit the assistant commissioner's description of low-income, inner-city residents. These applicants either did not qualify for the committee's program or appeared before formal approval had been given to the acquired property program. They were sent by the committee, twenty in number, to the Counseling Service and were later interviewed. FHA could not impose a cloak of confidentiality.

Due to the limitations of sample size, computer review was not feasible. Considering the limitations of the study, those portions of the questionnaire amenable to review were examined closely not to determine statistical significance, but rather to check the committee's theoretical and empirical observations.

The Counseling Service gave as the "best example of a person making effective use of what FHA had to offer," the story of Mrs. Tate, a fifty-two-year-old black school teacher, the provider for her family. Though bitter because a factory had bought the home she rented and the rest of the entire block for a warehouse, Mrs. Tate thought she found help through the Counseling Service. She wanted a ten-room house in the same general neighborhood for herself, her two children, and her partially disabled father. She told the counselor that she could not pay any substantial sum of money. She had no equity in her former home since she had been renting. The counselor showed her a picture of a single home that appeared to meet her needs. The white realty company that handled the property was called and an appointment made.

The agent, a white man, came to Mrs. Tate's home. He was forty-five minutes late. The property seen was, in Mrs. Tate's words, run-down. She said, "There were squirrels sticking their heads out in the eaves. The structure was out of line. I had a closed-in feeling. There were too many partitions. The yard was in terrible condition. It would have taken $2,000 to $3,000 to get the place in decent shape."

The agent did show Mrs. Tate other houses, "but he didn't understand my problem." To Mrs. Tate that seemed to mean not that the agent was unfriendly or even unsympathetic. The agent seemed to think that Mrs. Tate desired to buy a home from a white person. The agent was willing to accomodate Mrs. Tate but her desire was not to buy a home from a white person but rather to buy one that met her family's need. The race of the previous owner was immaterial. The agent was of no further value to her.

The house Mrs. Tate finally decided upon was one that she found on her own. It was located in the neighborhood where she lived. She thought the price of the home, $13,500, fair, even though a joist was broken and the fireplace had partly settled.

To Mrs. Tate, however, the Counseling Service had been most valuable. Through expert guidance she was able to determine what she could afford. Indeed, before she bought the home, she called the service and asked whether, in view of the information that they had, she could handle the asking price. Having determined Mrs. Tate's financial capacity, FHA was willing to extend a guarantee in terms of insurance on the home, thereby allowing financing. Probably, however, the signal contribution of FHA was the sense of security she derived from being assisted by someone who cared. She had only glowing remarks for the counselor, for his concern, and for his desire to serve.

Yet, for all this there remained some rather substantial questions. One point was developed by Mrs. Tate herself. When asked how the services could be improved, she said, "I'm concerned. I'm an older person, and I wonder what will happen to the home in the event that anything happens to me. I can't buy insurance for myself. Do you think that FHA could help me?"

By telling her that she could afford a home of the type purchased, Mrs. Tate was brought to a marginal point in terms of her purchasing power. This is not to condemn the Counseling Service for the assistance rendered. Mrs. Tate would have sought a home with or without the Counseling Service. The more fundamental question is whether more sophisticated financial assistance could have been rendered. Could the title to the home have been taken in the name of Mrs. Tate's son who was in college and working, thereby affording the possibility of obtaining insurance?

Still another problem was presented as a result of the interview. The Counseling Service assumed that Mrs. Tate was more or less wed to her neighborhood. Yet when Mrs. Tate was asked, "If you could have obtained the same kind of house for $1,000 less in a white neighborhood, would you have taken it?" the answer given was yes. In the course of discussion relating to her answer Mrs. Tate explained, "I assume that I have to pay a premium if I move into a white neighborhood. This I am unwilling to do."

Even accepting the nature of discriminatory practices in the real estate market in Indianapolis, the FHA could have provided Mrs. Tate with a reasonable alternative if she could have access to FHA acquired property. At the time of her interview, December 7, 1967, FHA held a home comparable to that which she purchased. The selling price of this home was $8,500, $5,000 less than the one she bought. This, of course, does not include the then more favorable interest rates that could have been made available at that time to Mrs. Tate through FNMA financing (six and three quarters percent for a thirty year mortgage) as contrasted to the conventional financing that she obtained (seven percent for a twenty-five year mortgage).

Mrs. Tate concluded the interview by saying, "I have told everybody in my neighborhood about the FHA Counseling Service. Curiously, they don't seem to believe me. They can't believe that anything as good as this can exist. People in my neighborhood are very bitter."[3]

In some respects the facts relating to Mrs. Tate were typical. Most of the individuals interviewed were between twenty and forty-five. Over half of the families had between one and four children in grade school. Their desire for better schools, better play areas, and companions for their children were significant reasons for seeking a home. For instance, one couple stated the neighborhood in which they were then renting "is very run-down. The school children have to cross the railroad tracks to get to school and there is only one guard, although the teachers sometimes do watch them."

At the time they sought counseling, most people were renting. After discussing their situation with the FHA counselor, however, all but two decided to try to buy a home.

Half of those questioned said they wished to move for personal reasons. Eight of the twenty individuals were moving because of public project displacement.[4] Again, over half of those interviewed felt they wanted to move quickly either for personal reasons or because of a forced deadline. Only two wanted to remain in the neighborhood where they were living because of friends and relatives. The actual neighborhood was of no concern to three families. Twelve families, however, stated that they wanted to move out of their neighborhoods for reasons that ranged from "I wish to be near my employment" to the frank statement that "the neighborhood I live in is very similar to a ghetto. . . . It's a bad atmosphere for children." Most of those seeking a new neighborhood seemed to be looking for a better environment in which to raise their families.

When the applicants went to the counselor, only three already had homes in mind. Two of the three did not tell the counselor about the homes because "the counselor seemed too busy talking" or because the individual realized after discussion with the counselor that the home was too expensive for him. The rest of those interviewed had no particular home in mind on their visit to FHA.

The FHA counselor, however, during the first discussion with at least twelve clients, reached a point of discussing specific homes for sale. Because of the design of the Counseling Service, as contrasted to the acquired property program, an appointment is made with a broker for an individual to see only one home at a time, thus minimizing competition between brokers over clients. Most of those who actually made appointments to see homes were disappointed that they could choose (from photographs) to see only one. The obvious reason for this disappointment was the preference for a greater choice. One man said, "There were other homes I wanted to see. In order to look at them, I had to take time off from work. I could do this once, but I couldn't do it several times." In its effort to satisfy the real estate industry, FHA was paying a price. The benefits of the service appeared to be watered down. Applicants are tied to job schedules; they are not free to come and go without loss of needed income.

Only six of those interviewed made appointments with real estate brokers through the Counseling Service; five looked at homes; the sixth met with the broker but found the home locked. On the whole, the six seemed to have had a good experience with the broker. Only one attempted initial purchase of the home he first saw, and he was successful. The six represented only a quarter of those interviewed. Their fairly favorable experience with the brokers, however, and their desire to continue their search for homes to buy is some evidence of the good use to which such counseling could be put, especially if it were increased in scope.

As a matter of fact, answers to questions designed to measure continuing enthusiasm in the search for a home indicated clearly that to the extent service was rendered it was helpful. For instance, over three-fourths of those interviewed planned to keep looking for a home to buy. Only one person had given up. Well over half of those interviewed planned to keep in touch with the FHA to obtain further assistance.

There also were positive reactions to the Counseling Service itself. Eighty-three percent said the counselors understood their situation well; ninety-four percent felt the counselors wanted to be helpful; and all believed the counselors were friendly. Seventy-seven percent said they would recommend the service to others and thirty-three percent of the respondents had already made such recommendations.

Could the Counseling Service be improved? About one-quarter of those interviewed said the service needed no improvement. A single theme of suggestion, however, presented itself in the remaining replies; more service was needed. As to what kind of expansion was called for, thoughts ranged from the personal views, "They should keep in touch with me," or the "counselor could have called back," to the community-interested response,"They need better communication so more people could be aware of its existence—better publicity."

The service has potential as seen by the applicants. "They have the experience to tell a person what he can afford rather than just asking what price range he is interested in." The counselor can give "more information on hidden costs which might affect a person's reaching a decision whether to purchase or rent. For example, the point system, I felt, was not adequately explained." But the potential is yet to be developed.

Some individuals indicated that they would have liked a larger choice of homes. Some, like the gentleman who was told he could not afford the down payment on a home, said the service could be improved "if they could have some kind of service to help those who are in need of it . . . to find short cuts or ways to help with financial needs and so forth. Those who can afford it, can go to a Realtor. For the classes of people they should be helping they should make more of an effort to help than they are doing."

Despite limitations imposed by Washington, the Indianapolis FHA Counseling Service was operative. The sampling interviews, though few in number, pointed toward what could be achieved. For the people served, here at least was an opportunity to learn and perhaps to gain hope. Within tight boundaries was an opportunity to buy. Depth of service, however, was lacking, not out of employee desire, but agency ambivalence. Also, the housing market to which the applicants could be exposed was not open but closed. By agency fiat, the service accepted only what the brokers submitted, and the brokers were bound up in their own restrictive marketing practices.

The Counseling Service in Indianapolis kept no tally of where applicants moved. No racial density map was maintained. It was enough that homes were found. Here, too, the figures tell the story of an agency limited by many external factors and the story of that new class it has been pledged to serve. The upward-moving, low-income families coming through the Indianapolis Counseling Service from November 1967 through March 1968 numbered 357. Of these, twenty-three found housing. The Committee on Special Housing had been responsible for twelve of the twenty-three.

Nationally, Indianapolis production compared most favorably with that of other FHA offices. During the same period (November to March) "nearly 4,500 families and individuals who were having problems finding decent housing they could afford have been help-ed . . . through the housing counseling service," according to the assistant FHA commissioner for field operations.[5] By "helped" he meant that 4,500 applicants were interviewed. The crucial question is, how many found housing? "As a result of FHA's guidance, 165 families who came in for interviews are now buying their own homes. Others have moved into better rental housing. . . . The service has been especially beneficial to members of minority groups who comprise nearly two-thirds of those who have been personally interviewed. Some 362 applicants from minority groups have either rented apartments or bought their own homes as a result of the service."[6]

While so many of the people the committee interviewed indicated their need or hope for even more of this service, less than ten percent of those personally interviewed on a national basis found housing, either rental or purchase, through the Counseling Service. Why? What about those who were "helped"? What was the quality of the housing found? Was it any better than the best the inner city could offer? Could it really be? There was FHA's long established relationship with the real estate industry, known and workable. There was but a new, even embryonic relationship between FHA and the low-income consumer of homes. The Counseling Service did not keep a record of where people moved, although this was a vital element of information.

Segregation in Indianapolis

Segregation had left its mark on the Indianapolis community through action of the city council many years before. A "segregation of the races" law was enacted as a zoning ordinance with but one dissenting vote in 1926, the high days of the white-robed Ku-Klux-Klan in Indiana.[7]

The Klan had made itself felt. Eighteen elementary schools were set aside for blacks, and Crispus Attucks High School was constructed for black use only. Black children in 1926, even those a few months from graduation, were forcibly withdrawn from schools they had been attending and herded into segregated facilities. Until the time came when Klan power was broken,[8] whites were not to live in black areas, and blacks were not to live in white areas, "except on the written consent of a majority of the persons of the opposite race inhabiting such community."[9] Mayor John L. Duvall spoke for many in his message approving the ordinance. His words were soft; they had the spirit of rationality[10]

This ordinance is in the nature of a zoning measure. The tenor of the Act seems to be to preclude the possibility of either our White citizens or our Negro citizens obtaining any advantage, each over the other, in the matter of residence. I have discussed the measure with hundreds of our citizens, both White and Negro, and I have found many for the measure among both classes. It is likewise true that I have found much opposition toward it.

I do not believe there is any intention on the part of your honorable body to attempt to discriminate against any class, either White or Negro as such, in the matter of the establishment of a home-residence. It would naturally follow that if the City of Indianapolis is to continue to grow and prosper, that we should have in effect certain zoning ordinances. . . . In this connection I do not believe that it is amiss for me to quote Booker T. Washington, that great leader whose memory is so dear to the hearts and minds of the Negro race, who once said: 'In all things that are purely social we can be as separate as the fingers, yet one as the hand in all things essential to mutual progress.'

To those good folks and loyal American citizens who oppose this measure, I feel that if they study the Ordinance with an open mind and as the patriotic Americans they are, with an interest in their race, their home, their family, and their future, they will hail with delight this step toward the solution of a problem that has long caused deep thought and serious study by members of both our races.

In conclusion, I wish to say that the Mayor is signing this Ordinance, firm in the belief that it meets with the approval of the great mass of our people, in the interest of peace and happiness on earth and good will toward mankind, ever bearing in mind his sacred duty to the people he represents, regardless of race, color, or creed, and the supreme obligation that we are under the Almighty God.

Though the policy of segregation was broken by 1968, the act of segregation remained. Now given a choice what would blacks in Indianapolis opt for? More precisely, what did those coming into contact with the Committee on Special Housing want? In three sets of interviews conducted from December 1967 to June 1968 a sampling of forty-five blacks, committee applicants, were questioned—in advance of their choosing any property for possible purchase—about their preferences regarding neighborhood racial balance; their estimate of the relative cost of comparable housing in white and in black areas; and, finally, what they would do if they could find comparable housing at fair prices in all white neighborhoods.[11]

Only three of those interviewed wanted to live in an all black neighborhood as contrasted to six who would pick an all white neighborhood. Six again would select a neighborhood that was one-quarter black, as against two who would choose one that was three-quarters black. The largest number, sixteen, or thirty-seven percent of those interviewed, would select a neighborhood that was half black. Finally, ten, twenty-three percent, said race was not the significant question in choosing a home; they were concerned with the quality of schools, transportation, and proximity to employment.[12]

The blacks interviewed were not inclined toward separation of the races. The zoning ordinance of 1926, which legalized the black ghetto and structured a black school system, would not have been acceptable to the majority of those who came before the Committee on Special Housing. Yet it must be stressed that the likelihood of a neighborhood holding at half black, half white was remote even in 1968. In Indianapolis the tipping point, the level at which whites—it is after all the whites who make the exodus—leave is far less than fifty percent. Supersaturation is more like thirty percent.

Of the forty-five interviewed, some sixty-four percent felt that a black would have to pay more for the same home than a white purchaser.[13] The interviewed group were asked what they would choose if they could buy the home of their choice either in an all black or an all white neighborhood at the same price. The replies were equally divided into thirds. One-third selected an all white area. Asked why, some answers were: "The area would be kept up better. . . . Often in a white area the trash man takes more care. . . . Environment is as good as the things in it. . . . Part of my nature is to be different. Race is used as a crutch. . . . The neighborhood is friendlier. Whites try to help you if they see you are trying."

Almost without exception the reason for choosing a white neighborhood was not related to being able to live next to a white. Those who showed a preference for a white neighborhood did so because of the qualities they thought that neighborhood would possess. Their concern was their home, not color. And again the rationale underlying preference for black neighborhoods had less to do with wanting to live near blacks per se than wanting to live in peace. Some typical comments were "I would rather not experience the discomfort of nonacceptance. . . . In Indianapolis there would be trouble with one Negro in an all white area. . . . I would be staying too busy making things look just the same or better than my neighbors. I'd be concerned with what my neighbors would say. . . . People are friendlier in Negro areas. . . . Whites stay in their houses. . . . The kids would have someone to talk and play with. . . . I'd have less anxiety about my adjustment."

It may be that the final third of those interviewed who would have selected either black or white neighborhoods more closely focused upon the deciding factor of all the groups. Race as such was not critical to buying a home. The same hopes and fears of whites came into play. Were the schools good? Would the children have space to play? Were the homes comfortable? Was the neighborhood cared for? Was the atmosphere relaxed and reasonably friendly? One of those interviewed dismissed the race question by saying, "I prefer to talk in terms of human beings."

The committee did not view its function as pressuring any black to move into an all white neighborhood. Nor did the committee accept as an absolute judgment, preferences of any sort made in advance of experience in shopping for a home. Many blacks came to the committee insisting that any home purchased must have a basement. This is what they were familiar with in the inner city. Suburbia had no basements except for homes priced above $25,000. Some real estate agents cited this as a factor in causing a self-imposed ghetto, saying "We give them what they want." The committee did not accept the rationalization.

Mr. and Mrs. Murray, highway displacees, insisted that they needed a home with a basement. The committee showed the few properties that met their requirements. Then a committee member took the Murrays to the eastern edge of the city where they went through a comfortable, new ranch home within walking distance to Murray's job. The committee representative was told, "Maybe we don't need a basement." The Murrays bought the home in the all white area.

The Murrays bought according to their desires and their felt needs. In their view, neither local nor state government had been of value to them. What they saw in the inner city was overvalued and inadequate. Neither the real estate industry or the FHA Counseling Service working in harmony with the industry could give the Murrays a variety of choice in decent homes at fair prices. The FHA-acquired property inventory was limited but even within its limitations there was variety in house style, location, and price. Above all, there was a reasonable assurance of adequate quality for a reasonable price.

Almost in microcosm the Counseling Service could provide the potential homeowner with a basis for comparison—at least for those dislocated by government action. They could compare price, quality, and financing of private listings made available to the Counseling Service with FHA acquired property. If the price spread between comparable inner-city and FHA's own suburban properties was not too great, the applicants might select the better buy and risk white harassment, thereby opening new areas to black citizens. Finally, of course, FHA could make perfectly clear the cash outlay required of potential purchasers not only in acquiring, but in keeping a home. This is a vital function, for to keep an area open the new purchaser must have the willingness and the means to keep his home.

4
The Indiana
Civil Rights Commission

The committee was staffed primarily by professional employees of the Indiana Civil Rights Commission. They were placed with the committee on a near full-time basis; one soon accepted control over committee field operations, the critical point of committee activity where applicants were sought and introduced to the acquired property program. The commission through its commitment of manpower had the means to significantly influence the committee's development. Whatever the paper policy of the committee organizers might have been, the reality of policy would be felt in practice, in the field where the personnel of the commission were centered. To understand the nature of the commission's commitment, and perhaps judge the degree to which comparable agencies in other areas might perform the same function for a Committee on Special Housing, it is necessary to study the Indiana Civil Rights Commission itself.

The "word" was that the Indiana Civil Rights Commission was an ineffectual agency, a symbol of tokenism, a gesture to salve the social conscience and reduce pressure, nothing more. The commission had its genesis in the Indiana 1961 Fair Employment Practices Act.[1]

Designated the Fair Employment Practices Commission, given an annual budget of $60,000, and armed only with the power of compulsory process, this agency was to effect the lofty legislative goal of "full utilization of the productive resources of the State to the benefit of the State, the family and to all people of the State."[2]

With what must be considered by any standard a limited staff of five full-time professional employees, the commission was to achieve its goal by making rules and regulations; formulating policies and recommendations for the governor and the assembly; receiving, initiating, and investigating charges of discriminatory practices; creating local or statewide advisory units and conciliation councils; studying the problems of discrimination; fostering goodwill among the state's population; issuing publications that promote goodwill; discouraging discriminatory employment practices by informal means, by persuasion and conciliation; holding hearings and calling witnesses; and, finally, cooperating with educational institutions in preparing programs of learning.[3] Quite a range of activity, but it all meant little if the law is measured only in terms of ability to impose sanctions. The new commission apparently could do everything with its miniscule staff except issue orders.

Recognizing its limitations, the commission began where there might be some hope for change—within the state government itself, where thousands were employed. The state could serve as a learning experience for private employers; the citizens could see the meaning of public policy.

The state government, however, could hardly be dealt with on a singular basis. Its agencies assumed a force of their own, and, as events unfolded, the policy of the executive was not necessarily that of the legislature. The commission began slowly. It requested only that the departments of state government supply information giving the number of blacks employed and a statement of departmental hiring and promotional policy.[4]

The response to this request for statistical information was less than satisfactory. The commission felt it necessary to request an opinion from the state attorney general as to whether it could compel another state agency to produce the required information. The attorney general said the commission could compel the departments to supply the information, but did not say how the commission could compel compliance.[5] The general assembly conveniently had provided for compulsory process but had eliminated the means for enforcing an order. Given the sometimes devious nature of Indiana politics, it is doubtful this was an error of omission. Left to its own devices the commission would have failed even to obtain information from the state of which it was a part.

The agency did not fail because Governor Matthew E. Welsh chose to have it succeed. As chief executive, all major agency heads served at his pleasure. Governor Welsh called a meeting of departments. They were told "the firm policy of my administration quite early." At the suggestion of his new commission executive director the governor appointed an equal employment opportunity officer for each department. "Still," said Governor Welsh, "some of the larger departments, and, therefore, the larger employers, would not comply. I had to threaten disciplinary action before the crust was broken. But it was broken. Chief among those reluctant to comply was the highway department." The agencies were told to cooperate.

Several years later Governor Welsh estimated that about 500 blacks found office jobs under his administration. He said, "Possibly, just possibly, that figure now in 1968 might reach 1,000. Our difficulty, once we set up the program was in finding the applicants—those who qualified." The state police and the conservation department could not find "qualified" applicants. The governor simply told each agency to disregard entrance requirements and find applicants who approached stated standards. Black state police and conservation officers were then hired. Then, as the governor later said, the process of quiet mediation that characterized the new commission and its executive director had meaning and effect.

These facts are in sharp contrast to the record of the legislative branch of government where the governor can exercise but minimal influence in its hiring practices. In 1968 the legislative council employed thirty-two persons. One is black; he is chief custodian. The council was scheduled to employ a black student-intern in the summer of 1968. The intern is the son of a leading black state senator.[6]

What if there had been another governor, one who did not want success? Would there have been a difference? Just as the head of the highway department might be dismissed at the pleasure of the chief executive, so, too, might the head of the Fair Employment Practices Commission be discharged. How meaningful, then, was the 1963 legislation that changed and enlarged the Fair Employment Practices Commission to a Civil Rights Commission? How much more power did it have when the General Assembly armed the commission with the weapon of the cease and desist order?[7] The governor in the final analysis held the power. He could have a weak, a strong, or a mild commission. Budget was not a significant factor if a governor had firm views on the direction the commission should take. After all, he appointed the commissioners and the agency's executive director.[8]

Understanding the conservative, temperate climate of Indiana politics, knowing the sensitivity of Hoosier politicians toward their constituents, strong executive action generally was not to be expected. The commission was to be given no inordinate powers, no significant funds. It was not to be given the kind of staff that would work outside the matrix of the community.

In this climate the General Assembly once again expanded the role of the Civil Rights Commission. In 1965, there was added to the commission's original act an amendment making equal opportunity in housing a civil right. Purchase and rental were brought under the ambit of the amendment. Made exempt, however, was the owner-occupant of a building with less than four units who chose to discriminate.[9] Reflecting moderation in the pursuit of integration, the General Assembly in 1967 permitted neighborhood groups to file with the commission "voluntary" plans to eliminate de facto segregation through a self-imposed quota system.[10]

For violation of the right to equal opportunity in housing, there was no Indiana-granted private cause of action, no individual power to go before agency or court and compel redress. Wrong was to be made right by the commission alone. Assume for a moment that there could be real enforcing power behind a cease and desist order and that the agency wanted to be a meaningful force. The executive and the General Assembly still were assured of temperate action. For fiscal 1967-1968 the agency received a total appropriation of $114,115, of which $95,840 was allocated for salaries or personnel services, leaving less than $20,000 for programs.[11] Compared with other states where civil rights enforcement may be in somewhat better repute, Indiana ranks near the bottom. Even Kentucky, having a 1960 population of 3,000,000, far less than Indiana's 4,600,000, appropriated $157,000 to its civil rights agency.[12]

The Indiana budget could be expected to indicate the quality and quantity of the commission's professional staff. Yet despite very low salaries, the budget determines only the number employed, not their ability. The executive director holds three degrees, including two in social ethics. His 1967 salary was $10,950. His deputy director has a B.A. and an M.A. from Hunter College. Her salary was $10,600. There is a professional staff of five and the half-time services of another. Each is classified a "consultant." Each has a minimum of a bachelor's degree. The highest-paid consultant earns $9,300 annually. The lowest-paid, a former minister who has a B.A. and a M.A. from Boston University, earns $7,900.

In directors' salaries, Indiana does not rank high in comparison with other states. Alaska pays its civil rights executive director $15,504; California, $19,518; Illinois, $15,000; Michigan, $19,000; Missouri, $14,000; and, New Jersey, $18,000.[13]

With its staff of five, the Indiana Civil Rights Commission has placed responsibility for an area of the state with each individual. There was little choice left to the commission in this matter. Greater Indianapolis could not be the single focal point of commission activity. Certainly commission services were needed in such areas as Lake County with the steel city of Gary where a black mayor was elected in 1967 over the active opposition of his own party organization. Of four staff members, the first is assigned to Northern Indiana; the second, Central Indiana; the third, Southern Indiana; and, the fourth, Northeast Indiana. Spread so thin, the commission had no choice but to emphasize its community relations role as contrasted to that of enforcement.[14] Its work assumed a pastoral quality. The formation of local human rights organizations was encouraged. The six that existed in 1961 were enlarged to twenty-two by 1965, many of which had full-time employees.[15]

The commission was charged to spread the word and let the community know that compliance with the law was expected. They were to involve the power sources in the work of the commission and thereby transform passive compliance into active cooperation. Such was the spirit of the times when the commission established a Housing Advisory Committee consisting not only of religious and civil rights groups but also the major representatives of labor and business including the real estate industry, banking, the chamber of commerce, and the federal government.[16]

The commission's deputy director said the Housing Advisory Committee "has been extremely worthwhile." When asked why and how, he replied, "It meets regularly. There is communication. There is active participation."[17] When asked what had been produced from these sessions, he answered, "Guidelines."[18] In 1965 the Housing Advisory Committee, with the assistance of the mortgage lending representatives, formulated "Guidelines for Non-Discriminatory Mortgage Lending Practices." One year later there were "Guidelines Recommended to Real Estate Brokers."

These guidelines were, at most, suggestions for group compliance that had limited effect. Discriminatory selling practices continued in 1968; housing segregation showed no marked decrease. Maps prepared by the commission itself demonstrate the point.[19]

There are examples that dramatize the restrictions of the ghetto at that time. On July 25, 1967, Stanley R. Resor, secretary of the army, as part of a national program relating to housing discrimination against servicemen, held a closed meeting of real estate, civil rights, and community leaders at Fort Benjamin Harrison, Indiana, located near the city of Lawrence in northeast Indianapolis. About sixty persons were present. The secretary was concerned about the 12,000 men, women, and children making up the twenty-one different commands that form Fort Harrison. More precisely, he was concerned about 1,124 families on long-term assignment at the post.[20]

Of this total, 623 families lived in off-post housing, a condition that the Defense Department encourages. Secretary Resor spoke bluntly. He gave the results of a questionnaire survey among men at the fort. Fifty percent of the white enlisted men found a place to live within five miles of the post. Yet the same held true for only twenty-five percent of the black enlisted men; the remaining seventy-five percent lived far from the fort. If a circle were drawn within a thirty minute commuting radius of the fort, sixty-nine percent of the whites would be inside, and only thirty-one percent of the blacks.

"Of the Negroes," said Secretary Resor, "who reported difficulty in obtaining suitable housing, half said that they had been refused rentals when vacancies were available—an experience with which only one out of eight whites had to contend. Half again as many Negroes as whites stated that difficulties in housing adversely affected their job performance. While nearly all the dissatisfaction of white servicemen was due to the cost of housing, only one Negro in five who had difficulty obtaining housing listed cost as his principal problem. Their difficulty, said nearly eighty percent, was the color of their skin."[21]

Secretary Resor was quite precise in letting the real estate men, most of whom firmly supported the Vietnam war, know why the "race question" was raised. There were more than 300,000 blacks in the service and 6,700 of them were officers. In the army in 1966, sixty-six percent of the blacks completing their first tour of duty reenlisted for a second tour compared to twenty percent of white servicemen. More than seventeen percent of the men in army combat units were black.

The number exceeded twenty percent for airborne units. Among infantry sergeants, "the backbone of our combat forces in Vietnam," twenty-four percent were black.[22] The commander of the army in Vietnam at that time, General Westmoreland, a man raised in the deep South, had praised the performance, responsibility, and courage of the black soldiers in his command. The general's words, repeated by the secretary, were spoken not only in Vietnam but also in his native South Carolina. They were carried and enlarged upon by the secretary of defense[23] and their political thrust was made absolutely certain by the president. Prodding Congress to enact a federal open housing law, President Johnson on March 27, 1968, expressed shock that black troops "can't live near the base where they have to train in this country."[24] Referring to a recent trip to Fort Bragg, North Carolina, when he saw off the 82nd Airborne Division, "more than half of whom were Negro boys going back to Vietnam for the second time," the president said these same soldiers had to "drive 15, 20 or 30 miles to get to their homes in the evening."[25] The president emphasized that this could not be tolerated.

The real estate men responded to the secretary of the army's speech with stunned silence. Finally one said, "We're doing our best. We let one into one of our buildings." Another man stood up and said, "They don't want to buy. They want to rent, and they make bad tenants. They're liable to be shipped out on a moment's notice." Another said, "Look, Mr. Secretary. I think I can say for all those present that we got the message. We know you have a problem. If any special case arises, if you need an apartment for any particular person, just call us. We'll find something, somewhere."

The pattern of segregation at Fort Bragg also existed at Fort Harrison. During 1967 and 1968 in all of Lawrence Township, which includes the city of Lawrence, there was a total black enrollment in the public school system of forty-four students. "These kids," said the Fort Harrison commandant, "probably come from families living in housing on the post."[26]

Where was the voluntary compliance of which the Indiana Civil Rights Commission was proud? Where was the cooperation promised by the real estate industry? Several months before a black state senator had made pointed inquiries relating to open housing directed toward assessing the activity of the Civil Rights Commission and the Indiana Real Estate Commission.[27] Only the Civil Rights Commission replied.

After more than a year the Real Estate Commission still had not answered.

The senator, through the state legislative council, asked: "Has the Civil Rights Commission established a relationship with the Real Estate Commission in furthering open housing?" The reply from this agency of voluntary compliance was revealing, "The Civil Rights Commission has taken the initiative in establishing a reasonably good working relationship with the Indiana Real Estate Commission. This includes the active participation of the Director of that Commission as a member of the Housing Advisory Committee of the Civil Rights Commission. The Civil Rights Commission, however, feels that more is to be gained through cooperation with the Indiana Real Estate Association and its 60 local real estate boards and some 2,000 realtor members. An officer of that State association also has served actively and cooperatively on the Housing Advisory Committee to the Indiana Civil Rights Commission. The Real Estate Association and some of its local boards have arranged meetings for the Director of the Civil Rights Commission to discuss the housing law and program with their members. The Association has also distributed through its members explanatory and educational material of the State Civil Rights Commission. In several instances, the Real Estate Boards have urged their members to comply with the law and to attempt to get their clients to do the same. On one issue, however, the association and local boards have maintained a firm position; namely, that desegregation should be brought about by voluntary means and through persuasion rather than by legal force."[28]

Real estate boards are frequently staffed by full-time directors who are controlled by an executive committee all too often composed and dominated by the few large real estate firms in the community. Consider the position of those who have been given the power to speak for the real estate industry. They ask for action by the industry rather than the agency, the Real Estate Commission, which purports to regulate through licensing. Yet the Real Estate Commission and its hearing officer are real estate brokers with ten years of experience.[29] The regulators and the regulated tend to be the same.

The Real Estate Commission formally admitted that it convened "informal conferences" to resolve disputes in those cases "where the facts will not substantiate any disciplinary action but where there are moral and ethical violations which are without the legal jurisdiction."[30] Not once was a conference held to discuss violation of the state open housing law. Not once were there rules promulgated to cause compliance with that law—even after Governor Welsh issued an executive order commanding compliance. (The order, however, came during the last days of his administration.) For that matter between 1949 and 1966 no new rules were promulgated by the Real Estate Commission. Evidently no need was felt.[31]

Official regulation took on the characteristics of self-regulation. It might well have been that these licensees who pride themselves on their "independence" wanted to insure their condition. These professional salesmen easily spoke the words of civil rights compliance, and the words were believed by the executive director of the Indiana Civil Rights Commission.

As late as June 10, 1968, the director still had hope for industry compliance. He told an Indianapolis neighborhood association that as many as seventy-five percent of Marion County real estate brokers favored open housing. The blame for segregated housing was still considered the fault of the homeowner.[32]

Secretary Resor's message of July 24 was not intended to be the beginning and the end to the problem. Although the secretary received little support from his audience, the president and the secretary of defense were determined to see an end to off-base housing discrimination.[33] At Fort Harrison, following Secretary Resor's address, the housing placement office was transferred from the engineer's building to the commandant's office. The order of the day was to obtain pledges of nondiscrimination from local apartment developments. Some progress was made. Some developers signed; they would take their quota. Still, the black soldiers did not move near the base in any appreciable numbers. In a confidential interview with a black officer based at Fort Harrison a few of the reasons became apparent. They ranged from there being "no real freedom of choice," to "the apartments were cheap looking . . . You heard your neighbors . . . There was no privacy." This officer bought a home in Forest Manor, a rapidly "changing" area in 1968.

Lawrence Township remained hardcore white. The new post housing office in the period from August 1967 to January 1968 effected no noticeable change. Still the Indiana FHA director said, "the order of the secretary of defense is there. The FHA is a federal agency holding title to homes. Isn't this an ideal situation for cooperation? Servicemen or civilian employees transferred to the fort are dislocated by government action. None could be more dislocated. Let's see whether we can help move things along." With that, early in January 1968, the FHA director telephoned the post housing office. In ten minutes he was transferred to four different people, none of whom chose to take the responsibility even to talk about the acquired property program. The fourth anonymous voice suggested that a staff member "can help you when she gets back from her vacation tomorrow. I'll have her call you for sure." The call did not come the next day or the one following.

The Committee on Special Housing decided to "go to the top" by calling the commandant. The committee was identified to the commandant as a group backed by a number of responsibile citizens, some of whom had attended the July meeting when Secretary Resor spoke of the need to provide adequate housing for black servicemen. The spokesman for the committee said that the group was in a position to aid the secretary and the commandant in the fulfillment of that mission. The colonel granted an audience. On arrival the committee representative was taken by the public information officer to the colonel's office where the commandant's deputy, his special services officer, and the fort's two housing officers were waiting.

After hearing about the committee's work, the colonel said, "The committee's plan sounds excellent. We have officers and enlisted men who could qualify as well as a very large civilian employee force. Right now, I instruct my housing officers to check all Negro personnel living away from the base as well as incoming persons. We will see whether they might be interested in buying a home. Frankly, I think FHA offers a pretty good deal." One of the housing officers, a civilian employee, spoke, "Our people want to rent, not buy. What will happen if they're moved out?"

The colonel answered, "If they're moved out, our housing office can help them sell the home to incoming personnel, or rent it, as the case might be. Furthermore, I see no reason why we could not help in maintaining the property pending any such sale or rental." Action was promised. Stories would appear in the post paper and bulletin. The housing officers would produce applicants.

The stories appeared as the colonel promised, but the applicants were not forthcoming.[34] "We only get the names of incoming personnel after they have arrived," said a young lieutenant, one of the housing officers. "By then most of them have found suitable quarters. Those who have not, must find something immediately. They can't wait two weeks for a home." When asked about those living in the inner city in inadequate quarters, the lieutenant replied, "We checked and found only one sergeant. He's living in a public housing project and doesn't want to move because he's making money on his housing allowance."

What had happened to the families mentioned by Secretary Resor six months earlier? Had they been relocated? Were they content? Had the housing office at the fort simply failed to carry out orders? Perhaps part of the answer came from a white officer interviewed by the committee, "That office is incompetent. The people there don't know how to help, and base personnel have learned not to rely on them for anything." In the seven-month period from January to July of 1968, the housing officers brought to the committee only one black and he had to have a home and move in within seven days, a challenge that the Committee on Special Housing could sometimes meet but could not in this instance. In the same period the housing officers worked closely with two white officers, one a major, to find a home. The major had three weeks. He selected and moved into a home in the city of Lawrence before leaving his family for overseas assignment.

Yet the people were there. A real estate broker told of selling approximately twenty homes to Fort Harrison personnel during 1967. From the finance center at the fort the committee received two civilian applicants. One was placed in Lawrence Township, and the family's three children caused the black school enrollment to rise nearly ten percent. A black sergeant on emergency leave from Vietnam reported to Fort Harrison. Independent of the housing office at Fort Harrison, he contacted the committee. His wife and three children were living in slum conditions in Barrington Heights, far from the fort. He asked if the committee could help him. The committee did help and his story illustrates the reality of Secretary Resor's message.[35]

Sergeant Dennen found his way to the committee through an indirect route. A fifteen-year career soldier and Korean War veteran, he had returned on emergency leave from Vietnam when his stepmother died. Two weeks before his return to Vietnam, late in January, he received a frantic call from his sister, Mrs. Wilkins. While her husband was at work and her two daughters were sleeping, a constable had come to her home and demanded that she leave immediately. Acting apparently on the instructions of a rental agent and accompanied by a mover, he walked through each room although he did not have a court order.

Sergeant Dennen, a quiet, thin man of average height, went to the

Wilkins' home immediately. He was met by the constable who was "fingering" a revolver he had no legal right to carry. "Listen, boy," said the constable, "don't give me any trouble. I pay your way with savings bonds." Sergeant Dennen replied, "They don't call me 'boy' anymore. You know something else—that revolver doesn't scare me. I was near the Cambodian border January 1 when they came after my platoon with machine guns. No sir, that revolver doesn't bother me one little bit."

The constable and the mover left, though promising to return with a police officer and a court order. The sergeant did not relent. Maybe his sister could be evicted, but there was a proper way of doing it. "The courts have processes," he said, "which have to be followed. These processes were being misused by the people authorized to enforce them. If that constable didn't know how to act responsibly, he had no right to the job."

The sergeant called the judge advocate general at Fort Harrison, the Legal Aid Society, the mayor's office, and the civil rights agencies. It was Saturday, however; there was no advice and no help until Monday. "Do civil rights take a break from 4:30 Friday until Monday morning?" the sergeant asked. "My sister needed help. It's a long weekend when a place to sleep is involved."[36] It was a long weekend for the Wilkins and Sergeant Dennen because the constable returned with what appeared to be a court order and the family was evicted. The children went to stay with other relatives; the sister and brother-in-law moved in with the sergeant; and the Wilkins' furniture was placed in storage.

On the informal advice of a school social worker the family came to the committee a week after their eviction. The committee considered them displaced because the totality of their experience seemed to make their eviction unlawful. Within six hours they had selected a home that they moved into about two months later. The sergeant came to the committee not only to give the story of the constable—in the hope that something might be done—but also "to see whether the committee could help" him. "There was so much hope and enthusiasm that . . . seemed to be [transmitted] . . . It sort of gave my sister and her husband a new outlook on life . . . the peace of mind they so much desired."

Living in Barrington Heights was not for the sergeant's family. In Sergeant Dennen's words, this apartment came "as close to a tenement as Indianapolis has." The Barrington apartment was taken only as a last resort. Before his first tour in Vietnam the sergeant looked for a home and "ran into the same walls I always run into." There were those who refused to sell to servicemen or those who demanded "unusually high rents or interest rates." One broker did take a $400 down payment on a home that was vacant. Days turned into weeks but no closing date was set and the sergeant's time for departure neared. It became apparent that the broker had no intention of closing. With effort, the sergeant had his money returned before he left for Vietnam. For six months his wife unsuccessfully sought a better home than Barrington.

What was the sergeant looking for in a home? Perhaps he was unrealistic. The sergeant answered that he wanted the best possible schooling for his children. He worried about where his children play and with whom. He was concerned about their safety and that of his wife while he was away from home. He wanted a safe and peaceful neighborhood.

The committee showed the sergeant several homes on the day he visited its office. Two he liked. One was in a highly integrated neighborhood; the other was in an area that the Indianapolis Human Rights Commission had labeled "violence potential." The sergeant selected the second home. When asked his reasons he replied, "It's roomier, nicer. It has a full basement for the kids to play. It has a fenced yard."

Having selected the home, the matters relating to closing went forward. A credit check disclosed numerous debts that, while being maintained on a current basis, nevertheless heavily taxed the sergeant's income. The commandant at Fort Harrison was called. "Here is exactly the kind of man Secretary Resor wants helped," he was told. "How about making him a member of the fort credit union, consolidating his debts through a single low-interest loan, and enabling him to purchase the home?" Within twenty-four hours the deed was done and discussed at lunch that day when the commanding general of the Fifth Army visited the post.

There was nothing hidden. The committee made no secret of the sergeant's purchase in the "violence-potential" neighborhood. Gene Slaymaker, a respected and responsible news reporter for WFBM-TV, a Time-Life station, interviewed the sergeant in full uniform in front of his home. The significance of the purchase, "north of 38 Street," long a black-white dividing line, save in certain enclaves, was discussed, and the sergeant's exact address was given. The committee was mentioned as well as its individual representatives. What would happen?

Nothing happened. The next day the home was still standing. Despite the publicity, committee representatives received no threatening calls then or thereafter. Maybe part of the reason rests in Sergeant Dennen himself. Asked on television if he worried about his neighbors, how they would treat him and his family, the sergeant said unemotionally, "No, I'm not worried. I intend to respect my neighbors' property. I expect them to do the same." Here was a man confident of himself, sure where he was going and why.

In an earlier interview, when Sergeant Dennen told of the constable's action, he asked: "I wonder why I should be in Vietnam fighting for other people's rights if my own family isn't secure." His sister and his wife reasonably secure, the sergeant returned to Vietnam at the height of the Tet Offensive. "He usually doesn't write when the going is rough," his wife said. The committee nevertheless received not only a handwritten letter of thanks but a promise of help on the sergeant's return.

The story of Sergeant Dennen demonstrates the frequent irrelevance of organizational activity designed to achieve civil rights broadly and open housing particularly. The colonel relied on a housing office that did no more than supply listings. It took no personal, affirmative action to demonstrate the opportunity that existed. It did little but utter platitudes of change. It could show the Pentagon a stack of signed pledges that had no real meaning to those seeking homes. The imagination and initiative of command came from those who could command, from the president, the secretary, or the colonel. Encountered directly and specifically, such as the request relating to the credit union, command could respond. From below, however, there seemed to perk the arrogance of the passive, general orders followed to the letter so that their spirit was emasculated.

When the sergeant and his sister were most in need of help the Indianapolis Human Rights Commission and the Indiana Civil Rights Commission were represented only by an unanswered telephone. It was Saturday. The vigor of self-regulation did not generate sufficient energy to project itself through the weekend. Only the presence of a determined combat veteran inhibited a constable acting on direct orders of a rental agent. Paper guidelines had only organizational validity. The Indianapolis Real Estate Board could say to the Indiana Civil Rights

Commission, the NAACP, or a mayor's commission that it was trying. But did the board speak for its members? Were the members as committed as the board? Did the articulation of organizational compliance serve as a means to avoid confrontation and individual compliance? The significant factor is how broker X treats customer Y? How are guidelines applied? What does the Civil Rights Commission do to insure compliance in individual cases? Are complaints solicited? The facts indicated that relatively little was done.

Indianapolis Metropolitan Enforcement

At the city level of government, however, came another answer. The executive director of the Indianapolis Human Rights Commission said complaints were solicited; a law enforcement unit existed within the commission. "Help yourself," the agency brochure proclaims, "to better housing."[37] Both city and state laws, like those throughout the nation, guarantee each citizen's right to choose the house he wants to buy or rent without discrimination. The Human Rights Commission administers the city's open occupancy ordinance and receives and investigates all complaints of housing discrimination. "If you have a problem, phone the commission." Phone, and wrongs will be made right, is the implied promise. With a professional staff of five, a 1967-1968 fiscal budget of $59,384, and a commission of twenty-five appointed by the mayor and city council, complaints are invited.[38] With an ordinance mild in tone and weak in substance, complaints are solicited. With an ordinance that requires first efforts toward concilia- tion or on failure, then public hearings with all the panoply and difficulties of adjudication,[39] only to result in a finding of violation that may be referred to the city attorney for further action, complaints are solicited.[40] If the city attorney decides to litigate and the trial and appellate courts sustain his position, there is no redress of grievance. There is only the penalty of a fine of not less than $100 nor more than $300 and costs.[41]

To insure compliance, to encourage the free submission of com- plaints the city commission has among its staff of five a housing coordinator obtained in mid-fiscal 1967. All too well the committee recalled the coordinator's publicly proclaimed warnings of danger in the streets, "The people are being stacked like wood. . . . Either have open

housing or face explosion." The committee's director of field operations replied, "Here are homes. Where are the people being stacked like
wood? Bring them in. See whether the Committee on Special Housing
can help. Then after the FHA supply has been exhausted, talk to us
about a job not being done." The housing coordinator was silent, but
the executive director of the Human Rights Commission stated, "We'd
like to help the committee, but we have a job to do here first. I haven't
got the manpower to spare either to find people or show homes."[42]

Activity had indeed picked up at the commission. In the last half of
1967 the agency received eight housing complaints. From January to
June of 1968 eighteen complaints were filed. Twelve of these were
successfully resolved, "not simply conciliated," emphasized the executive director.[43] What does "successfully resolved" mean? It means that
the complainant was satisfied. He either obtained the housing in
question, comparable housing, or was "otherwise" satisfied, perhaps by
being able to be shown through a home, a right that had been denied
him previously.[44]

The executive director of the Human Rights Commission was
militant in asserting rights seemingly granted by ordinance. He, unlike
the Committee on Special Housing, was not particularly concerned with
a conflict-free approach to a problem. He was not afraid to see anger
vented, and, to some extent, through his agency he offered a vehicle
more constructive and far less destructive than the anger of the streets.
In a meeting of the commission he did not hesitate to ask for a small
appropriation to pay for a newspaper ad to help the Committee on
Special Housing. The sound and fury of that meeting was not lost on
real estate interests present who opposed the appropriation request.[45]

There are limitations to enforcement machinery, particularly when it
is inherently weak. Eighteen complaints was a substantial increase but it
did not bring free housing or even additional housing.

Contrasting Roles: The Indiana Civil Rights Commission

The head of the state Civil Rights Commission, totally committed to
the ways of peace, found only a limited role for adjudication, for
formal enforcement machinery. He candidly stated, "The State Civil
Rights Commission, like similar commissions in other States with longer
experience in administering housing laws, realizes the many limitations

of the enforcement procedures provided in these laws with respect to acquiring satisfactory housing for those seeking the commission's assistance. One of the most obvious difficulties is the length of time required. It is almost impossible to investigate a complaint, schedule a hearing and issue an order within 60 days of the date a complaint is filed (as required by statute). With a staff of five and a Commission of five members which meets one day per month, the number of such hearings and orders possible is quite limited. It is equally convinced that it should operate primarily through education, persuasion and conciliation."[46]

His assessment accurately reflected commission work. In the five-year period from 1961-1966, the agency handled a total of 856 complaints for all categories: employment, public accomodations, housing, education, and miscellaneous matters. Of this total, there were only eighty-six housing complaints filed in a state with a population of more than four million where residential de facto segregation is patent.[47] Since being given the power to impose sanctions the state commission has issued two cease and desist orders.[48] Both applied to South Bend. One concerned public accomodations and the other was related to private housing. A year elapsed between the complaints and the orders. Both complainants were unsatisfied. The woman was no longer interested in joining the health club. The black policeman denied the house of his choice found another. Neither complainant seemed as interested in a cease and desist order as he was in having his grievances redressed at the time of injury.

Voluntary compliance was the only tool realistically made available to the commission. The executive director tried persuasion, talk, and even pleas for self-regulation in open housing. He seemed to be a moderate and unemotional man, but when he saw labeled on a map over 100 houses scattered throughout the county, he became excited.

At a meeting of the Urban League Housing Advisory Committee on February 19, 1968, a committee representative spoke, as the associate director of the league had requested, on "some specific plans for zeroing in on repossessed properties during the next month."[49] Among those present were the executive director of the state Civil Rights Commission, the director of relocation for the Indianapolis Redevelopment Commission, the mayor's chief administrative assistant, and church and social service leaders, a total of about twenty persons. The committee representative concluded, "This program can succeed.

Homes are available now. We must know, however, those who need the homes. We don't have the list of names of those dislocated by highways, parks, and code enforcement. We've had to search them out. We need help in showing the homes. We have now only a single man able to provide the individual attention necessary. All the help needed for success can be and ought to be provided by the relocation office. The committee's work is a function of relocation."

The director of relocation replied that he and his staff were busy. Applicants wanted to rent, not buy. The relocation office looked on the FHA properties as "an excellent resource." With that the committee was politely dismissed. The mayor's chief assistant said nothing. He had to leave, but as he passed he whispered to the committee representative, "We'll be in touch."

The head of the state Civil Rights Commission, however, was not unmoved. Sitting next to the director of relocation, he turned and spoke, "For years we've been waiting for the opportunity presented by this program. Now that we have it, we are not going to waste it. I think you have an obligation to find the people and help them see that these homes can be theirs. My agency thinks this program is worthwhile and we're giving manpower to see it implemented. You should, too." This firmly felt opinion expressed a view that prompted the executive director of the Civil Rights Commission to find potential buyers himself during his off-duty hours. His interest did not stop until the applicants he found had moved into their new homes. To him the Committee on Special Housing had a program that offered agency and staff a choice of methods. It made available the opportunity for affirmative action that could prevent discriminatory treatment and in the process drive a wedge into the crust of the restricted housing market.

There was some reevaluation from the director of relocation. He brought four black women, who seemed to have social work training, and his white male assistant to another meeting "to listen and help." For the committee the session was frustrating. The staff repeated what their supervisor had said earlier. There aren't buyers. Nearly everyone wants to rent. The staff showed no temerity. They weren't sure the FHA homes were good. A committee member said they could see the houses for themselves, and then added, "In the final analysis the success of this program depends upon you. It's your responsibility." One by one each of the four women said, "I do not want that responsibility."

Open housing was law for Indiana. Statute was reinforced by

ordinance in the city of Indianapolis. Agencies had been established to implement what the legislatures had ordered. Yet the tools of enforcement were crude at best. Agency budgets were minimal so there were necessary limits to investigation, to obtaining the facts relating to violation. Sanctions were difficult to apply since administrative hearings were required before court enforcement could be sought. The relevant government agencies were forced to rely upon voluntary compliance that was easy for real estate interests to accept in word but not in deed. There were few positive programs the agencies could use that would permit meaningful compliance with statute. There were in Indianapolis, as in most urban areas, thousands of inner-city people, most of whom were black, being displaced by highway construction and urban renewal. There were funded agencies such as the highway department and the Indianapolis redevelopment commission charged with the responsibility for helping those displaced to find homes. Yet the area of search for new housing was confined to an ever narrowing market in the inner city. There was no effort to expand available housing by reaching toward those areas that had been closed by discrimination. Even when new housing units, accommodations in once forbidden areas, became available through the FHA-acquired property program, relocation authorities were not disposed to use them. Instead, it was the state Civil Rights Commission that took up the new mechanism as a means of fulfilling its statutory goal.

5

Relocation in Indianapolis

The setting for the committee's program should have provided a sound environment for success and a model for other urban areas. As a community Indianapolis seems to be much like other medium-large cities. It has a growing population concentration with the attendant problems of an inner city being developed as a service area and constricted as a source for housing. In 1967 the population of Indianapolis was estimated at 796,000, a gain of nearly 100,000 in seven years.[1] With a broad-based economy made up of such companies as Eli Lilly & Company; P. R. Mallory; Allison Division, General Motors Corporation; Homes Instruments Division, RCA; Ford; Chrysler; and Western Electric Company, a steady expansion is expected to yield an additional population gain of 195,000 between 1975 and 1985.[2] About a quarter of the population of Indianapolis is black, a percentage that will rise in the future; most of these individuals live in the inner city where they are caught in a housing squeeze.

Interstate highways were being slashed through the city, making it readily accessible to other industrial areas such as Cincinnati, Louisville, Chicago, and Detroit. The more transportation improved, the more appealing Indianapolis became as a site for corporate development. The more corporations and their skilled labor and executives entered into community life, the more the city changed. The sleepy downtown area, once a reserve for black dwellings, awoke. Banks bought land and built new offices. Hotels and a convention center were constructed. The state universities increased their facilities significantly. All these developments caused housing displacement in the inner city that was compounded by an influx of semi-skilled and unskilled labor, often black, into the area to fill new jobs.

For Indianapolis, the housing squeeze is tight. Somehow the community must open or burst. The "Metropolitan Indianapolis Housing Study" reported: "At this time [1968] an estimated 25,000 ill-housed metropolitan households have immediate housing needs and in humanistic terms desperate housing needs. Provision for this human need no later than 1975 will require 7,000 units in addition to meeting all other basic source needs within the eight-year period."[3]

To meet at least that portion of the housing need created by government, the state of Indiana and the city of Indianapolis established relocation offices to find new housing for displaced inhabitants of the inner city. The committee on Special Housing assumed that the FHA acquired property would be seized upon and quickly consumed through the vehicle of the relocation offices. This did not happen for a number of reasons, not the least of which was the attitude of the relocation agencies.[4] Agency officials did not dispute the scope of the housing need, but they had their own interpretation of what the inner-city displacee desired and perhaps what he should be given.

Whether the relocation officials were correct depended in part on the nature of those displaced and those to be displaced, particularly the young people who would be starting new families and whose needs would shape the direction of community action. "In the seven years between 1960 and 1967, it is estimated that the number of young adults in metropolitan Indianapolis, the age group between 18 and 24 years old, increased by 26,000 persons. This was more than twice the increase in their age group in the entire previous ten years between 1950 and 1960. The significance of this trend to housing demand is obvious. It is in this age group that the bulk of new household formation takes place. . . . looking ahead, it is anticipated that these trends of rapid growth among young adults and only modest growth in the older adults (25-and-over) will continue into the early 1970s."[5]

These newcomers are black as well as white. They are the babies of the Second World War. They are the veterans of Korea and Vietnam. Many are high school and college graduates. They are one step further removed than their parents from the past. They are a significant part of 130,000 who made up the black population of Indianapolis in 1967, and they will be an even larger percentage of 158,000 blacks who will be part of the greater Indianapolis community in 1985.[6] Above all, these newcomers are people making important decisions. They are deciding the destiny of their families and of their community. There are stories enough to illustrate their mood.

A black veteran of Korea, a committee applicant displaced because of highway construction, was told by an FHA counselor that he could not afford the home of his choice. No stretch of his current income would make the purchase economically possible. The veteran replied, "I'm tired of little bites. I want to take a big bite for a change. I'll get a second job. I want that home, and I'll have it." And so he did. He was not afraid of the strain on his family or himself. He added, "I'd rather work hard for something, than be forced to live like a pig. I can't keep a family like that." This thirty-year-old man, a father of three school age children, took a second job as a janitor in addition to his first job as a custodian at Chrysler. He happened to move into an all white area next to a school the NAACP had threatened to boycott because it was underenrolled and all white. He was received as a neighbor by his neighbors. He was a man who had had enough of slums, crowded housing, and tomorrow.

This man dramatized a fact that Indianapolis statistics clearly delineate. The cold, formal language of a scientific study rob that probe of its sense of human frustration, of unfulfilled desire, of the need and pain that are the blood and muscle of these statistics. The study nevertheless, developed facts that the city planners have still to digest—the population of Indianapolis continues to grow but not for all segments of the community. Although between 1960 and 1967 the overall number of adult persons per household declined, there were sharply different trends between the black and white households. The number of adults per white household dropped, but until the tight credit days of 1967 new housing units for whites continued to be available in generous supply, and the white families in Indianapolis found homes. This was not the case for blacks. While the number of adults per white household continued to decline, between 1960 and 1967 both total and adult population per black household increased.[7] The black housing market tightened substantially and the squeeze was felt by increasing numbers.

Large-scale clearance of occupied black units by urban renewal and highway construction cut deep into the supply. During the decade from

1950 to 1960, approximately 9,470 housing units were removed from the market. Of this total, 6,180 units were demolished by governmental action or permit. The largest percentage of housing loss occurred in the substandard areas in which low income groups have traditionally lived. From 1960 to 1967 an estimated 7,600 units were lost to public demolition alone, and again slum areas, especially black ghettos, bore the brunt of the brunt of the loss.[8] Most of the available housing stock in the area (both new and used) was not open for black occupancy. In the face of sharp increases in the young adult population and in black income generally there was a clear restriction on new household formation.

How tight is the squeeze? In 1967 there were 35,000 black households. By 1970 there will be 38,400, an increase of 3,400 new families who will be seeking homes.[9] This figure does not include those who will be displaced by government action such as highway construction, urban renewal, and university expansion. It says nothing of industrial or service organization growth and consequential housing destruction in the inner city. In the three-year period from 1965 to 1967, 4,141 families and 220 individuals were displaced by governmental action. "Still to go, if one carries the projection ahead as far as five to seven years, are 5,213 more families."[10] In 1967 metropolitan Indianapolis had reached only the halfway point in the process of governmental removal.

The expanding black population had been more tightly compressed than ever before. The potential for violence was rapidly increasing. A lid had been placed on the black housing market. Black families with higher incomes had no place to go so they stayed where they were when they could. Their housing was not available to those with lesser income. There was a repressed demand that blocked a filter process that, in turn, would have opened new housing.[11] "This breakdown in the filter process not only means the thwarting of demands on the part of Negro families already in standard units and looking for something better, but also results in much higher levels of substandard occupancy for Negroes than for whites of comparable income capacities."[12]

In March 1968, firm estimates were made of the effects of repressed demand.[13] Looking at similar income groupings between whites and blacks and comparing the differences between white and black standard housing between the income groupings, the differences may be explained in terms of housing discrimination. The study report reasoned that with the same income, blacks would be expected to aspire to the same proportion of sound housing as comparable white households. "The fact that they do not achieve this proportion, or even appear to aspire to it, can be reasonably ascribed to the *stark* fact that standard housing is not generally available to them."[14]

In 1960, before government began any significant redevelopment in Indianapolis, there were 5,250 more blacks than whites living in substandard housing units. More than half were families whose income in 1960 was under $4,000. The remainder were scattered: 1,100 more blacks earning from $4,000 to $6,000 lived in substandard housing as contrasted to their white counterparts; 900 more earning $6,000 to $10,000; and 250 more earning more than $10,000.[15] Eighteen percent of black households in Indianapolis were substandard even in 1960.[16] The study, conservative in its estimate, assumes a repressed demand in 1967 of 5,000 housing units resulting only from discrimination. There are other factors that highlight, even increase the demand. The study does not note the effect of increased earning power. It does not consider that the factory worker of 1960 made $2.26 an hour working a 39.7 hour week while in September 1967 he made $2.85 an hour working a 40.9 hour week.[17] The man whose annual wage approximated $4,700 in 1960 jumped to more than $5,800 in 1967.

The state and the city of Indianapolis seem to have moved with painful reluctance to meet the housing need. Within greater Indianapolis the state highway department operates five relocation offices solely for those dislocated by highway construction.[18] Their ostensible function is to help ease the difficulty of dislocation. The state went so far as to allow compensation for moving expenses to aid in the effort at placement. But the state also vested power over relocation in the highway department that defied Governor Welsh on equal employment.

The *Indianapolis Star* reported, "More than eighty percent of the houses and apartments listed for rental at the relocation offices are offered through the agencies that own and manage slum property. . . . Several of these houses have no heat. Others have no bathrooms."[19] At the state level, no effort is made to insure that listings meet minimum code standards. Curiously, "freedom of choice" is cited as official justification for the job that is being done. "We can't force a man to better himself," explained Charles Sheets, then chief of the department's division of land acquisition. "If he wants to move into an outhouse, that's his right."[20] The dislocated have been moved by the state to homes with broken porches and unpatched roofs, to homes with rats in the basement and vermin in the kitchen.[21]

The state is doing its job. Quarterly reports are filed on state relocation advisory assistance by the division of land acquisition with the resident division engineer of the bureau of public roads. For a state agency anxious to get on with the job of construction, equipped with five well-staffed field offices, the statistics are revealing. This is the agency whose employees have first contact with the dislocated. Its employees knock on doors of homes that have been condemned. They ask if assistance in relocation is desired, and fill out questionnaires (RAAP Form Number 1). From January 1 to March 31, 1968, a total of 367 households in need of new housing were visited. Only 220 asked for assistance. Of these, only sixty-four accepted the housing offered by the state. For the quarter ending December 31, 1967, a total of 538 relocatees were reached but only 281 sought assistance. Of these, only ninety-one were placed by the state.

Of the ninety-one relocated for the quarter ending December 31, 1967, a period immediately before the FHA acquired properties program was launched, twenty were white and seventy-one nonwhite. Four were homeowners and eighty-seven were tenants. Sixty-one held homes valued at less than $6,000 or paid rent of $60 or less. Thirty, however, held houses valued from $6,000 to $15,000 or rented at $60 to $110 per month.[22] These people might have wanted to put money into a home of their own; they might have looked at the FHA acquired properties if they had known about them.

The highway department refers difficult cases to the Indianapolis Redevelopment Commission. The commission, unlike the department, has standards that go beyond the "outhouse" principles of freedom of choice. Dwellings must be in safe, sound, sanitary condition. The commission handles more than those displaced by highway construction. It has been given responsibility for code enforcement and park project displacement. In the year and a half from June 1967 through April 1968, the relocation office of the commission undertook to work with 696 families and 220 individuals. By April 1968 it had relocated 466 families and 155 individuals. It was left with a "balance on hand" of 230 families and sixty-five individuals.[23] A seven year projection indicated the bulk of the commission's work was yet to come.[24] The commission's executive director, whose agency is funded in part by the federal government, asked for increased monies and staff in 1969.

Specifically, he wanted to double his relocation staff of nine as well as his budget.

The Redevelopment Commission, like the highway department, is apparently confined to listings in the inner city. Although it is more selective than the highway department, it has not opened the housing market; the filter process has not been able to work and repressed demand increases. This is not to say that the commission is unconcerned or that it has not sought to stimulate an expanded market, but that the primary interest of the commission has been concentrated on the inner city and particularly on the rehabilitation of rental properties.[25]

Otis Bryant, the Indianapolis relocation director, told the committee, "Most of the people who come to us don't want to buy. They want to rent. Those who do want to buy usually find homes on their own."[26] None could dispute the truth of what Bryant said in those exploratory days of September 1967 before the FHA program was announced. Those who had the money, the knowledge, and the desire would find the best housing available in a shrinking market. If necessary, they would pay the premium demanded by a market reflecting demand in excess of supply.

"Look," Bryant continued, "there are a lot of Negroes who had been homeowners before, and now that their homes have been taken for the highway, they aren't about to consider home ownership again. These people—at least many of them—have lost up to twenty percent on their investment. The state would pay them no more for their homes." When asked why there was a loss and if the people were entitled to fair value, Bryant replied, "Yes, but many of these people paid a premium to buy their homes, and the state isn't about to make up that premium." Homeowners were becoming renters. Maybe these were the kind of facts that led the Redevelopment Commission to stress inner-city enlargement of the rental market, a task in which, according to an unpublished Metropolitan Plan Commission survey, they were joined in 1968 by twenty-eight private, charitable groups.

But what if these people could buy good homes at fair prices in stable neighborhoods of their choice? Would this make any difference? Bryant, a black, who had lived in Indianapolis many years, replied, "Sure it would make a difference. Negroes would move out of the ghetto if given a chance." Then Bryant went on to tell of a friend who only a few months before had moved eight blocks north of the

Thirty-eighth Street dividing line. He told of a cross burned and garbage dumped. "Still, I think Negroes would freely move. My friend has every intention of staying just where he is."

Bryant dealt in the present, not the future. There was a known housing inventory to which blacks could move without the additional worry of neighborhood harmony. Bryant knew that these homes were in sound repair. He operated within his agency and his responsibility was directed toward those who entered his doors. He might have had an interest in the total market but his job was relocation, a function certainly more elevated than the highway department's removal. Bryant had listings. The fact that those placed diminished the available supply and caused inner-city rentals to soar thirty-two percent because of highway construction was not within the jurisdictional ambit of relocation.[27]

While relocation offices worked in the inner city, individuals and organizations at every level within the community also planned and acted to expand the inner-city market. Religious groups united. New names quickly became familiar: Housing Opportunities Multiplied Ecumenically, Incorporated (HOME), Interfaith Housing, and Pride. They raised monies that the federal government through a variety of programs matched. With $350,000, HOME hoped to rehabilitate and rent thirty-nine units.[28] Interfaith Housing with as great an expenditure had opened and filled forty-two rental units and twelve sales units under contract. The rentals ranged from $60 to $90 a month. Four major programs, including Interfaith Housing, hoped to make available 150 units by the end of 1968. Between January 4, 1968 and June 1, 1968 the Committee on Special Housing lost eighty-seven units to the public market because it could not find the people who needed homes.[29]

Richard Lugar, the young Republican mayor with a business background seemed to grasp the limitations as well as the benefits flowing from the scattered endeavors of charitable groups. Organization and cohesion were needed. The mayor's Task Force on Housing and Relocation as part of the already existing Greater Indianapolis Progress Committee, manned substantially by citizen-volunteers, lawyers, businessmen, and religious leaders, as well as those professionally concerned, was given as its chairman an extremely competent corporation lawyer, Wayne C. Ponader. They met in the mayor's conference room on the twenty-fifth floor of the city-county building. The records of the meeting state that Ponader reviewed the primary goals of the Housing and Relocation Task Force: to coordinate and assist the present efforts of various groups to establish housing for low and and middle-income families in Indianapolis; to determine and initiate additional housing programs in appropriate areas of Indianapolis to supplement existing relocation programs caused by highways, redevelopment and present housing programs.

"He discussed the preliminary goals which have been accomplished in (1) determining the nature and extent of the present housing problem in Indianapolis; (2) determining the housing plans and proposals of the governmental bodies and private organizations and groups presently working in this area; and pointed out that it was now time to (3) determine in what specific areas this Task Force can facilitate and assist the present housing programs of those organizations presently involved."[30]

The mayor gave direction and stimulus to the cohesive organization that appeared to be developing under the shelter of the Task Force. Thousands of new housing units were needed, not more public housing, but housing constructed by private enterprise—backed perhaps by the federal government. The conservative community could only laud the efforts of one contractor who "put up 1,000 FHA financed, low income units in a year."[31]

It was not surprising that the mayor endorsed the project of the J & W Construction Company to build 200 low-cost houses ($10,500 to $12,900) on scattered lots in the inner city. Indeed, the mayor was in good company, the project received a two-million-dollar backing from the Teachers Insurance and Annuity Association of New York.[32] "I hesitate to endorse any firm, but this company is making a civic contribution," Lugar publicly stated. "They have been particularly aggressive in buying vacant lots, many covered with weeds and junk, and turning them into attractive tax-producing properties. . . . These homes are fine-looking and well-constructed and an asset to the neighborhoods where they are built. They are shoring up the value of surrounding homes as well as giving us a tax base where we've had a vacant lot. And I understand the company is ready and able to build several hundred homes as soon as they can find buyers and lots. . . . Copenhaver [the builder] is evidently a very imaginative businessman. *And I particularly endorse his concentration in the inner city.*"[33]

Less than a month later the mayor attended the Indianapolis

Low-Income Housing Luncheon and Display sponsored primarily by the Mobile Research Corporation of the Midwest.[34] Indianapolis was introduced to instant housing, modular construction, a product of mobile home technology. On display were multi-story homes produced in Vicksburg, Mississippi, at less than $10 per square foot against conventional costs of $13.50 per square foot. Single family units that could be assembled on site within eight hours were also shown. Already cities around the country were responding. The modular industry was being considered for urban renewal.

The primary thrust of the power structure was the inner city. The young Mayor seemed determined to right the wrongs of dislocation. Yet he also seemed wary of any effort designed to free the housing market. "Anyone," said the mayor before the Indianapolis Hebrew Congregation during the winter of 1968, "who stands for and pursues open housing, walks a mined field. He walks dangerous ground." Help from the mayor would be given conditioned on relative safety.

The Committee on Special Housing was already established. Persons dislocated by government action were receiving preferential treatment in purchasing FHA acquired property. Media began to report and endorse the work of the committee. The powerful WFBM stations of Time-Life gave a firm editorial endorsement in February 1968.[35] Two weeks later the committee was represented on the mayor's Task Force on Housing and Relocation.[36] Put in terms of preferential treatment for dislocated persons, the program appealed to the imagination and aggressiveness of both the mayor and his housing chairman. They asked why shouldn't the committee be given lists of all those dislocated by government action? Why should the committee be compelled to spend so much of its energy finding the dislocated when local and state governments have the names and other pertinent information in their files? Why shouldn't VA acquired property also be made available on the same preferred terms as FHA acquired property?

Harold Hatcher, executive director of the Indiana Civil Rights Commission, discussed this last question on behalf of the committee with local property management officials of the Veterans Administration in April and May of 1968. They, in turn, asked Washington for advice. The answer was that there was no justification at the time (May 1968) for such a preferential program since qualified buyers were not using a significant amount of FHA property. There was an indication, however, that a kind of local preference might be given to any proposition submitted by a displaced person on VA acquired property.

In assisting the committee, however, the mayor drew a sharp line between finding homes for those dislocated by government action and a free housing market. The mayor was not about to venture into any scheme that seemed a naked attempt to create what the community might consider open housing. He made this clear in discussion relating to other institutional sources of property such as corporations. His reasoning included and went beyond any general concern over white reaction; there were power sources that could not in his view be ignored. Referring to the possibility of open listing of corporate acquired property, the mayor asked, "What do the real estate brokers think of the proposal?" More precisely, the question should have been, "What do those few Realtor leaders of the Indianapolis Real Estate Board who market the bulk of corporate and white residential listings think of the proposal?"[37]

The role of the white-dominated real estate board could not be ignored. It operated as an influence on the role city, state, and federal government might play in housing. It was therefore necessary to know the measure of real estate industry sensitivity. Would those who dominated the real estate board resist government initiative in moving toward a free housing market? Specifically, how would the Indianapolis Real Estate Board react to the FHA acquired property program?

The queries were important. The FHA program could be dissolved by government order just as it had been established. The possibility could not be overlooked, for the real estate industry had a deeply rooted, close relationship to government, far greater than that of any Committee on Special Housing. On the other hand, there was positive potential for cooperation with the industry if it accepted the acquired property program. The real estate industry was in a position to translate the reality of the committee's program and its impact to its white principals as a part of their selling decisions.

The industry did not respond immediately or clearly. First came the proper words, the language of public-spirited, law-abiding citizens, sounded vigorously by the executive director of the Indianapolis Real Estate Board. Replying to an outline presentation of the FHA project, before the Housing Advisory Committee of the state Civil Rights Commission, Jack McMahan, the board's executive director, stated, "The overwhelming number of Realtors are in compliance with the open housing laws. It is wrong to charge them with discrimination. We are doing everything possible to cooperate."

How were the Realtors cooperating? Mr. McMahan was direct. He said that the Indianapolis Real Estate Board had wanted to cooperate with FHA and its Counseling Service that had been established initially on an experimental basis in Indianapolis and fourteen other cities. After all, the real estate boards in those cities were cooperating with FHA.

Among the fifteen experimental cities were Milwaukee, Baltimore, and Washington, D.C. Milwaukee probably had a more in-depth program than most. In the first seven weeks the Milwaukee office obtained 400 listings from seventy brokers. By FHA's own estimate seventy-five percent of the listings were in black areas and twenty-five percent in white areas. Two hundred and seventy-seven applicants were interviewed; of these 148 were black and 129 white. In the relevant period six offers to purchase were made.

For Baltimore, the District of Columbia, and Saint Louis, the first month of operations were discouraging. In Baltimore the real estate brokers had not provided listings. Though twenty-two applicants were interviewed, no application for mortgage insurance resulted. In the District of Columbia fifty-nine of sixty-seven applicants were black. One person had been able to either rent or buy. In Saint Louis ninety-four applicants were interviewed. No application for mortgage insurance resulted.

Carmen Pasquale, FHA assistant commissioner for field operations, reemphasized FHA's relationship to the real estate industry:[38]

> FHA encourages the support and cooperation of the real estate community in the program. After FHA counseling, applicants are referred to real estate brokers, builders, and apartment managers if the applicants are able to buy or rent standard, private housing. . . . Participation by the real estate community in the housing counseling program is voluntary. FHA encourages participation and welcomes listings for sales or rentals from the industry to facilitate FHA referrals to industry participants. FHA's policy is to not accept listings from individuals who are seeking to sell their own houses without the benefit of the services of a real estate broker.

There was a sense of partnership when the FHA assistant commissioner in charge of field operations emphasized FHA use of brokers, "Last year [1967], for example, we paid some $30 million in broker's fees on FHA-owned homes that were sold by private brokers."[39]

FHA was there to help the brokers, who, after all, only had limited time to serve the low-income families who formed the greater number of those coming to the Counseling Service.[40] Brokers were civic-minded, but they also had to think of profit. These same brokers, moreover, were interested primarily in sales, not rentals, and they could not deal with the applicants who were in need of public housing. "The FHA, being part of the Department of Housing and Urban Development, is in a position to have the capability to refer families who need the service to other programs of HUD or other community resource services."[41]

The Counseling Service was to be run with existing FHA manpower. The middle-income families who received primary attention and the huge construction projects involving large federal allocations were to continue to receive priority. "The program is not going to be a waste of manpower or add to the cost of operation of local insuring offices. We have competent personnel in our insuring offices who are highly qualified to perform as housing counselors and can undertake to do so easily in addition to their regular duties."[42]

McMahan had called his counterparts, staff officials of other real estate boards in cities where FHA had a Counseling Service, and he reported, "We found out that the service was okay, that we could cooperate with it." The real estate board voted to make its multiple listings available if individual homeowners agreed. That is, each listing broker asked the property seller whether there would be any objection if the home were listed with FHA. In doing this the broker made it plain that if the home were listed with FHA any sale would have to be on a nondiscriminatory basis.

Literally hundreds of homes were to be made available to the Counseling Service, according to McMahan. But the real estate board reconsidered its action. It withheld sending the listing received because the FHA acquired property program eliminated the broker. The Indianapolis Real Estate Board as a matter of principle believed that licensed brokers should be used in the sale of property. Until FHA revised its position the board would withhold listings.

At the time McMahan spoke, before experience and data had been acquired, one could agree fully that brokers should be involved, if properly controlled, in the priority use of FHA acquired properties. One then could accept the board's action on principle.[43]

McMahan carefully explained that very few members of the board dealt in any substantial way with FHA acquired property since that was a field reserved to specialists. He seemed to be offering a basis for negotiation and possible cooperation in achieving a free housing market. The committee representative accepted what he thought was a basis for discussion. After stating that business, after all, was not the province either of charities or social service agencies, he added, "Let's shape a proposal that will be acceptable." McMahan said, "Fine. I suggest you contact Dave Morley, the Realtor who does handle a great deal of business of FHA repossessed property. See what he has to say. We'll work together. I'm always available."

Within two hours, Dave Morley, a professional broker in his forties who viewed the license he held as including public responsibility, met with a representative of the Committee on Special Housing. "Let me assure you," he said, "not all real estate brokers wear suede shoes. Many of us are professional. We are in business and that business calls on us to safeguard the interests of our clients." Morley spoke of a real estate practice without discrimination. It was a firm for which he had worked that "opened" Forest Manor to blacks. He, personally, had made many sales to blacks in white areas but only on the basis that that was where the person wanted to go. "I never forced anyone to integrate."

Would Morley cooperate? Could a relationship be established that would permit the weight of the real estate board to be thrown behind the committee's program? Answered affirmatively, the commitee could turn over its function to the real estate industry and become no more than a kind of civilian review board slowly fading away as the Realtors' practices changed.

Morley proved his word. He was handed a problem by the committee. For months, a white couple had been trying to help their maid, a thirty-seven-year-old black widow with six children, find a new home. Almost a year earlier there arose the possibility of public housing because the widow, who had come to Indianapolis from a share-cropper's existence in Alabama, earned only $115 weekly including a monthly pension from her deceased veteran husband. Her home was a shack with a coal-burning stove as a source of heat. She lived near railroad tracks where there were no signs to warn her children as they walked to school. The white couple sought help from a militant black minister who made promises but did nothing. The committee did not have a house large enough and priced low enough to accommodate the widow.

The white couple expected little when Morley was introduced. Yet within twenty-four hours, the widow saw a lovely seven-room Veterans Administration repossession in an all white area. Within another twenty-four hours, her proposition had been submitted by Morley who had presented the widow's credit profile in a somewhat more satisfactory light, stressing her stability in relation to her debts. Within three weeks the widow and her children were moved from their shanty.

"I don't expect any violence," said Morley. "It's a stable neighborhood." No violence came. The eldest son of the widow soon was king of the block, the children were happy in school, and the widow came to know her neighbors. Not far away, only a five-minute drive, were her white employers who had developed respect for the white Realtor from whom they had expected so little.

Morley and the Committee on Special Housing in consultation with McMahan shaped a proposal to bring the brokers back into the acquired property program. "Frankly, when that happens you'll see that we will do a better job," Morley said. "Why, given the chance I could sell every piece of property FHA has. I know people and property. That's my business."

There weren't thousands, hundreds, or even tens of dislocated persons knocking on the committee's door. Yet, the dislocated existed. If the profit motive would stir the brokers to do the job of placing the people and thus aiding in freeing the housing market, so much the better. Once the brokers were admitted to the program the hundreds of real estate board multiple listings would be released, thereby providing another vehicle for accelerating the market opening process.

Within the ranks of the committee there was excitement. HUD officials listened in disbelief.[44] Could it be that the real estate board really wanted to cooperate? Could it be that the board desired a free housing market? Why McMahan even accepted the "rightness" of the proposal involving corporation-owned property. Granted it might be embarassing for the board to do anything in active support of that suggestion, at least formal opposition would not be forthcoming. Perhaps the chamber of commerce or the mayor would carry the ball.

The proposal for changing the FHA acquired property program was drafted and the two real estate men were told, "If it meets with your approval, it will be submitted to HUD with the committee's endorsement." They read and agreed. The proposal had as its core simple revision of the FHA regulations relating to acquired property available to the dislocated. The committee recommended that the regulations be changed to read "commission may be paid" on the sale of FHA acquired homes.

This would allow a lever of discretion to be exercised by each FHA field director. Brokers would be used and paid to the extent they comported themselves with the spirit of the dislocated program. McMahan and Morley agreed but asked how the proposed program would work. When asked for suggestions one Realtor replied, "Controls must be exercised. You want people who are responsible." The Realtors themselves established the criteria for the program. Only brokers with five years' experience should be permitted to sell under the dislocated program. Each broker should have an office. This would eliminate the part-time salesmen and bring to the program only those who had vested interest in real estate as a profession.

All those who would qualify by the Realtors' standards should be invited to participate, but in so doing, they would have to enter an agreement to handle FHA acquired property on a nondiscriminatory basis. While such an agreement had long been in existence, it would assume special meaning under the proposed program. A roster of qualified participating brokers was to be formed. Applicants would continue coming to the committee to be certified as dislocated and shown listings, but would then be sent to brokers on a rotating basis. Any broker selling property under the program or finding a prospect would have to bring the applicant before the committee for certification and a credit check. The procedures would have permitted close checks on participating brokers for the committee would know the applicant and determine property location by means of a current racial density map for metropolitan Indianapolis.[45] For the broker, the committee would be useful. He could point to the committee or FHA as the motivating force for any black introduced to a white neighborhood. He would only be doing what the government ordered. The government could be the scapegoat. Perhaps even more meaningful for those few brokers who had made substantial sums in the sale of FHA acquired property, there was the assurance of "first come, first served." The first broker before the committee with a qualified buyer and a designated property would have his commission assured on sale. He would no longer have to compete with ten to twelve bids in a public lottery.

Should problems of discrimination arise, provisions for sanctions were available. The local FHA director could strike the guilty broker from the participating roster. The committee would not make any arbitrary recommendations to the FHA director. The facts first were to be presented to the committee, one of whose members would be a Realtor who was an official of the Indianapolis Real Estate Board.

This, in sum, was the proposal for revising the FHA acquired property program. It had agreement in principle from McMahan and Morley. Together with an entire outline of the committee's project, the proposal was to be forwarded to HUD, specifically to the office of the secretary. "To back up what we've proposed, to demonstrate our good faith," the committee's executive director said to the two Realtors, "why don't we run an open house? Let's not just limit ourselves to dislocated persons. Let's compare the effectiveness of the brokers to that of the committee's volunteers."

It seemed an excellent opportunity. Only a month before, in cooperation with FHA, the committee ran a widely-publicized open house. For two weeks front page stories appeared in the black newspaper, the *Indianapolis Recorder*. One typical article read: "Are you forced to move because of highway or park construction? Has your home been cited for code violation? Are you in need of housing? Homes can be bought at fair prices throughout Greater Indianapolis. Come to the Committee on Special Housing. It will be open on Saturday and Sunday from 10:00 A.M. to 5:00 P.M. for you." FHA employees agreed to work during the weekend. Applicants were met at the FHA door by committee members. Homes were shown to those interested. Drivers were available to allow physical property inspection of rehabilitated homes.

Once interested and after a preliminary committee credit analysis, the applicant was taken to one of seven FHA volunteer counselors to learn realistically what he could afford. The applicant then returned to the committee. If interest was still sharp and if the applicant, according to the FHA counselor, appeared to be able to afford the home he selected, it was set aside pending rehabilitation and credit and employment checks. For those who had earlier found a home and had the necessary verifications completed, FHA had staff members available to accept contracts and money.

Nearly sixty persons had come to the open house. After hearing about the program, forty chose to undergo counseling. Within two weeks, approximately twelve properties were set aside for prospective buyers, of which five were blacks moving into all white neighborhoods.

The committee felt a measure of success. The few individuals who happened to constitute the field workers of the committee knew or came to know well the people looking for homes. No one was treated just as an applicant with a number. All were treated as specific personalities with specific needs. The committee did not take the cloak of an impersonal organizational entity.

And the FHA staff who for so long had been removed from people with problems relating to inner-city existence, who had been confined to the niceties of the middle class, came to find that not all blacks were doomed by their own volition to live in slums. Some wanted more and were willing to work for it. One lady from FHA who initially did not want to work on the weekend said to the committee as the last guests left on Sunday, "Thank you for inviting me. I've seen something and learned something I'd not been aware of. I'd like to work again if you have another open house."

Not all was success, however. There were more than 100 FHA homes in inventory that were fairly priced and scattered throughout greater Indianapolis. But there were some applicants whose housing needs could not be met. For instance, there were only a few FHA homes with more than three bedrooms. During the first three months of the committee's operations a list was compiled of those applicants wanting, though not necessarily needing, a four bedroom home. From January to April 1, 1968, of sixty-two applicants twelve wanted a four bedroom home. With an inventory of seventy-one available units at the time there were ten with four bedrooms and one and a half baths. Of course, as applicants increase and inventory dwindles the same ratio might not be maintained.

Further, merely because there were ten homes for twelve applicants doesn't mean that the needs of ten families were basically met. These applicants would have to decide whether any of the ten units met their other wants. There were those who wanted a specific neighborhood in which no FHA homes were located. There were those who wanted higher priced homes. In seven months of operations (January to July, 1968) there were at least six applicants who sought and apparently could afford $18,000 to $25,000 housing. There were those who did not qualify as "dislocated" under the program, and there were those who doubted that the committee had decent homes at fair prices. After all, the committee was a strange sounding entity. Generally, people looking for homes go to a real estate agent, not a Committee on Special Housing.

Competition bringing full service would mark the second open house. With the cooperation of FHA and its employees who yielded another weekend, those wanting to buy a home would be invited. The committee would welcome all who came. Those qualifying as dislocated would be made aware of FHA acquired property as at the first open house. Those not dislocated would be directed primarily to brokers. All would go to FHA counselors to determine the price range of homes they could afford. The committee, for its part, would encourage all dislocated persons to see the attending brokers "to compare."

The participating brokers were each to be given a desk in a room separate from the committee. While the committee controlled the general traffic flow, Morley assumed sole responsibility for his fellow brokers. A sign stating "Broker Control Point" was to be posted. There Morley was to keep a roster of brokers in attendance. On a rotating basis, applicants were sent to a designated broker who was to maintain his own listings. If the applicant could not be satisfied, he was to be taken back to the Broker Control Point and assigned to another broker.

Morley and one of the few black Realtors, William Ray, were to join forces to implement the procedure and to contact the white and black real estate agents. Above all, Morley was to urge fair asking prices and insure against "junk listings," that is, the offering of dilapidated property. Finally, and this was most important, efforts were to be made to insure that members of the city's four multiple listing associations would be present. If this occurred then the hundreds of listings that McMahan referred to at the Housing Advisory Committee meeting would be available, including the listings in white areas.

Would McMahan agree to the open house? By themselves, Morley and McMahan discussed the proposition. The answer was yes. A new day seemed to be coming. A new approach, grasped by young businessmen, seemed to erase the ugly vocabulary and action of the past. The committee spoke of business and a free housing market not only in terms of social values. To the real estate men the committee spoke in terms of free enterprise, of breaking down restrictive business practices by permitting the exercise of a free choice by the consumer. The words seemed right for the Realtors.

Within a few days good fortune turned better. McMahan reported that he and representatives of the national headquarters for real estate boards were scheduled to meet with FHA Commissioner Philip Brownstein. "I hope to have an opportunity to tell him about the program here in Indianapolis," McMahan said. A committee representative told McMahan, "Tell him everything. Let him know that a new kind of cooperation has been found. Let him know of the proposed changes that we intend to forward."

McMahan left and promised to tell the committee about the conference immediately on his return to Indianapolis. McMahan returned, but no call came. A committee representative telephoned, "How did things go? What happened?" The answer was unclear and not at all direct. "We didn't have much of a chance to talk about the program," said McMahan. "I told Mr. Brownstein that the brokers were upset because they were out of this part of the acquired property program. It was a good conference. Phil gave me his card. He told me to call him personally if I had any questions in the future. He said I wouldn't have to go through any red tape to get an answer. He sure is a nice guy. I think everything is going well."

That was the last direct communication from McMahan relating to the Committee on Special Housing. He attended a meeting a few days later to review the final draft of the committee's proposal. Present were Dave Morley and the Indiana FHA Director, Allen Dale. McMahan gave the same summary of the Washington meeting, after he and Morley gave what appeared to be acceptance of the draft.

What happened in Washington, at least in terms of Commissioner Brownstein's understanding, became clear in a telephone inquiry from one of the commissioner's assistants to Dale shortly after the conference: "Is the Committee on Special Housing selling our acquired property? What the hell is happening in Indianapolis to make the Realtors so mad?" Dale answered that it was the committee that had proposed the dislocated persons program as it relates to acquired property. He described the committee as an organization of responsible individuals and groups, such as the Indiana Civil Rights Commission, and he said that the committee as such was not selling property, but committee members who were properly deputized were aiding FHA in the sale of property as required by Property Deposition Letter 129. He went on to specify that the program was helping inner-city residents and at the same time saving FHA money, and that no one was being paid any money whatsoever for the sale of these properties. It was at least the third time Dale had been required to identify the committee.

Neither Dale nor the committee members spoke with McMahan about the telephone call from FHA. McMahan's previous deep involvement with the committee was as if it had not been. But McMahan did not disappear completely. Many weeks later at a luncheon meeting that was attended primarily by concerned social service agency executives, a representative of the committee discussed private assistance and inner-city housing problems. Before the speeches McMahan came to the head table and said to a person concerned with rehabilitating inner-city housing, "A member of the Real Estate Board asked that I contact you to see what we can do to be of assistance." At the same time, a letter was sent to the Urban League in which McMahan offered to meet and set up lines for cooperation between the real estate industry and the league's Fair Listing Service.

McMahan appeared to shy away from the thrust of the program of the Committee on Special Housing. Perhaps there was sound reason in doing so. McMahan did not talk before the Housing Advisory Committee as an individual but as a representative of the Indianapolis Real Estate Board, an organization that had its own members who assumed varied positions of power. McMahan could in all likelihood do no more than the more powerful board members or officers would allow.

Nothing was said to Morley of the committee's growing concern about the real estate board. Morley had promised to cooperate, to show what could be done at an open house. The committee believed Morley was a man of good faith. It was in that spirit, despite what had occurred, that the committee proposals for change in the FHA acquired property program were forwarded to HUD as well as to certain major national organizations that had shown an interest in the committee's work.

Morley kept his word. He sought out brokers, black and white. He reported to the committee, "One broker called me and asked what this was about. He wanted to know what listings to bring. I asked what he had. He read the addresses. I said, 'Forget it. We don't want junk property.' He answered, 'That's half of what I got!' I told him to bring the other half."

Great effort went into getting members of the multiple listing associations. Morley put days of work into the effort. Finally, at the last minute, he could say, "They'll all be represented." The committee was to have the advantage of the hundreds of listings referred to by McMahan.

Allen Dale called a press conference on April 17, 1968, just a few days after the murder of Dr. Martin Luther King, Jr. On that day the headline of the *Indianapolis News,* the city's only afternoon and evening paper, was "Open Housing Drive Planned April 27-28." The lead paragraphs read, "Realtors, real estate agents and prospective home buyers will join forces April 27-28 in an attempt to find homes throughout the city for purchasers regardless of race . . . [the committee] said the occasion, which would be a tribute to Dr. Martin Luther King, would entail a meeting of real estate representatives from Indianapolis and Marion County and prospective homeowners in an effort to make available all prices of homes for anyone interested."[46] The *Indianapolis Recorder,* WFBM, and other radio and television stations carried the story prominently.

The Indiana Civil Rights Commission had earlier made available on a near full-time basis an administrative assistant. Files had been shaped for the committee's director of field operations who knocked on doors whenever and wherever an applicant wanted help. FHA properties had been carefully plotted on a large map and their state of readiness noted.

At ten o'clock on the morning of April 27 the committee's chief social work consultant and the administrative assistant sat at the reception table. Records were to be maintained for in-depth follow-up interviews. On one side of the office were six FHA staff counselors. A room with four tables had been assigned to the committee's four fully active field workers.

Although only two medium-sized Realtor firms participated in the open house, at least six Realtors and twenty-five brokers, including two sub-division contractors, sat behind the Broker Control Point.[47] The committee made a few preliminary inquiries about the brokers' listings. When asked if they carried many listings, the Realtors stated they had at least three or four hundred. Asked if they were to be shown on a nondiscriminatory basis, the answer from one was "Absolutely. That was the agreement with Mr. Morley." When asked how many of the properties they had available for showing in the multiple listings (which then numbered nearly 4,000) were in all white neighborhoods, the reply was "We didn't do too well." When asked for an estimate, there was a long pause. "We estimate that we may have twenty-five properties in all white areas." Of 4,000 multiple listings, no more than four hundred decent homes at fair prices had been screened for nondiscriminatory sale. Of these, only twenty-five were in all white neighborhoods. The estimate was not made by a skeptical committee but by white Realtors who knew they were not to be checked.

How meaningful then was the possibility of FHA receiving the multiple listings of the real estate board? What was the import of the "hundreds of properties" that might be made available to the Counseling Service if FHA revoked its broker-exclusion proviso in the acquired property program? For that matter, could the acquired property program have offered a rationalization for not making known the limitations contained in the checked multiple listings?

How accurate was the statement that a majority, even seventy-five to eighty percent, of all Realtors wanted to and were complying with the city and state open housing laws? Not one of the city's largest Realtor firms chose to be present at the open house. Not one of those Realtor firms handling corporate acquired property chose to attend. Not only did they stay away, but the proprietor of one of the most influential residential and industrial Realtor firms said, "I have no intention of cooperating. I intend to do nothing until the federal open housing law forces me to do so, and then I will think about it."

What of the Realtors present at the open house? Surely they had not only evidenced a desire to comply but had supported the state and local housing laws. Again, consider the facts. At a meeting well in advance of the open house, the executive director of the Indiana Civil Rights Commission had said, "When you're looking through your listings for those where the owners have checked 'FHA,' have agreed to let the property be listed with the FHA Counseling Service, how about doing something else? You know our state open housing law exempts only owner-occupants. Property which is vacant must be sold on a nondiscriminatory basis. This could be added to your list." It was not added. Only FHA-checked property was included in multiples brought by the brokers.

There were, however, twenty-five brokers or contractors present, and they were not there to waste two days in a symbolic showing. They were there to sell property. They would exercise their best efforts to effect sales because only then would profit be made. Even if the brokers were not terribly interested in a free housing market at least these professionals could help put people in decent housing.

Fifty-three persons came to the open house. All were encouraged to see the brokers. Nearly all took advantage of what lay behind the Broker Control Point. The applicants were not timid. Many went from broker to broker in a kind of supermarket shopping under one roof. Three applicants saw as many as five brokers each. What were the results? Did the brokers help? Was the venture profitable?

Random interviews with three Realtors, a contractor, and two brokers produced practically the same comments. They thought that the open house was good, but that better publicity was needed to attract more people. A contractor and a Realtor then took the initiative. One said, "Next time let us help with the publicity. We would be happy to prepare and pay for advertising."

Morley felt a sense of satisfaction. Experience had been acquired. He thought that at least three propositions (offers to buy) had been written, and, perhaps most important, for the first time black and white real estate brokers were in the same room working together, trying to make sales, and in the process trying to show that private enterprise was better than committee enterprise.

Despite the clarity of the publicity, not all of the guests came to buy homes. They received, nevertheless, all possible help with problems relating to housing. Mr. Pound, a black, had seen one of the committee members several weeks before. His very large home in a stable black area was in the process of insurance company foreclosure. The committee aided in staying the suit and arranged a method of repayment. Pound could have sold his home and bought other smaller quarters for his wife and five children, he could have continued living as he had, or he could have taken his structurally sound but deteriorating home and rehabilitated it. He chose rehabilitation. He came to FHA to see what could be done in the context of his income.

The FHA counselor to whom he was sent said, "I don't really see how we can help. This man is in pretty bad financial shape." Pound was taken to another counselor more closely involved in the committee's program. "Yes, perhaps we can help. I could send you to a bank vice-president who helped us before, but why don't you try to get a loan yourself? If you fail, come back. There isn't any sense in using our last resource unless we must."

The committee asked William Ray for advice. There was no hesitancy. "Yes, there probably is a way. Several insurance companies have made available money for inner-city rehabilitation. This falls in that category. The money is being administered by the X Bank. Go to Mr. Jackson and tell him I sent you. Here is my card. If there are any problems, please feel free to call me."

In the final analysis, whatever the brokers thought, whatever the committee surmised, the success of the open house had to be measured by those attending, the potential buyers. Two to three weeks after the open house a team of interviewers trained by Mrs. Kaplan visited those applicants who had any contact with brokers at the April 27-18 open house. The sample was small and the results not definitive, but the interviews highlighted some revealing facts.[48]

Initially, eighteen applicants who saw both the committee and the brokers were interviewed. A later group of seven applicants who had visited only with brokers were also questioned. The seven were not tallied with the initial eighteen. In all respects but one, independent review showed the seven to be in such close agreement with the rest that, with the exception noted, the following summary describes the entire group, nearly half of those attending the open house.

Who were the applicants? What were their ages? How many children did they have? Were they renters or owners at the time of the open house? How had they learned of the open house? Those who saw the committee were young. Their median age was thirty. Most had two children in grade school, and, perhaps as significant as any other factor, most were renting at the time of the open house, which they had heard about through their newspaper. Though living in the inner city, they were not apathetic, worn-down slum dwellers. Their apartments were clean, their furniture well cared for, and they were interested in improving their living conditions.

The committee interested them. Interviews with FHA counselors helped all to decide to try to become homeowners rather than renters. Their motivation in moving, in changing status, was either compulsion or desire and sometimes the combination of both. Some were forced to move because of public project displacement. Others wanted to move for personal reasons such as: "I want a better school for my kids." "This neighborhood is too rough; it isn't safe." "I'd like to better myself."

Brokers told eleven of the initial eighteen about homes for sale in an area where they wanted to live. Ten of this group had arranged appointments with brokers following the open house, and all ten were shown homes in a neighborhood where they wanted to live. Eight said they liked at least one home well enough to buy it. Of these, seven signed offering propositions and tried to make purchases. One proposition was accepted; one was rejected because the prospective buyer was unable to obtain financing. Three propositions were rejected for reasons that were unclear but not related to price and two remained unresolved three weeks from the date of submission.

So three weeks after the open house, with the help of the brokers only one family had found a home. Of those who had not found a home seventy-one percent intended to continue their search. Eighteen percent said they had "had enough," and they were going "to give up looking." Forty-eight percent planned "to get in touch with the committee for more help."

What do the sampling figures mean? It is here that a difference between the group of eighteen and that of seven becomes apparent. Without a single exception the seven serviced by brokers alone were not satisfied with the assistance received. They had not found a home. Three did not plan to contact a broker again. Four had not at the time of interview (three weeks after the open house) received or initiated contact with their designated broker.

Why was there such a difference in response between the two groups? Obviously with a limited sampling no reason can be offered as causative, although speculation is possible. Why did fifteen of eighteen feel that they had a positive experience with the committee even when many had not found a home of their choice? Why did so many in this group want to continue contact with the committee? Some of their comments were: "The committee gave me valuable information as to what price range I can afford, what to look at from the quality aspect, and legal information on real estate transactions. . . . They've opened my eyes to the problems of buying costs and other factors. . . . The committee was more helpful and personal. The broker was only interested in making a sale and couldn't care less." One man said that because of the committee for the first time in his life he realized he could move into any neighborhood he could afford. One woman said, "The committee did make it seem possible to buy a home. They at least have given us hope."

There was conviction in the words. By Sunday evening seven FHA properties had been set aside for qualified buyers pending rehabilitation of the houses. As a result of the open house, another five homes were set aside within the following three weeks. Compare this with the one accepted broker proposition.

Why was there such a difference? Were the brokers simply attempting a show? No, the brokers present wanted to sell property. That was why they were there. They conducted themselves as they did in their regular business. If anything, they spent more time and showed more patience than they would have with their regular customers.

There were, however, major points of distinction between the couple who would walk into a broker's office in the normal course of events and those who visited the committee. The fact that they felt a need to come to the committee was no small matter. The weekend visitors had been renters. They were young, not yet familiar with the experience of major debt obligations—though nearly all of the applicants had debt problems. They were people who doubted their own abilities, individuals with many questions as to whether they could own a home of their own. They had a flickering hope when they crossed the FHA threshold. That hope had to be nurtured and allowed to build to enthusiasm through understanding. There was a financial, legal, and, above all, a psychological gap that the renter had to leap. And he had to want to leap the gap. The committee was there to show him that he could make the jump. The committee did not simply show homes.

For what they did the brokers could not be criticized. They acted as their training and business interests dictated. The facts were, however, as the assistant FHA commissioner had earlier stated.[49] Brokers might be civic minded, but low income families could not generate sufficient profit in relationship to their problems. The FHA Counseling Service was established for these people. The applicants before the committee, like those who came to the Counseling Service, belonged to a class of people who had gone unnoticed. They were neither middle-income nor poverty-stricken. Rather, they were people approaching a bridge. On their bank was all that the inner city can yield. They were people about to make a choice, to stay with what they knew or cross over to the unknown, the seemingly shining land of middle class.

The committee dealt with those in the nether world, people who had a gross family income of $6,000 annually, people who had stable jobs, but who had not yet learned to unwind the tangle of credit problems. These were the wandering dispossessed who visited the committee.

Those dislocated by government action in the inner city were most hard pressed for adequate housing. Government and private organizations were responding to that need in terms of the inner city. Yet try as they might it seemed unlikely that enough new housing could be constructed to meet the immediate demands of thousands. It was not unusual, therefore, to see some government agencies acting as formal conduits for landlords of dilapidated inner-city property; these agencies accelerated the process of slum development. There were few who sought the advantages that a free housing market might bring in opening new housing in other areas of the community. Certainly the white-dominated real estate board was not among the few. But even if the Realtors chose to comply with the open housing law, it is doubtful that at this point they could have spent the time and made a profit by serving the inner-city renter in his transition to homeowner.

6

A View of the Committee and its Methods

There was a need that had to be met. The committee had what it thought were tools for the job; a solid, ongoing housing inventory would be made available each year. The citizenry could not escape; at some point they would have to accept the obligations as well as the privileges of the city. The capacity of blacks to move throughout Metropolitan Indianapolis, it was hoped, would aid in sealing the doors to a system of two societies and release the forces for an open society.

It was not enough that blacks could move. They had to know that they could move; they had to know they could exercise the right that was theirs. The white community had to know that this right was alive and growing, not a dead legalism, an idea reserved for brotherhood week luncheon speeches. Human rights are not made lasting solely by organizations, slogans, or sporadic dedication. Only their assertion by men, by the consumers of justice, vest the rights that are claimed.

Who within the black community would come to a Committee on Special Housing? No ordinary home buyer would seek the assistance of a committee, whose name alone meant little. A home buyer would want and obtain the services of a real estate broker. Neither those who could afford the premium that had to be paid to move out of the ghetto nor those who already were homeowners would ask for the committee's services in terms of FHA acquired property. A few who were curious, or bargain hunters, or who had been frustrated in efforts to enter a particular neighborhood might inquire of the committee.

There were needs that could not be fully met by the committee. The displaced persons program, after all, was merely a legitimate means to a far broader end. The committee was not in existence merely to ferret out the displaced and find them housing. That was only its function as it related to FHA acquired property. The committee also envisioned aiding persons, black and white, renters and buyers, to fulfill their housing desires in freedom. None who called upon the committee were to be turned away. Yet the disturbing fact was that the typical middle-income consumer who had been a homeowner not only would tend to shun the committee as an organization but would resist any institutional approach. As a consumer, he would rather take his chances with brokers, who stood as symbols of the affluent community.

In striking toward a free housing market, the committee, however, did find a new consumer group. Young couples, mostly black ghetto residents, who were renters living in uncomfortable quarters began to arrive. They did not come out of social conviction and a desire to integrate the community, but because they had problems for which solution seemed difficult. Many felt the real estate industry could not help them. This was a reason why brokers were not invited to participate in the third open house on July 6, 1968. Still, for the plethora of publicity given its program the committee commanded no special attraction even for those most in need. As a device, the committee, its name, and its organization were palatable to the white community and to certain groups within the black community. The committee was a conflict-free mechanism. It operated a program to aid the displaced, not merely black people. It functioned not for the purpose of integration, but for the exercise of free choice, to allow blacks to stay in a black community—if that was their desire. It was a project of no single group. It was not dominated by the Urban League, the Baptist Alliance, the NAACP, or the mayor's Task Force on Housing and Relocation. It was a Committee on Special Housing open to all. It had a name and dialectic unfamiliar to the community at large, it could not be slotted, placed in an easily recognizable social service or civil rights pigeonhole.

The committee structure, however, achieved no positive results other than creating a climate of neutrality. It softened any thrust from the racist right and inhibited factional fights among often divided black organizations, at least in terms of using the committee's work as a focal point for criticism. Neutrality, however, demanded a price. Until its goals and capacity became known, strong cooperation, the willingness to use the committee's program as a "resource" was not forthcoming from social service, community, and most of the private civil rights groups that were apt to have contact with the people with problems, those who might turn to the committee.

Applicants did not rush to the committee. In fact, at the start of the committee's operations and during the first few months, very few came. Those who did come were reluctant, for they came when there seemed nowhere else to go. It was not that they knew the committee had something to offer. One applicant said he came "expecting the same runaround, but just maybe there might be help." There was even a certain anger demonstrated by many of the applicants in their initial contact with the committee. This anger tended to surface in the personal encounters at the three open houses; it did not show itself in the same way in the telephone contacts. There were no doubt many reasons for the anger shown by some applicants, but whatever the reasons, the committee accepted the anger and reacted with a desire to help.

In this kind of a context, how could the committee in its operations draw tight organizational lines? How could standards of firm definition be established for those who qualified as displaced? How could the committee refuse service to any when its believability was so tenuous?

It could not risk referring special problems to other appropriate agencies for handling. It did so only once. A young white Appalachian couple with two children came to the committee for help. They were deeply in debt and faced with making a choice between public housing and buying a house. Making that choice depended upon the results of in-depth credit counseling that might lead to a plan of debt consolidation. A committee worker who was a professional staff member of the state Civil Rights Commission had put nearly thirty hours into working with Mr. and Mrs. Bennett. A home had been selected. Then the committee sought the aid of the social service organization that was charged with rendering credit advice. The organization was asked if the Bennett's debts could be consolidated and a total family budget created.

It took nearly a month to obtain an appointment for Mr. and Mrs. Bennett with the social service agency. Further, once there, the young couple was told: "No budget can be worked out until after you move into your new home. Only then will your expenses be known." The Bennetts chose public housing. They could not chance the unknown without help. No criticism of the social service agency is intended. It was subject to the limitations of budget and manpower. The committee's work, however, was with people who had real and immediate problems, and the problems could neither be separated from the people nor placed in limbo until someone, somewhere, found the time to be of service.

Except for one point, the committee was left unstructured: People were to be served as individuals. People were to be served at their convenience; office hours were forgotten and the committee became mobile.[1] People were to be given the opportunity to choose and to know fully the price that had to be paid for the choice made. There might be social value in a free housing market, but it was individual choice, not imposed principle, that would establish the market or see it remain merely an idea.

If people were to be served, they first had to be found. The committee did not wait for knocks at the office door. Committee field workers were given complete freedom and corresponding responsibility. The committee existed to expedite the task of the field worker. Policy was not shaped in advance of experience, and the primary interpretation of experience was that given by the field worker.

The title of director of field operations was given Orville Gardner of the state Civil Rights Commission as an afterthought. Potential buyers were not aware of Gardner's title or of his position within the committee, but by word and deed he gave the impression of a capacity to make decisions. His first hurdle was to kindle the flickering interest conveyed by a telephone call. He was to let the person at the other end of the wire know that homes were available and that the committee was composed of individuals who were concerned for that person's welfare and ready to help. No applicant had to take time from work to see him.

Properly deputized as a relocation officer, Gardner carried in his pocket a mimeographed copy of the local code enforcement regulations. No unnecessary preliminary sifting took place. A few questions coupled at times with visual observations and he could make the needed judgment on displacement qualification. He made an effort to keep an applicant from feeling that he was being stamped, categorized, and, if he proved himself worthy, processed. The committee had access to homes. There was a dearth of those displaced by government as committee applicants; yet the statistics pointed to an enormous need. Until the number of applicants became greater than the available supply of homes, committee approval and legal support were given for a broad definition of dislocation. With the help of outside counsel who later joined the committee came the interpretation of dislocation in specific cases: Soldiers transferred to Indianapolis from other posts were judged dislocated by government action since government had forced the move.[2] Those forced to leave public housing because their income reached beyond the outer limits and unable to find adequate shelter were considered dislocated. Those living in unsanitary conditions that they themselves could not reasonably control were termed dislocated. Mr. and Mrs. Edwards, for example, owned a once pleasant home near a highway construction site. Earth and lumber had been piled high around them, and rats bred in packs. Despite numerous calls, the state refused to do anything. The director of field operations was given opinion of counsel that the Edwards were dislocated.

Counsel opinion was also requested to determine the status of those who had been placed in inadequate quarters by the highway department's relocation section. The opinion given was that as long as the applicant had been dislocated at some point in time, he would qualify as dislocated until he found decent living quarters. Similarly, the committee recognized broader environmental problems. There were areas in the city with extremely high crime rates. There were families who could not allow their children outside safely and could not keep them inside because space was too limited. It is an obligation of government to provide adequate police protection, to aid in freeing neighborhoods from the threat of violence and to help keep the streets safe. A thirty-year-old mother of three said, "I need a bigger and better place for my kids. I want them to feel they have a home so that they'll stay off the streets and the trouble that's there." She qualified since her neighborhood was one of trouble and violence.

In matters of tight interpretation, though the applicants were unaware, memoranda on dislocation were written. In the scope of its interpretation, the committee was not reckless. There were real estate brokers closely following committee activity. Sometimes committee workers were followed. There were incidents in which brokers went beyond the point of observation. Some brokers reported alleged infractions of Property Disposition Letter No. 129, the regulations governing acquired property, to the Property Management Division of FHA. Four times committee workers were charged with entering homes before rehabilitation work was completed. Only once did this take place, and then by mistake. Finally, there were incidents of harassment. Homes were rehabilitated, but on two occasions while showing committee purchasers through to make their final inspection, dirt had been carefully sprinkled in the living rooms. It was enough to discourage the buyers. It was not enough to inhibit the committee but it did necessitate greater preparation.

The committee had to remain flexible, but it had to create structural and administrative rules such as that setting the order of priority for purchase if more than one person selected a single home.[3] This, coupled with the required credit checks that the committee ordered for all applicants, forced a modicum of centralization. There were rather obvious advantages. Not only could the committee know and survey the properties available, but it could also determine who the applicants were, their backgrounds, and how they came to the committee. A measure could be taken of the extent to which other agencies concerned with housing took advantage of the program.

The committee did nothing to impair the use of FHA acquired properties as a "resource" by other housing groups. The first qualified applicant asking for a particular property would have that home set aside for him. The committee could provide useful information feedback to other agencies, and it could judge with some certainty the impact of the program on the community. Against a current racial density map, FHA acquired properties were posted. Arrows marked the homes from which applicants moved to their new domiciles. Files were kept on properties lost for want of qualified dislocated buyers.

To enter the ranks of the open committee, only two criteria had to be met: a willingness to help establish a free housing market and a capacity for work. Around the large square table of the FHA conference room in Indianapolis, the committee met as often as twice monthly. Organizational representatives and interested persons were invited. Individually, city and state relocation officers were asked to attend. Black and white leaders, conservative and radical, were asked to sit, listen, talk, and act. The program was theirs.

Problems were discussed openly. FHA personnel were given the chance to educate the committee to the ways of an agency and in turn to be educated. With particular problems, generalization yielded to pragmatic handling. Blame for mistakes was not the center of discussion. The paint on Mr. Lane's home peeled only three months after occupancy. Could anything be done? What preventive measures might be taken in future cases? Three months after Sergeant and Mrs. Dennen selected their home rehabilitation had not been completed. Why had there been such delay? Mr. and Mrs. Brooks came in for their closing. They didn't understand the "extra" costs, the sums beyond the down payment. They were very upset. Wouldn't it be better to have a committee member present at all closings? For that matter, wouldn't it be good for all committee field workers to have a clear idea of what a closing involved? Mr. and Mrs. Cook selected a house. The cost, however, exceeded by at least $1,000 Cook's current purchasing power. Cook asked the committee whether taking a second job could resolve the problem.

The fact that the questions before the committee were specific and that all present were moving toward the common end of answering the questions, does not mean an absence of conflict. There was routine at FHA and it seldom fit the urgent needs of the purchaser. The committee could have acquiesced to the regimen of the agency. The committee could have tried to slowly induce internal change within the agency.

The committee was composed in part of individuals who would have felt more comfortable avoiding conflict and pursuing consensus, insuring safety even at the loss of success. There were those among the committee who thought it better to caution purchasers of the limitations of FHA rehabilitation, rather than fight again and again, in case after case, for sound repair. There were those among the committee who thought it better to "warn" all applicants at the point of initial contact, that money must be in the bank before listings would be shown. There were those among the committee who wanted "good" credit risks only, who wanted to deny Cook the opportunity to buy the home of his choice by taking a second job. "This," one said, "might exacerbate the very stresses which could fragment the family."

There were, however, others on the committee and in addition, there was the Indiana FHA director, who had the power and inclination to see a free housing market take shape. The questions posed in conferences were to be answered not in terms of allowing for bureaucratic convenience, nor for the security that comes from insuring against any possibility of mistake. Questions were to be answered in terms of serving the people.

The paint should not have peeled three months after the Lanes moved into their newly rehabilitated home. Three months was an unreasonable length of time to repair the Dennens' home. The basement of the home selected by the Reverend Wilson should not have been left cluttered with trash. A door in the Preston's home should have been put on hinges, not nailed shut. There was no room for compromise on these facts. On advice of counsel, the committee took preventive measures. Under Item H of the contract of sale each material defect in rehabilitation was noted. Under the terms of Item H, the home would be purchased only on the condition that the stated repairs were made. The committee's director of field operations began to list defects, sometimes photographing them.

The FHA staff complained that too many items were being listed. "Rehabilitation," said one staff member, "does not mean total repair. It only means that the home will be placed in safe, sound, sanitary repair. Nothing else. You should tell people that homes generally should be taken as is. You must remember that we send inspectors out to look at homes following rehabilitation. We would know if there were anything really bad." FHA, the personnel in Property Management emphasized, could reject the conditions stated and discard the offered contract. It was evident that they were disturbed to see the committee use Item H. It made their routine somewhat unsettled not only in terms of making needed repairs, but also just in knowing that the committee, too, was becoming familiar with the intricacies of the agency.

"Maybe we're promising too much," said a committee social worker. "Maybe we ought not say anything about the repair of the home. If people like the home, let them take it." The suggestion, though realistic, was rejected. Dale stated that as a matter of policy FHA is obligated to try to improve neighborhoods. It "is not in the business of creating or ignoring neighborhood blight." The old standard was changed by the FHA director; now each acquired home was to be placed in a state of maximum repair, not just safe, sound, sanitary condition. Families should be able to move into the home without doing a thing. It should be a home in which they have reason for pride. It should be an incentive to the rest of the neighborhood to upgrade property.[4]

The committee began to grasp the reality of rehabilitation. In metropolitan Indianapolis FHA spent from $600 to $1,500 rehabilitating each of the several hundred homes acquired annually. In 1967 approximately $200,000 was paid to individual housing contractors. Modest homes of five rooms, typical of the FHA acquired listings, having between 900-1,100 square feet would be painted at a price of about $500. Not infrequently the committee found that although the rehabilitation contract called for two coats of quality paint, a spray gun had been used to apply a single, cheap paint cover.

The contractors were not conducting charitable enterprises. They were taking substantial profit.[5] There was leverage the government could use. It was paying the bill for property that it owned, and it could demand performance for money paid. A mild measure of imagination coupled with action could end what often appeared to be exploitation of government by private enterprise. Why should the committee accept the status quo and why should the committee or FHA be oversensitive to the feelings of contractors?

Within the committee, with the active cooperation and participation of FHA's Indiana director, there was an array of talent capable of resolving problems. Mr. Nelson earned $7,000 annually. He was married with three children. "I like the homes that you have, but do I have to go through a credit check?" The committee found that Nelson had several long-overdue debts totaling more than $1,000. No home could be purchased until his debts were reduced. Counsel was sought, and an alternative was given Nelson. With a bank loan, an attempt would be made to compromise his debts. Once the compromise was accepted, a credit check would take place.

Mr. Woods, a semiskilled worker, earned about $8,000 annually. One year before he came to the committee, a friend, a real estate agent, offered to help him with his tax returns. The offer was accepted, and the friend completed the necessary returns incorrectly. The result was that Woods' tax return reported a federal tax deficiency of $1,200 despite the fact that his employer withheld tax, that Woods was married and had three teen-age dependents, facts that his friend neglected to consider. Woods, like Nelson, preferred to forget, if possible, the $1,200 debt, at least until he bought the home he "had to have." After being asked to "please tell us everything. Only then can we help," Woods told the Indiana FHA director on a wintry Saturday afternoon, "I only owe about $700 in bills." This he said although he paid five dollars for a credit check that revealed the truth.

"Damn it!" said Dale when the credit report came in. "Why did he have to lie to us? We ought to let him stew in his own juice. Look at the trouble and time spent in finding a home for him. We accepted what he had to say without question. Now look at his debts. What the hell are we going to do?" There seemed little choice in terms of the committee program. Dale and the committee met again with Woods on the Saturday following his first visit. Patiently the details of the credit report were presented. Woods was given a copy of the credit check. The facts were in the open. A home had been selected. An offer was made to obtain free counsel to file an amended return for Woods, and, in the interim, work out an agreement with the Internal Revenue Service. "That is wonderful. I sure will call the lawyer as soon as I get home," Woods said to the committee representative. He was told "Don't worry about calling him. He'll call you. Just be sure to give him the information needed.".

Woods was sold the FHA home only after a check with the volunteer counsel. The lawyer had called Woods and an appointment had been scheduled to get the needed information. The lawyer seemed confident that most of the tax deficiency could be eliminated if the facts were as stated. For four months Woods lived in his new home. All appeared well. Then the committee representative who worked with Woods received a midnight call, "I hate to bother you after the trouble you went to. I almost feel like I'm begging, but would you cosign a note for a small loan for me. I need money to get food for my family." "But you have a job," was the answer. "What happened to your paycheck?"

The Internal Revenue Service had taken Woods' paycheck in garnishment, not some of the paycheck, but all of it. Why? Didn't Woods have counsel? "Well, I decided not to use him, but to pay off the debt myself. I was paying twenty-five dollars a week, but I missed a few payments." Woods did not tell the lawyer that his services were no longer wanted. Another telephone call disclosed that each week since the lawyer accepted the case he had called Woods only to obtain an evasive reply. "Look," said the lawyer to the committee, "I'm willing to help. I'm not charging a fee, but for me to do anything, the client has to cooperate, and he's not doing that."

Total garnishment brought cooperation. The committee representative did not sign a note, but did compel communication between Woods and his lawyer. The garnishment was lifted. An amended tax return was filed. Woods found that there was recourse other than evasion and escape. He found in one instance that he could work within the system that seemed so demanding. It is not known whether Woods will accept the system or whether he believes his experience was the exception rather than the rule.

Mr. Smith, a man about forty years old, nervous often to the point of frenzy, earning nearly $12,000 annually from three jobs, felt trapped. He purchased on contract a home that was in poor condition. He didn't hold title to the home, he merely paid on a contract. If he defaulted, even in a single payment, the contract holder could force his eviction, either seeking rescission, or payment. Smith told the committee: "They haven't been fair. They [the contract holder, a firm possessing many inner-city properties] tell me my payments are $110 a month. I pay; then they raise the payments to $115. That's not right and the damn place isn't worth $110 a month. It's a hellhole." The single-spaced, small type contract called for specific payments of $110 a month. The sum was to include taxes. The contract holder merely passed on the tax increases to Smith without the legal right to do so and as a result the monthly payments were hiked.

Everything Smith said was true. Indeed, by any standards the home of Smith was unfit for human habitation. By FHA standards in terms of building code enforcement he qualified as displaced. It could be argued that, possessing an equitable interest in the home, and a contractual obligation to put it in decent repair, the certificate of eligibility should not have been issued. Sound repair of Smith's house, however, would have meant payments as great as the cost of the home.

Smith could have responded by a legal challenge to the unilateral contract change or he could have attempted to sell the home at a price that would have allowed full payment to the contract holder. Either choice would have freed Smith from the obligations he had assumed, but Smith chose neither. He elected not to pay anything for several months, and the contract holder chose to evict him.

"What am I going to do? " Smith asked. "I have to be in court tomorrow. The company told me that I would have to get out before that or they would throw my things on the street. They shouldn't have a right to do that. I have to find a home for my family. I have to find a home now." Within twenty-four hours the committee found Smith a rehabilitated FHA home.

Within the same twenty-four hours counsel entered an appearance on behalf of Smith, and the contract was challenged.[6] Within the twenty-four hours, assuming the accuracy of the credit information given by Smith, pending a credit check, FHA permitted him to move into a new home on a lease basis.[7] Unfortunately, Smith was grossly inaccurate in his credit statement. The few hundred dollars in listed debts grew to a few thousand following the credit check. Smith "forgot" that he owed many of the bills that he soon found had to be paid if he were to remain in his home. Like Woods, he seemed afraid of the system, able to face it only with evasion, although he eventually did seek legal counsel.

With organized assistance, including outside counsel, Smith was taken a long way in resolving what seemed to him an overwhelming problem. He found that the law could work for him as well as against him. He found that contracts were not always adhesive. Smith found technicians in the system willing to render assistance. He also found that he could not stand both within and without the system at the same time. He could not have the best of both worlds. He had to choose. The committee might have made the choice somewhat easier. The committee's capacity to act promptly and its ability to produce concrete results might have demonstrated to Smith that living within the system was possible.

Committee workers attempted to do more than react to problems presented by qualified applicants. They reached out to the community in pursuit of a free housing market, and elements within the community responded. Individual whites in the Butler-Tarkington section were willing to lend interest-free money to stabilize their neighborhood, the city's oldest heavily integrated area. Two such loans were made, although in both cases the buyers insisted on paying the prevailing rate of interest. White buyers were found for blocks that had become heavily black. Lawyers drafted the instruments of loan in accordance with the desires of the parties and fees were not charged. The committee's director of field operations, wearing his other hat as a staff member of the Indiana Civil Rights Commission, saw the new purchasers situated. Another step had been taken toward a free housing market, toward allowing individuals to move in accordance with their desires. There was some indication that the committee contributed to the decision of a leading national life insurance company to reinstitute mortgages in Butler-Tarkington because, as one company official stated in July of 1968, "The neighborhood has stabilized. In our view there has been a demonstration of pride of ownership. We don't like to grant residential mortgages where panic selling or large housing turnover is prevalent. We don't know what will happen to the neighborhood."[8]

The committee had incentive for direct action provided in no small part by lawyers and law professors who formed a part of the group.

Their philosophy was one of decision, not delay. Their training, and education, premised so often on cases and controversy, was that of viewing a single state of facts and driving toward an answer expeditiously. Lawyers do not relish uncertainty as it might apply to their cases and to their clients. Intellectual uncertainty and abstract problems might be enjoyable, but in battle lawyers prefer to know the lines of conflict with as much certainty as possible.

In the drive for a free housing market, however, the law-trained persons had much to learn. Their approach might energize, but it was also limiting. Lawyers took cases in which problems could be brought into focus and resolved by decision. Then the lawyers moved on to the next case while the client lived with the decision. "Remember this," said the deputy director of the Indianapolis Urban League, "long after a particular case is resolved there will be others like myself working in this community. We have to live with the people and organizations that are here." The Urban League official was concerned about the people and the community. She wanted change that would be lasting. Understanding the institutions that were deeply rooted in the community, she knew that they frequently were staffed by professionals who prided themselves on their expertise. It would be better to win cooperation than to conquer it. Decision might be compelled but the anger, the frustration, and the humiliation of the "professional overruled" cannibalized such a victory.

The lawyers consulted did learn. On a hot July day, an FHA official called a committee lawyer: "Mr. Garrett has been working with the Counseling Service for about six months. For thirteen years he has been buying a home on contract from the West Insurance Company. It is nothing more than a chicken coop. The fellow is crippled, has several kids, and lives off a pension. The state condemned his home, but only offered $600, and Garrett paid $6,500. If he walked away from his property now he would owe about $3,000. We helped him find a home on the private market. Evidently Garrett did walk away from his home because he just brought in some court papers to us. He has to appear tomorrow in court. What should he do? "

The contract between Garrett and the insurance company was examined and measured against the complaint that sought specific performance—the payment of $3,000 owing on the purchase price. The lawyer for the insurance company was called, "Why bring suit? Why not let him walk away? He hasn't got any money, except maybe a few hundred dollars. The complaint is like beating a dead horse." Counsel agreed but answered, "But we evidently have been given no choice by the company. The company officials are really angry. They made it very clear that they hope for bad publicity from this case. They want the community to know the company is sick and tired of these leeches who take modest but decent property, destroy it, and think they can walk away—and especially those who think they can walk into another home and do exactly the same thing. They have to learn to accept responsibility. That's the way the company feels. We're on a retainer. Personally I want to work out a settlement. Do you have any suggestions?"

The lawyer had in his file a picture of the "chicken coop" one year after the contract had been executed. It appeared to be a modest but decent home. The lawyer also had a picture of the home taken shortly before suit was filed. It appeared to be a "chicken coop." Whatever the value of the home had been at the time of contract—and there was substantial question as to the $6,500 price tag—it had dropped significantly. The company, possessing a large portfolio of inner-city mortgages, marked the deterioration to malevolence, to a desire to destroy. "And just because Garrett happens to be a member of a minority group doesn't mean that he should be able to get away with that kind of destruction," the lawyer quoted the company officers as saying.

For the lawyers, however, the contract and the complaint raised nice issues. It was possible to argue the invalidity of the contract and the material deficiency in the complaint. It was possible to give the company a major legal battle in which the company itself could be placed in jeopardy. It was quite a temptation to go to court, to let the company live with its decision of trying to make an object lesson out of its experience with Garrett. The temptation was heightened because of the company's power position within the inner city. A favorable decision for Garrett might benefit many others holding that company's contracts.

The committee lawyers hinted at this in their discussion with the lawyer for the company, but it was only a hint. Their primary thrust was in another direction. The message of the Urban League was not forgotten. The lawyer for the insurance company got this response from committee lawyers, "We agree with the company in principle—if the company means that decent homes sold at fair prices should not be destroyed. We agree that proper responsibility legally assumed should not be tossed aside. We are willing on behalf of the company and the Committee on Special Housing to stress these points before the Indiana director and the Counseling Service of FHA. We will do so in your presence, if the company so desires. The company is after a principle rather than a man, and we agree with the principle as stated. There is room for the company, the committee, and the FHA to work together to see that responsible people get decent homes that meet their family needs at fair prices."

The lawyer for the company accepted the stated position. Garrett would know that he, like Smith, could not both contract out and contract into the system at will. From the viewpoint of the committee's program, what would happen if the company found good buyers for its properties? What would the company's attitude be if the buyers paid on time and maintained their homes? Would the company be willing to improve new properties and invest more money in the hope of greater return? Doesn't it follow that the more property turnover, the greater the number of defaults, the less willing the company would be to bring its homes into good repair? If the company's inner-city portfolio should change dramatically, if it were made stable, would there be a softening of management's position on the disposition of its homes and financing in suburbia? There was a desire to answer Garrett's problem, and there was hope that a long-range program gain through dialogue might be obtained.[9]

The committee lawyers learned that there were other areas in the exclusive domain of social workers. Lawyers might find the means to compel the Marion County Redevelopment Commission to produce its lists of dislocated families, but staff and agency cooperation in establishing a free housing market was a different matter.[10] The committee, however, was well supplied with those who understood such agencies. The committee was composed in no small part of highly skilled social workers. Two of its members had graduate degrees in social work coupled with deep experience. With them were others who could speak the language of the social service organizations. The executive director of the Redevelopment Commission was disturbed over the possible lack of responsibility on the part of the committee until he learned from the deputy director of the Urban League that the committee members had educational and vocational backgrounds equal to the best of the city's social service organizations' staffs.

The executive director of the Redevelopment Commission, in a general way, again was asked to use the FHA program as a resource. He said he would.[11] Specifically, a black staff member of the commission was invited to committee meetings. He participated in planning the committee's third open house, Freedom Weekend, on July 6, 1968. He was given a desk as a relocation officer at that open house. Applicants were funneled to him. He saw, and most important, experienced, the committee in operation. He became involved. At the end of the open house he left tired but pleased, for people had been served.

There were specific personal matters in which the social workers took a primary role. For all, they helped to smooth the move to a new home and a new condition from renter to that of owner. For blacks moving into white neighborhoods, there was, when the new owner so desired, an effort made to smooth the way. Brief biographies were distributed. There were times when neighbors were upset. The Committee worker listened while emotion was vented. The occasion arose only once when the Committee worker sensed the possibility of violence from the invective heard. Increased police patrol was sought beyond the routine period. Weekly calls were made once the family moved into their home. Ministers in the area were contacted.

There were sometimes deep personal problems where the law-trained committee workers could listen and restate program principle, but then had to yield to the delicate discretion of committee members with social work orientation. A couple in their thirties with two children moved into a neighborhood termed "violence potential" by the Indianapolis Human Rights Commission. The move went well. Several neighbors welcomed the family, some were overbearing in their welcome, so enthusiastic were they in boasting of having a black on their quiet street. Many of the welcomers expected the family to mirror their own middle-class values. Children were not left unattended during the day until they were teen-agers. Liquor was consumed in moderation. Parties were held quietly. Extramarital affairs were conducted with discretion; a lover did not pound on the door of the house at 2 A.M. when the husband was away. Relatives might visit or stay for awhile in a crowded home, but they did not bring their appliances and store them in the back yard.

The committee did not screen its applicants to determine what values black families would or should hold important. In the context of credit capacity, the committee simply showed homes and allowed a process of natural selection to occur. The committee was interested in free choice; it did not promise pleasant neighbors or tranquil neighborhoods. In its follow-up service with the black couple in their thirties, however, the committee found rumblings; it found talk, gossip, ingredients that could produce an explosive reaction. What, if anything, was the committee to do? Suppose a white Appalachian family were guilty of the same violations of middle-class standards. What would happen? If the noise of a party were too loud, or a lover shouted too loudly, the police might be called. Neighbors might talk. Neighbors might move if the situation seemed bad enough to them.

Even if the committee had the power to impose sanctions, which it did not, did the committee have the duty or the right to inject itself into a neighborhood problem because the family happened to be black? The white lawyer members of the committee simply said, "There ought not be a double standard. Our concern is freedom of choice. Yet, we're white men. We're not sure we are able to judge what ought to be done here." The matter was delegated to the black members of the committee. They decided to select one of their number to talk with the black woman whose husband was so often away on business. The one selected was not to lecture or warn. He was only to describe what was happening in the neighborhood. The woman would have to make her own decisions.

The committee heard problems, not as a formal body but as individuals from whom the committee's director of field operations could seek help. The committee was a reservoir to be used. In the final analysis, it was the activities of the director of field operations that best represented the committee's work, its usefulness, and effect. The load the director carried was heavy, particularly in the context of the desired personal, intense relationship with the applicants. From the time the state Civil Rights Commission joined the committee's program through May 1968, a period of more than three months, the director handled 128 applicants. In that period, he was heavily involved with sixty-eight families. By his evaluation, which is conservative, forty-two families were settled to their satisfaction. From the view of the Civil Rights Commission, eighteen were well-settled in terms of "fostering integration." Ten of the eighteen were placed in FHA acquired properties. In the stated period more than twenty-five percent of those with whom the director had heavy contact moved into all white areas. More than sixty percent of the sixty-eight were settled to their satisfaction. Of forty FHA acquired properties either sold or set aside by June 24, 1968, five were held for white families, all of whom were to move into all white neighborhoods, and fourteen properties were designated to blacks who were to move into all black neighborhoods. Not a single white family of the five showed the least interest in homes located in integrated neighborhoods.

In assisting FHA, the committee said nothing of the quality or the price of the home to potential buyers. Using the one-line property descriptions tendered by FHA, the committee could drive the applicant to the home, look in the windows, and wait for rehabilitation. The committee could not state the asking price. It only could give a price range since final price would not be known until rehabilitation was completed.[12]

In a legal and realistic sense the committee was an intermediary for the FHA. The committee was a kind of affirmative manifestation of that agency's Counseling Service. Once an applicant was interested in a home, after the credit check had been ordered and the certificate of eligibility issued, the committee, usually through its director of field operations, would aid in completing an FHA form offer to buy. Where questions of income capacity seemed unclear, the committee would hold a preliminary conference with an FHA counselor. "Generally," said the director of field operations, "I'll just sit there and let FHA and the applicant try to work things out. I won't say anything unless the facts don't seem to be coming across. The decision on credit is FHA's decision, and I won't argue so long as the credit decision bears a relationship to the program. I haven't really had to do much arguing because the FHA counselor seems as anxious as anyone to see his agency's program succeed."

The question of whether a home would be sold after an offer was submitted usually did not arise. An offer without conditions generally was accepted, but there always existed the power within FHA to reject. There was one case where the FHA counselor and the committee disagreed. The committee recognized the credit risk involved, but the family of Mr. Haines, a black, was large, and there was an eight-room home in excellent repair available, one of the few large properties brought into FHA inventory in the first six months of 1968. Haines needed and wanted the home, which sold for $16,500. As Haines earned about $7,500 annually, the home was about $500 a year more than he normally could afford. Haines was willing to take more of his income and put it into housing. The FHA counselor felt the Haines would be "stretching themselves too thin." The committee aided in submitting the Haines' offer to buy; it was rejected, and the property, located in an all white neighborhood, was sold on the public market to a white purchaser.

The director of field operations worked from an office in his home. The committee's office at the Urban League was used as a clearing house and information-gathering unit. Work with the applicants took place in the field. The director's heavy involvement with sixty-eight families by the end of May, jumped to more than one hundred by the middle of July. Routine seemed a necessity, but effective operation demanded flexibility. In the absence of a budget permitting employment of more professionals, volunteers seemed a possible solution. Many came forward only to step back when they found that time, effort, and patience were required in great abundance. Volunteers were of value only in limited functions. They could attend standard, uncomplicated closings. They could provide transportation for applicants to and from the director's home. For those highly motivated applicants who had confidence in themselves and knew rather precisely what they wanted, volunteers could drive them past some of the listed properties for a "windshield" inspection.

A measure of help began to be given to the director who spent much of his time patiently convincing an applicant that perhaps the committee could be of assistance. From those already placed came referrals. Typical of those who brought others before the committee was this comment, "We can tell about the committee better than it is able to talk about itself. Our friends will believe us. You just make sure they qualify and show them the homes. We'll do the rest."[13]

Referrals came, particularly from black families. By June 25, nineteen black families had moved into their new homes. Of these, eight families referred others to the committee after they "first talked over the committee's program" with their friends and relatives.[14] Often the referrals were multiple. Wilfred Brooks referred his daughter and two friends. All found homes. Brooks lives in an all white neighborhood. His daughter, her husband, and child, found a home in an all white neighborhood a half mile from her father. One of the friends selected a home in an all white neighborhood, the other in an integrated neighborhood.

The brother-in-law of Mr. Andrew Wilkins, whose story was told earlier, came to the committee. He found a home in an all white neighborhood although Wilkins had decided upon an all black neighborhood. The brother-in-law, Sergeant Dennen, referred his sister and brother to the committee. One received substantial financial guidance, the other delayed purchase until she "could save some more money for a down payment." Wilkins did not stop with his family. He referred his job supervisor, a black, to the committee. The supervisor selected a home within three weeks.

The work of the committee did not end once the contract for purchase was signed and the way smoothed where necessary for a black into an all white area. The committee was there on moving day to insure that the utilities were operative, that furniture was moved, and that there were no added problems relating to rehabilitation.

Once moved, the people, black and white, often called upon the committee if trouble later arose—even though the trouble was not directly a part of buying the home. These calls particularly illuminated the need of this population group for sound business and financial counseling. Mr. and Mrs. Parsons, newly married, bought furniture for their new home. They purchased the goods for cash, a most unusual circumstance, from an inner-city furniture company conducting a "going out of business" sale. The company delivered different merchandise than that bought. Parsons was refused the right to return that which was sent and receive his money or obtain the designated furniture. "What should I do?" he asked the committee. A call from the committee counsel resolved the matter. Parsons had his money refunded within twenty-four hours. He bought new furniture. This time, however, he shopped stores that he hadn't entered before, such as Sears Roebuck and the J. C. Penney Company.

There was no sudden dash toward a free housing market. The elements that could form to create such a market were all present; there was an existent supply of homes priced and financed fairly, and the displaced persons seemed to be a readily identifiable group of consumers in need and able to afford the available housing. There was a trained staff anxious to match buyer with property. The elements that should have fused, according to paper theory, did not. The displaced, numbering in the thousands, could not be found. The relevant agencies that possessed their names would not tender them, nor make strong use of the FHA acquired property program. Individuals within each displacing or relocating agency were sought out by the committee and urged to observe committee operations, to test committee capability and credibility. Some did, but formal cooperation from the agencies was not forthcoming.

For the committee the way was slow. Those few who could be found in need of homes had to be served as individuals. This took time. It was not enough to help a man find a home. In making what probably is the most significant purchase in the lives of most people a great many other problems—often related to credit—first had to be worked out. Even after this was done the individual assisted frequently sought further help in dealing with his new role as homeowner. To some extent the committee found itself in the role of providing continuing education, meeting multiple goals in the effort to achieve what it thought was the simplistic end of a free housing market.

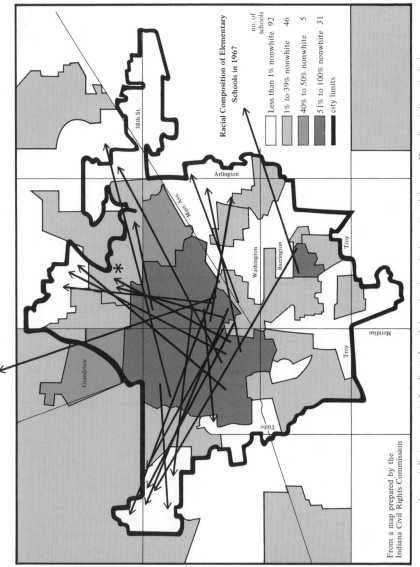

Racial Composition of Elementary Schools in 1967

	no. of schools
Less than 1% nonwhite	92
1% to 39% nonwhite	46
40% to 50% nonwhite	5
51% to 100% nonwhite	31
city limits	

38th St.

Mass Ave.

Arlington

Washington

Barrington

Troy

Meridian

Troy

Tibbs

Grandview

From a map prepared by the
Indiana Civil Rights Commission

Arrows indicate movement of applicants from their previous inner-city homes to outlying areas. Heavy lines indicate city limits.

* indicates a largely white area with partial integration. Scale: 1/2 inch equals 1 mile.

7
The Applicants

According to staff time charts, providing individual attention some-times meant as much as forty working hours for a family. This did not include time spent seeking applicants out, the time the committee spent checking whether appropriate forms had been returned, time spent by the FHA counselor reviewing and passing upon income capacity, or time the lawyers spent helping to resolve credit problems. What results did the heavy time expenditure bring for the nearly 200 persons who were reached by the committee between January 4 and July 15, 1968? [1]

By July 15 forty-five homes had either been sold or set aside.[2] An estimated eight to ten additional homes were to be selected or set aside by August 1.[3] Of the forty-five home total, twenty-nine families had moved into their homes and lived there for at least a month. Given the opportunity to select a home from a large inventory, where did the twenty-nine families, black and white, move?

> Twelve black families moved into all white areas, most of which were not adjacent to the inner-city ghetto.
>
> Two black families moved into integrated neighborhoods that were defined as significantly less than fifty percent black.
>
> Ten black families moved into black neighborhoods that were defined as more than fifty percent black.
>
> Five white families moved into all white neighborhoods.

For those who had set aside property a similar distribution took place:

Eight black families were scheduled to move into all white neighborhoods.

Two black families were to move into integrated neighborhoods.

Four black families were to move into black neighborhoods.

Two white families were to move into all white neighborhoods.

The majority of the purchasers were black. Of forty-five families selecting committee homes, only seven were white. Each of the seven moved into an all white neighborhood. Four of the seven had been homeowners before they came to the committee. Several were aware of the "bargain" prices available in the purchase of FHA acquired property. They came to the committee simply because there were decent homes available at fair prices and they wanted them. The white group contrasts sharply with the black purchasers.

Consider the figures on black purchases. More than half, twenty out of thirty-eight, selected homes in all white areas; four chose integrated neighborhoods, and fourteen black neighborhoods. Given the opportunity, there were blacks willing to move away from the inner city, willing to take a chance—if it can be so viewed—on living away from other blacks. The committee's marked racial density map indicates the extent of the chance they were willing to take. The lines of movement show the homes in which the applicants lived and those to which they moved. There are few moves that did not take the person from his old neighborhood to another neighborhood many miles distant.

Of 200 persons who had any contact with the committee nearly twenty-five percent found homes. What of the remaining 150? Were they being served? Did they find value in the committee's program? Nine who had homes set aside withdrew. They asked that the property be released. Seven were black and two were white. Of the nine, five withdrew because they themselves feared the "financial burden." Two went to the point of closing but could not bring themselves to sign the instruments of obligation. The remaining two "just had to wait too long to get into their home." One said, "I was told the home would be ready in sixty days, and it's been ninety days. That's too long."

The nine, however, were less than ten percent of the 150 remaining contacts. What of the remainder? By July 15, were all or most being served? Did they still want to be served by the committee? Had they found alternative housing? In follow-up interviews, the committee sought answers. "Mr. Jackson, did you have a chance to look at the listings? Is there anything we can do to help? Could we provide a car?

Have you further need for the committee? Have you found another home? Where? How did you find it? Are you pleased with the purchase?" These were the kinds of questions that allowed the committee to sift and maintain an active list of applicants.

By July 15 about a third of all those coming before the committee, a total of sixty-seven persons, had terminated their contact with the committee. Why? Were they dissatisfied with the committee, with its program or with its inventory? Had they found a better answer to their problem? Twenty-four of the sixty-seven had purchased a home on the private market. At least seven, all black, bought from brokers because FHA inventory was "too low-priced." Some comments were: "The homes weren't large enough." "We wanted a $25,000 home on the Northside, and you didn't have it."[4] The twenty-four constituted the largest group within the sixty-seven. Several among the twenty-four had been homeowners before dislocation. Each black purchaser on the private market, however, bought either in an all black or integrated neighborhood. Not one of the twenty-two blacks among the twenty-four bought in an all white neighborhood. None appeared dissatisfied with the committee. The typical response was, "At least you cared."

The next largest grouping among the sixty-seven were fifteen families who were tempted by the committee. They saw homes they had not seen before. They understood these homes could be theirs, but, for a variety of reasons, they did not choose to act. They wanted time to think out their situation, or they wanted to see whether they could make their own arrangements later on. To some the committee might have had an aura of government, and that could mean public housing. To others the committee might have induced fear of the unknown. Were the committee homes sound investments? If they were so good, why weren't they being sold by private real estate brokers? The story of Mr. Owen, one of the fifteen, may illustrate their thinking. Owen, a black dislocated by government action, inspected several FHA homes, but nothing seemed to please him. One day, however, he saw an FHA home in an integrated area on the southside. "There's a lot wrong with this place but all in all it's a pretty good home. I'm just not sure what to do." He did nothing, and the home went on the public market for sale through brokers. He visited the home again. There were white and black viewers, and there were brokers writing propositions. He asked for a proposition to be written for him. Among six bidders he won in the public drawing. The home did not seem to have as much wrong with it since he bought it through the more conventional FHA program.

Another group of fifteen dropped from the committee program without any opportunity at that time of moving toward home-ownership. In each instance income capacity and debt obligation combined to keep them in the position of renter. Three of the fifteen were on the brink of bankruptcy; their low rent was too high. The committee assisted them in finding public housing.[5] The committee worked with each applicant until housing was found or the applicant withdrew.

Still, twenty-five percent of the applicants were placed. Forty-five homes were found. Putting aside any social commitment on the part of FHA, consider the economic facts of the committee's first seven months of operations. The agency was able to dispose of more than $500,000 in FHA inventory at no cost to itself. The agency saved significant sums in the sales. Every home sold through the committee had the same price as if it were placed on the public market. Yet FHA paid no commission. In seven months the FHA was able to count $25,000 that it did not have to pay based on its normal five percent commission to brokers. It was also able to save on advertising expenditures. The committee's program had the indirect effect of funding the federal government. Perhaps there was some recognition of the committee's value when the FHA asked for committee comments regarding the acquired property program and the Counseling Service.[6]

Forty-five homes were found, mostly for blacks. Who were these buyers? The committee knew who they were as individuals. They knew their faces, their families, their problems. They were told repeatedly by FHA Property Management personnel of the risks the buyers and the committee were taking. "These are good people, but they have credit problems. You're not going to be doing them, the committee, or the FHA any good by moving them into homes they can't afford. Let's face it, almost all of your people [the committee applicants] are not very good credit risks." The committee tended to believe the warning. It tended to accept the individual with a poor credit history as the stereotype committee applicant. It tended to maximize the individual's problems and minimize his strong points. For all this, however, the committee did not relent in helping these very people find homes. While the committee had to accept FHA judgment on credit capacity since FHA was the agency selling its own property, it did however press for full understanding, for consideration of a man's motivation and potential. The committee felt that its actions very well might create additional problems but that the opportunity for a person to make a choice to fulfill his own life was worth the chance.

In six months of operation the committee had not yet compiled the data for a credit profile. It would order credit checks in compliance with FHA regulations. The reports went directly to the FHA Counseling Service. There they were read and interpreted against the detailed report made by the applicant on Form 2900, the petition for mortgage insurance. The files were confidential, often considered so confidential that the applicant himself would be denied his own credit report.

Each committee applicant was encouraged by the committee to disclose fully all relevant credit information, "Tell the FHA the truth. You'll only hurt your own chances for the home by leaving anything out. If the FHA doesn't get the information in the form for mortgage insurance, you can be sure that it will get everything in the credit report. If you tell them the truth, they'll be in a better position to help." Neither the committee nor the FHA Counseling Service tampered with the facts. They did not engage in the common practice of mortgagees who on completing Form 2900 in private transactions made assets for closing, such as household furniture, appear to have a greater value than they actually had.

The committee had knowledge of only some facts evidently applicable to all of its black purchasers and it had impressions as to others. The committee knew that every black purchaser of a home in an all white area had been a renter before. It knew that except for a few instances all the black purchasers had been renters. It knew that as renters the applicants were undergoing a major change. They were becoming members of the property class. The committee sought to smooth the transition. Strenuous efforts were made to keep the costs of a home purchased at the same level as the apartment rented. Individual patterns of consumption and debt payment were reviewed with the applicant by the committee and the FHA Counseling Service.

Perhaps this was proper, helpful, even necessary. There was unanswered, however, the question of comparison. Were the committee purchasers greater credit risks than those applying for mortgage insurance in private transactions? Three law students, one with knowledge and experience in statistics,[7] the second in social work,[8] and the third in product value analysis,[9] shaped a study design under committee direction to answer this question. The Indiana FHA director approved the design and called on his staff to gather the necessary data without the use of names. Two groups, CSG and FHAG were created for the purpose of measurement. The first CSG consisted of twenty-seven families, most of whom were black and had either bought or had homes set aside for purchase under the committee's program by July 1, 1968. The second FHAG consisted of a random sampling of twenty-seven families who had applied for FHA insurance in private transactions from January 1, 1968 to July 1, 1968. Recognizing the historic approach of FHA in serving the middle class, the likelihood is that most of the FHAG were white. The data obtained were nearly complete. In a few instances interpretation was needed to make estimates. This was seldom required and took place in two categories: years of employment and assets available for closing. Where the files did not set forth employment tenure, an arbitrary one year was provided. Where total assets available for closing were not listed an estimation was made based upon number of years employed, annual income, neighborhood, and similar files.

While considering the comparisons, recall the committee's fears and FHA staff warnings.[10] The CSG male applicant was 38.4 years old, significantly older than the FHAG counterpart's 31.3. Similarly, the CSG female applicants averaged 6.2 years older than the 'FHAG (35.4 years of age compared to 29.2). The oldest reported head of household for CSG was 57 compared to the FHAG of 53. The youngest head of household for CSG was 21 against the FHAG of 18. The committee had before it older applicants—those who might be considered somewhat more settled in their lives.

There were 2.4 children for each average CSG family, compared to 1.7 in the FHAG. The frequency distribution found the heaviest CSG concentration of 1 to 4 number of family dependents contrasted to the FHAG highest level of 1 to 2 children per family. In both groups nearly all families had children. There were four CSG families without children; compared to two FHAG. All FHAG applicants were married. This was not so for CSG families: 21 or 77.8 percent were married; 3 or 11.1 percent divorced; 3 or 11.1 percent separated, single, or widowed.

Against this background of age, marriage, and family, who were the heads of household? Did the supposed predominance of female heads of black families reflect itself in those coming before the committee? The FHAG had a population of 27 families with 27 male household heads. The CSG with the same population had 22 male household heads and five female, or 18.5 percent of the total. While there was a variance between groups, it certainly cannot be said that the CSG population was dominated by female breadwinners. There was an indication, moreover, that the CSG was highly motivated in moving economically upward as a family. Eighteen, or 36.4 percent of the CSG females worked, brought in additional family income, compared to four, or 14 percent working in the FHAG.

Did the CSG woman have to seek employment? Were their husbands earning significantly less than the FHAG? Were their family obligations substantially greater? The statistics were revealing. The average CSG male applicant earned $621 a month compared to $597 for the FHAG applicant. There was a difference of $24. The CSG male earned more than the FHAG. When the income of husbands and wives were totaled the variance was sharper. Family income for CSG averaged $854 monthly, that of FHAG, $760, for a difference of $94.

Committee applicants as families earned over 12 percent more than those who sought FHA insurance in private transactions and were considered safe risks in the judgment of FHA personnel. Still, this in itself was not a full contradiction of government experience. It might be reasonable to assume that although the committee applicants earned more, they might be transients, holding jobs briefly then leaving. One FHA representative stated, "People should have motivation, a stake in the community before we agree to grant insurance." To FHA and the committee, each with its own concerns and its own stereotype drawn, the comparison of job duration brought surprise. CSG males were on the job 3.7 years longer than FHAG applicants, and CSG females worked 3.4 years longer than the FHAG females. Were the committee applicants without motivation? Did they lack staying power? One explanation offered was, "Well, you know how it is. These families have credit problems. They may make money, but they spend it. They're forever in debt, and you can't buy a home that you can't afford." What were the credit characteristics of the committee applicants? Was their relative family income and employment stability offset by debt obligations? These were the findings: The average CSG family had 3.3 accounts open at the time of application; the FHAG, 2.9. There were no reported bankruptcies in the FHAG but there were three in the CSG, representing 11 percent of the total. The three had been adjudicated bankrupt in 1963, 1964, and 1966 respectively.

Did the past of the three, the 11 percent, stain the remaining 89 percent? Consider the frequency distribution in number of installment accounts outstanding at the time of application. The median was three accounts for the CSG group; for the FHAG, five. With the CSG sample, of 90 accounts, 40 represented finance companies, a percentage of 44.4. The FHAG group had 25 open finance company accounts for 31.2 percent. The largest concentration by type of account in the FHAG was that of department stores and this represented 27 of 80 open accounts or 33.7 percent of the total. The CSG had only 15 open department store accounts or 16.6 percent of the total for that group.

Although committee applicants had fewer open accounts than FHAG applicants had, there was concentration in finance companies. Purchases were funded this way rather than through charge accounts or banks. Committee applicants had only 10 percent of their total open accounts with banks; the FHAG had 20 percent. Since banks chargs lower interest rates than finance companies and banks solicit small business, why didn't the black committee applicants use the banks? Were they poorly informed? Did they feel banks were not intended for their use? How often did a black customer have to wait while his identification and account were examined by a bank teller before a ten dollar personal check would be cashed? How often did a black domestic insist on payment in dollars "because it's just too hard to cash a check?"

The finance companies welcomed black customers for there was profit in dealing with them. The committee applicants compared favorably with the FHAG in making finance payments when due or before. Eighty percent of the CSG were prompt; 81.5 percent of the FHAG. Where CSG dealt with banks or department stores, however, a different pattern of repayment was demonstrated. All FHAG bank accounts were paid on time while only 66.6 percent of the CSG could make such a claim. The remaining 33.3 percent ranged in tardiness from 120 days after the account was due to a point where suit for collection was considered necessary. Similarly, 92 percent of the FHAG paid their department store accounts on time compared to 66.6 percent of the CSG. A total of 26.6 percent, almost all of the remaining CSG, paid 120 days after the due date.

Why was there a difference between payment patterns with finance companies as contrasted to banks and department stores? The study did not give the answer. One could only speculate. Finance companies generally required weekly payments, while banks and department stores billed on a monthly basis. Weekly charges could be met by each weekly paycheck. Monthly charges required saving and a budget. For 33.3 percent of the CSG, who were late on bank payments, the regimen of weekly payout could be assumed more readily than the monthly bills that so often are paid by checks drawn on banks. The black dealing with a finance company often enters weekly with cash. He doesn't pull coupons and send checks. He isn't attracted to the banks. Time after time the committee had to request that a checking or savings account be opened so that down payment money could be deposited to insure the verification required by FHA. The black applicants kept their money at home where it could be seen, taken, and spent.

Whatever were the reasons, 33.3 percent of the surveyed committee applicants had some poor payment habits. Did this mean that they were poor credit risks? In terms of FHA standards the primary test to determine credit risk is willingness to pay as reflected in credit reports. Yet, the CSG, despite some poor payment habits, earned more and owed less than the FHAG. Now consider their total debt.

Two families in both the CSG and the FHAG had no debt at the time of application. For those remaining the comparison was pointed: the CSG average total debt was $1,333; the FHAG, $2,696. The committee applicant had a total indebtedness that was less than half that of the individual seeking FHA insurance in private transactions. For the CSG and the FHAG the most recurrent frequency of debt distribution was in the $0-$500 category. For both groups this represented 37 percent of their total population. Not only did the committee applicant earn more and owe less than the FHAG, the same committee applicant had lower monthly payments—despite the use of finance companies. Excluding housing costs, the CSG paid $72.74; the FHAG $78.11.

With less owing, the CSG had less to show when assets were added and compared with the FHAG. Utilizing raw figures and averages the FHAG held an asset ratio of 5.29 to 1 over the CSG. Included as assets "available for closing" were: household goods, furniture, personal property, and cash. Average assets for the CSG were $1,613; the FHAG, $8,545. The figures have meaning but the extent of that meaning should be tempered. Information for FHAG was derived primarily from the Form 2900, the application for FHA insurance, prepared by authorized mortgagees who knew that the greater the asset position of the mortgagor the better chance there was that insurance would be forthcoming. For items such as furniture, household goods, and personal property FHA could impose no check on stated figures. The committee, however, had no desire to inflate the applicant's position. There was deep concern that the applicant buy only what he could afford. Toward this end applicants were cautioned repeatedly to state only the truth to the FHA Counseling Service, which aided in preparing the Form 2900.

The care of the committee and the conservative nature of its applicants reflected itself in the homes purchased. Among the CSG 55.5 percent experienced an increase in housing expenses as a result of purchase; the FHAG, 85.1 percent. Housing expense decreased in 29.6 percent of the CSG cases, compared to 14.8 percent within the FHAG. While each of the FHAG cases changed in some direction, there was no change in expense in 14.8 percent of the CSG cases. Looking to the frequency distribution, the largest concentration of CSG increase averaged $30.73 monthly; the FHAG, $49.65. Where decrease took place, CSG averaged $25.37 monthly; the FHAG, $10.75. In no instance did the CSG pay more than $126-150 monthly for housing expenses after purchase. More than 50 percent of the FHAG exceeded the CSG upper limit. The CSG bought homes that averaged $12,070. The FHAG bought homes that averaged $15,044. The FHAG took more expensive property, paying on an average 24.6 percent more for their homes than the CSG. Of the purchase price for the CSG, 96.1 percent was amortized, compared to 95.2 percent for the FHAG.

What do the statistics indicate? If the FHAG were the "safe" risks— and they were according to FHA—were the committee applicants so different? The typical committee applicant was on the job longer, earned more, owed less, had smaller monthly payments, and wanted a less expensive home than the typical "safe" FHA applicant. It is true, however, that almost 34 percent of the committee applicants had some bad payment habits, but the income capacity was present to rehabilitate. They were not hard-core unemployed; they did not suffer from heavy debt. They simply had not formed the habits for repayment, and the community banks might share some of the fault for that.

The thirty-four percent with some bad payment habits was not the sixty-six percent. Why did the majority of the committee applicants carry the FHA staff imprimatur of bad risk? Was it because 28.72

percent of the CSG men were unskilled and didn't wear a white collar, as contrasted to 3.7 percent of the FHAG? Did it have to do with color? Did it have to do with stereotypes? The statistics raise deep questions concerning the exercise of agency discretion. The statistics certainly point to the need for the FHA to search out the facts before assuming conclusions.

Applicants and Home Ownership

A free housing market does not come in a day. Those who were in effect creating it out of their own personal desires to own homes were being reached. Some might call them pioneers. The committee preferred to think of them as families wanting their own kind of good life, nothing more and nothing less. Not a single applicant, not a single black, wanted a home simply "to integrate." The committee applicants who bought homes were people beginning to cross a bridge from the inner-city ghetto to middle-class suburbia. They walked the bridge slowly. Whether they moved on toward a different life or turned back was their choice. The committee was there to help during the first crucial months of transition from renter to homeowner. The committee was there also to observe—without invading privacy. The committee understood that a free housing market comes about in part because of the determination and willingness of the new homeowners to stay.

The committee's chief social work consultant drafted a questionnaire to be administered one month after the new homeowner moved.[11] Under her direction and instruction, a team of interviewers representing the committee called on twenty families who moved into FHA acquired property under the dislocated program. Included in those interviewed were twelve black families in all white areas and three white families in all white areas. The remainder were black families in black or integrated neighborhoods.

No effort was made to limit evaluative contacts to blacks entering all white neighborhoods. Such an approach would have no relevance to a free housing market where the thrust is not integration but affording to the consumer demonstrable freedom of choice. As homeowners their reactions were vital, even the black family in a black neighborhood. Their confidence could blossom. Their newfound status could affect the neighborhood and, more important, when the family looked for another home as most American homeowners do seven years after purchase, the confidence gained might be reflected in an easier move and perhaps a move to a different kind of neighborhood.

"Continued evaluation is necessary," said Mrs. Kaplan, "as a means for assessing the usefulness of the program and as a means for highlighting procedures or policies which need modification as the program expands and as the real estate market undergoes change. Continued evaluation is necessary also for the personal benefit of each family already served by the committee. In the process of growing from a new homeowner into a comfortable member of a community, there is the possibility of families meeting problems which alone they cannot surmount. Someone must then be available to put the family in contact with those people whose particular knowledge or resources can help deal with the problem. . . . The follow-up interview deals primarily with the move itself; with the initial steps the family takes toward adjustment in the new situation, and with the family's thought and feelings about the process which brought them to their state of homeownership."[12]

First discussed with the families was the move itself, how and with what ease it was accomplished, and, through the eyes of the families questioned, how the neighborhood reacted to their arrival. Committee interviewers made their own visual observations. Did the families look settled and comfortable a month after their move? Only two families seemed substantially unsettled. The remaining families both looked and said that they were well settled.

The move itself went smoothly for most. Four families used professional movers. The rest either moved themselves or had friends help. The large majority of the twenty interviewed moved on a weekend and spent about a day doing so. Their neighbors had ample time to observe them. There were no rushed midnight moves by the black families into all white areas. Three black families received offers of help from their white neighbors ranging from an offer to babysit to the use of telephone. When asked how the neighbors reacted to their moving in, only one black family commented on a negative incident— that of a door slamming, which the black family in the all white neighborhood thought hostile. Seven black families in all white neighborhoods expressed neutral attitudes such as "no problems," "nothing special," "no reaction noted." For the remaining four black families in all white neighborhoods there were positive responses: "Our neighbors called on us." "We speak in passing." "They're very friendly." "Our kids get along real well."

None of the twelve black families in all white neighborhoods voiced fear in making their move. None was greeted by overt violence or harsh words. The only incident reported initially was that of the door slamming. All moved into low-middle income housing, $12,000–$15,000. Their neighbors were not affluent professionals; they were the skilled and semiskilled workers. Their homes did not have the high middle-class isolation of large lots separating neighbors. The committee applicants moved into homes that were close to others. Still, their white neighbors voiced no anger and some even were friendly. What does this say for the violence that did not occur? If moves could be made in low-to-middle income areas without unduly upsetting white residents, could the same be done in high-income areas?

The twelve blacks questioned did not appear especially brave. They were in search of a home, and each found one that happened to be in all white areas. Most indicated by word or reaction a sigh of relief when the move was completed and their white neighbors accepted the fact.

It was this acceptance that might have lent strength to the two black families who faced incidents later in the summer. One had what seemed to be a small cross burned on his lawn; the other had eggs thrown against his front door. The violators did not identify themselves but ran away. Neither family attributed the incident to neighbors. Each said the incidents must have been the work of "outsiders." After both incidents neighbors expressed their regrets to the families. For the family subject to the cross burning there was no repetition. The husband, father of two children, said, "Nothing more has happened, but it looks like a long, hot summer. We intend to stay. We like our home." That was early in June 1968. By August 1, 1968 the summer for that family had cooled considerably; the outsiders had not returned. The family did not stay because of police protection or because they felt safe. The Indianapolis police were called after the cross burning. The patrolman answering the call said to the family, "If they try that again, hold them, and telephone us." "Hold them with what? The end of a shotgun? " asked the husband.

The second incident was more disturbing but was accepted with calm determination by the black family involved. Eggs were found splattered on the front door. The police were called; extra patrolling was promised. Two weeks later during the early morning hours on a

Saturday, more eggs were thrown. At breakfast the family received a telephone call. Mr. Bridges, the head of the household, who had said nothing of the incident to outsiders, reported the conversation. The caller said, "I understand you're having a little trouble." Bridges replied, "No. There hasn't been any trouble." "Well," the caller said, "if you do have any, let us know. We'll come out and blow up a few of those white homes. Then they'll leave you alone." Bridges, who held a second job as a security guard, identified the voice as being that of a black—at least that was his firm opinion.

The next day during the early morning hours more eggs were thrown. There followed the same call. Bridges asked, "How can I get in touch with you if there is trouble?" "Don't worry about reaching us," was the answer. "Just put a story in the *Recorder*. We'll find it." Bridges went to church that morning. His minister, a black inner-city Baptist, said, "I understand you're having some trouble. You want to tell me about it?" Bridges' reply was, "No. There's been no trouble."

What had happened to the promised extra police protection? The committee was told that at the highest level within the police department, it had been decided that extra protection could no longer be afforded. The rationale was that "a black man moving into an all white area deserves no more protection than the last white man in an integrated area." The decision seemed to bother only the committee. Bridges expected little. He was determined to stay. In fact, his daughter's family had purchased a house through the committee within a half mile of his home.

For a month following the last egg throwing nothing more took place at the Bridges' home. Still, even against the background of the two incidents there seemed no relationship between "outside" difficulty and enjoyment of their new homes. Mrs. Kaplan stated, "We discussed with all those families interviewed their feelings about their new home itself. With only one exception, all the people were quite pleased with their purchase. The single exception, a white career army officer, found his home too small 'but sufficient for the temporary use' he had in mind. Aside from the army officer all others said that living in their homes was as they expected—and even better. Some reactions were: 'I'm proud of it.' 'We're happy with it.' 'It draws company,' and 'friends and families are pleased and often impressed with what we bought.' "

Except for that of the army officer, the new homes compared most favorably to the dwellings in which each family previously had lived.

Time and again the response given the interviewer was that the acquired house was just what the owners had wanted. Usually the owners liked their new homes because they were more spacious, provided better play areas for children, and were cleaner and easier to keep clean. Most of the families, having found better living conditions, wanted to improve their homes after only a month of occupancy. They had plans that they freely discussed with the interviewers. Some wanted to plant more flowers or repaint. Others skilled in carpentry and redecorating had begun more substantial improvements. Mr. Connors had in a month converted his garage to a family room, the only one in the neighborhood. The families were involved in creating a home to suit their needs and personalities as well as in maintaining their particular share of the neighborhood in as fine a condition as possible.

Neighborhood responsibility was deeply felt by the twenty interviewed. They compared their homes to others around them. All said their home compared "at least equally" to those around them. Twenty-five percent of those interviewed said their homes were nicer than others in the neighborhood. One put it this way, "My home overrates them all. It gives me a good feeling when I pull up in front of my house."

A home of pleasing quality did not mean satisfaction with the FHA promise of rehabilitation. More than seventy-five percent of those interviewed were dissatisfied with the repair done. Plumbing and wiring were often defective. Paint had begun to peel and crack. Tiles and windows were broken. Workmen on occasion neglected to clean up. In one instance, the city's Health and Hospital Corporation demanded additional home improvements.

Until the Indiana FHA director ordered a new policy for rehabilitation that went beyond "safe, sound, and sanitary condition," the families encountering difficulties met only middling to poor success in causing FHA redress.

Many of the repair complaints, however, reflected the purchasers' newness as homeowners. They expected near perfect repair. They expected door knobs to be tight, not wobbly. A single tile loose in the bath sometimes prompted a complaint. These kinds of complaints seemed to reflect the families' inexperience with homeownership. The committee recognized a need to let those who bought know that they might have some preliminary tasks to perform before they began major improvements.

Moved, settled, repairs made, what of life in the neighborhood?

How well acquainted had they become with their new neighbors? In their eyes, how were their children adjusting to schools and playmates? How involved were they in the community? Did they join nearby churches? Did they use neighborhood stores? Did they hold to the ties of friendship in the ghetto.

Summarizing interview results, Mrs. Kaplan wrote: "Every family interviewed was pleased with its neighborhood. Most frequently heard was the comment, 'It's clean and quiet.' Cleanliness and peacefulness were highly valued. Perhaps the impressions are summed up best by the mother who said, 'It's a friendly, nice, quiet neighborhood with small children around. It's good for raising a family.'

"In general, each person interviewed felt that the rest of the family and their friends were 'delighted' with the change, with the new home. There was an exception. Friends of the family subjected to the 'cross burning' said they were 'crazy' to remain. The family decided to stay.

"In all but two situations the families met some of their neighbors and found them, for the most part, friendly and welcoming. One black family in an all white neighborhood was invited by a minister to join the nearby church. The same family, at the time they moved, were asked to a neighborhood party. Some of the relationships tended to deepen, to take on a continuing character. A black lady joined her white neighbor to start a sewing group. Those on less friendly terms (two families) with their neighbors were so by choice or because busy work schedules simply prevented socializing. The remainder felt they would become more friendly with their neighbors 'as time went on.' Their neighbors had, as one woman stated 'made me feel welcome.' The twenty families liked their new situation much better than the old."

The experience of the children was good. The new schools were better than the old. "The teachers are more interested." "My son was challenged by math for the first time and has caught up now on multiplication and division which were not being taught in his previous school in the same grade." For the most part children played together well. The two families who chose not to socialize reported that their children "stayed mainly at home." Another family said one of their children, a teen-ager, "went around mostly" with former companions. Two families reported incidents; their children faced abusive language. The response of the two families typifies the attitude of the committee applicants who moved to all white neighborhoods. One mother merely said, "Well, you know how kids say things. They'll work it out." The second mother elaborated. Two preschool children came to her home and asked innocently if the "niggers could come out and play." The mother nicely sent them home telling the two "there aren't any niggers here." She asked the two to tell their parents that her boys could play with them sometime. The two preschool children later returned, asked, and were permitted to play with the boys.

The twenty families were settling into their neighborhood. They were using some local stores and taking advantage of the social groups There was no rush to shift shopping from the old stores to the new. Where new stores were frequented the reasons given were convenience or improved product quality. Half of those interviewed continued to shop chain and discount stores following an already established pattern of price and quality comparison. A few noted that the small neighborhood stores sold at higher prices than they were willing to pay. One woman, however, said that "In the little corner store children are not cheated when they go to make small purchases as they were in the Barrington area."

Sixteen of those interviewed belonged to a church when they moved. Of these, three were considering membership in a nearby church for convenience. One family, blacks in an all white area, however, seemed to be responding even more to the extremely warm welcome extended by a local pastor than the factor of convenience. The remaining thirteen families were not considering change. They had affiliations of long duration and strong personal ties with congregants and ministers. Mrs. Kaplan said that this could have been expected since "the church is the very familiar, supportive, and secure 'haven' in a stressful time of personal change as well as the source of the friendships already established. One might wonder if more changes in church affiliation will occur as time passes and these families establish relationships to and within their new neighborhoods."

Five families, including three blacks in all white areas, had been introduced by neighbors to community social activities, ranging from coffee gatherings to neighborhood associations. The five enjoyed and were continuing their participation. One black woman, a former War Against Poverty professional employee who purchased a home in a largely black area, hoped to start a block club. A housing development was being constructed. She wanted to be sure "that neighborhood values were maintained." This was a woman who had been displaced by interstate highway construction. Five families were not aware of any neighborhood social groups. Ten were sure there were none. Of the twenty interviewed, only three indicated an unwillingness to join in neighborhood activities. Their reason? Lack of time.

Each of the twenty interviewed praised the committee. It had served them well. Often their comments were centered on the committee's director of field operations. Summarizing, Mrs. Kaplan wrote, "If we draw no other conclusions from the comments made regarding the Committee's service, we feel justified in stating that previously there had been an abundant lack of personally tailored attention on the part of those with whom these families did business. Said one new homeowner: 'I like the Committee because we were treated with extra special care. Although it was business, it was friendly and relaxed.' "

Committee Program and the Housing Market

Those who purchased FHA property evidenced a desire to stay in their new homes. The extent that they will do so is the key to a free housing market. Mrs. Kaplan wrote: "We have demonstrated that a free housing market can be established legally, but it will endure only if those of a community are convinced of its applicability to themselves and to their neighbors." The committee, through the wide publicity given its program, hoped that real estate brokers, particularly black real estate brokers, would understand the economic benefits that might be theirs. They had the opportunity to see an FHA director committed fully to a free housing market. They had the opportunity of seeing white areas open. Homes that had been denied them might now be made available. Perhaps a white broker holding a listing in a formerly all white neighborhood would consider a proposition and fee sharing if a qualified black buyer were brought to him. The neighborhood had been broken; it was no longer totally white.

Even more important, the committee hoped that the property lost to the public market, the homes not taken by committee applicants, would be seized upon by black real estate brokers. The homes were being placed in excellent repair and sold at fair prices. Those brokers who had not been aware of the supply of nonrestricted listings before knew of them by January 4, 1968, the start of the committee's program. Not only was there newspaper, radio, and television coverage but the Indiana FHA director had announced the program at a meeting of the Indianapolis Real Estate Brokers Association.

The potential that could have been exploited was significant. From

January 4 to July 19, 1968, the committee had 195 properties available for sale on a preferential basis to dislocated persons. The committee lost 118 properties to the public market. Of these properties, ninety-seven were in all white areas; five were in integrated areas; and sixteen were in all black areas. The overwhelming number of the homes placed on the public market were in precisely the areas where the black real estate agents claimed exclusion.

What did the black brokers do? Did they use the listings made available? During the period of January 4 to July 19, 1968, black real estate brokers accounted for four sales. They were successful bidders on slightly more than two percent of the properties available, and their success reflects their willingness to take the time to find a prospect, write a proposition, and sit at a table while the open lottery takes place. The complaining black brokers indicted themselves. They shared in the responsibility for the denial of a free housing market.

The black brokers, however, denied this. On July 20, 1968, their organization launched "a campaign to eliminate unlicensed persons and agencies from the real estate profession. . . . The campaign, according to Mrs. Edna Johnson, (chairman of the Ethics Committee, Indianapolis Real Estate Brokers Association), is designed to eliminate unlicensed governmental, private persons and agencies from 'the practice of real estate and engaging in competition with licensed professional agents in violation of the Indiana Real Estate License Law' . . . In one step of the program, the organization has asked the Federal Housing Authority to return all the FHA's repossessed properties to real estate brokers for sale."[13] The other step, vaguely defined, seemed to be "more justice" in the handling of discriminatory housing complaints lodged with the State Civil Rights Commission.

These black brokers were hostile to the committee's program of using FHA houses to establish a free housing market. They were opposed to the committee's helping to bring about the type of market that on a long-term basis could only work for the benefit of the black brokers.

When asked what reasoning sparked the action of the black brokers, one of them said angrily, "You're taking customers away. You're taking property away." Those served by the committee, however, were not the customers of brokers, black or white. This was demonstrated by the broker attended open house and by the attitude of the applicants themselves. Even after giving the black brokers some private listings in all white areas, the brokers had not sold the properties.

Was there another, deeper threat to the black brokers? Their listings, after all, were limited. They were, by their own admission, restricted and confined generally to the inner city. The properties sold through the black brokers were limited in number and often poor in quality. Prices charged, however, bore a strong relation to demand. If the supply of homes were limited and the demand great enough, poor quality could have only a minimal effect on price. The committee had given black buyers something to compare with the inner-city property prices. Even if a black did not want to live in an all white area, he was offered homes there at fair prices. He might reasonably expect that a five-room house in suburbia costing $12,000 ought to cost no more in the ghetto.

Was this a cause for the anger of the black brokers? Did they see their livelihood as dependent on the continuance of the ghetto? Was it out of fear, then, that in the same attack on the committee and the Indiana Civil Rights Commission, the organization of the black brokers announced the positive move that it "has set up a new housing counseling service," which opened on the same day, July 27, that community groups, including the committee, had joined together for an inner-city open house?

Questions only can be raised. It may very well be that there is no rational explanation. It would not be the first time in the committee's brief life that institutional action came without apparent reason. Nor would it be the first time in the committee's life that black institutions appeared to work diligently against the interest of black people.

Those dislocated by government action formed a natural grouping of individuals in need of housing. Mostly black, though some were white, the nearly 200 dislocated who thought the committee might be of value were on the whole individuals requiring much personal attention in the search for a home. Yet of the forty-five who either selected a house or actually moved under the FHA acquired property program, all stood well as consumers, as wage earners, as stable families, in relation to a group, mostly white, purchasing comparable housing and seeking FHA insurance. The problems of the forty-five and, for that matter, the 200 committee applicants, were related in no small measure to adjustment to a new status, that of homeowner rather than renter. For those of the forty-five who had effected their move, on the whole, all went smoothly. They seemed content with their choices, which took some to black areas, other to integrated areas, and still others to white areas. The time seemed ripe for the private sector, namely the black real estate brokers, to accelerate the process of change, to press further in efforts to open the real estate market. This was not done. The black brokers were hostile to the committee. They seemed to prefer a restricted market where their role was clear and their profits would enlarge as thousands of displaced blacks grabbed for housing.

8
An Evaluation

In seven months the committee did not establish a free housing market. It demonstrated but did not actuate freedom of choice. The white community did not feel that escape had been eliminated. The real estate industry did not comprehend either the concept of a free housing market, or appreciate the changes that might be coming. The committee did not become so sufficiently rooted that whatever the reaction of the white community and the real estate industry, it, as an entity, could continue to help people find homes of their choice throughout metropolitan Indianapolis. Beyond FHA there is limited support for the committee. No effort had been made to open new resources to broaden the committee's housing inventory.

Despite these limitations, the committee did take a small step on a long road to a free housing market. People, black and white, have moved throughout metropolitan Indianapolis. In seven months, twenty black families chose homes that happen to be in all white neighborhoods. Blacks have moved and have given every indication of staying in the homes of their choice, and almost without exception their white neighbors have accepted the decision.

Twenty neighborhoods in which blacks had been denied entrance were changed. Whether the twenty white neighborhoods panic will be a question of conscience and reason and emotion. If the white owners wish to stay they will find support from the same state Civil Rights Commission that has staffed the committee. The committee assisted two black families in finding homes in one all white neighborhood. When a third black family bought a home through a real estate agent, the state Civil Rights Commission entered and helped the residents to form a neighborhood association as a means for communication and a method for stabilizing the neighborhood.

But if whites rush to move, that, too, is their choice. New homes will be opened to blacks. If white neighbors on either side of a black family decide to sell, for whatever reason, they may for the first time in that neighborhood's history, entertain thoughts of selling to blacks. The committee had one such experience. Also, when two black owners of homes acquired through the committee in all white areas had to sell because of new jobs in other cities the purchasers were black. A reason for this may be that the "committee" owners used black real estate brokers in effecting the sales. It should be noted that the sales occurred between July 15, 1968, and January 1, 1969.

A step has been taken. The FHA acquired property program provides the momentum for action that will come. Wherever white sellers may move, at some point, in some way, FHA may follow. For FHA is too much a part of the nation's housing market to be left behind. At some point, some of the newly acquired white homes will go into default, and the lending institutions will seek a return on their investment, the invocation of FHA insurance, and new listings will be made available under the FHA acquired property program.

The rate of progress, however, is not brisk. It is painfully slow. Blacks have not rushed to the committee's doors. The dislocated comprise a small portion of the black community. But even of the dislocated, numbering hundreds of families, the committee has attracted only a few. By January 1, 1969 the committee could list only fifty-two families who had moved under the FHA program. The committee, through FHA, holds a large inventory located throughout metropolitan Indianapolis. There were 195 homes available in seven months. Yet during the same period there were thousands of listings, held by white brokers, that were not open to the blacks.

The committee found itself outside the structure of existing social service organizations concerned with relocation of displaced families. The committee sought organizational cooperation and individual participation. In an effort to provide full service the committee strove to be cohesive; to become its own resource. For the committee there seemed no other alternative. It was better to serve some than none. Neither state nor city relocation offices seemed receptive to housing opportunities beyond the inner city, particularly when those opportunities related to home ownership. This view reflected the relocation officials own assumptions that inner-city displaced families desire to remain renters with slight inclination to leave their old neighborhoods.

The lack of full participation by relocation agencies hurt committee operations. Dislocated persons simply were not referred in any numbers to the committee. For that matter the entire FHA acquired property program was suspect. Without applicants in substantial numbers there could be only limited sales of property. Measured by a ratio of property sold to applicants the committee performed rather well in comparison to the private real estate market. With approximately 200 applicants the committee aided FHA in setting aside forty-five properties. For about every five persons with whom the committee worked one set aside a home. With how many persons must a real estate broker have contact before an acceptable bid is forthcoming? The number certainly would not be less than that of the committee.

The difficulty encountered with relocation officials in Indianapolis need not occur in other cities. In Fort Wayne, Indiana, the head of the city's relocation agency was asked to participate in establishing a Committee on Special Housing. The invitation was extended by a businessman well known and respected in the community. Without qualification the city official offered his support. In Gary, Indiana, the same support came when the invitation was made by the state Civil Rights Commission.

Relocation agencies can have a vital role in making the FHA program effective. Their cooperation should be sought, but it should be understood that cooperation must be placed in a context. The committee was not designed as an entity from which applicants are referred elsewhere. The committee was structured for action. The cooperation of relocation agencies will serve no worthwhile purpose unless it is enlisted in the cause of action, in an effort to serve those dislocated by government.

In this regard cooperation must encompass the multiple tasks assumed by the committee, which to the applicant probably were difficult to categorize. To the applicant the committee both was and was not a real estate broker. The committee had the objective view of a broker. It was interested only in helping the applicant find a home of his choice. The committee, however, made no profit; it received no commission, the single legal criterion in Indiana for defining one as a broker or real estate salesman.[1] The committee's director of field operations did not act as a salesman. His concern was twofold: making sure the applicant knew he had an opportunity to buy and shepherding the applicant through the procedural maze to purchase.

To the applicant the committee was an amalgam of broker, relocation office, social service agency, lawyer, and friend. To operate effectively, the elements had to stay in balance, with the focus on the field worker. There was hope that within the committee balance might be maintained. Outside the committee, problems could be expected. Black brokers, rationally or irrationally, felt challenged. The Redevelopment Commission bordered on open opposition to the committee. Social service agencies did not fully or openly use the committee as a resource. The city government through the office of the mayor informally extended support but never publicly gave the committee the security of its endorsement.

It will take time to bring together brokers, relocation offices, and social service agencies and to convince them that a free housing market will work in their interests. Forty-five families are not enough to bring significant change. Time is needed for the forty-five to be enlarged to a hundred and more. Each new move-in adds a molecule of strength to an incipient free housing market.

Categorized both as a "holding operation" and a "pilot project" the Urban League gave the committee further financial support five months after the FHA program was established. In doing so, however, the Urban League found itself in a quandary. As an organization it is not service-oriented; it is more concerned with education. The committee, however, educates by action. This the Urban League recognized in its submission to the United Fund: "The most significant part (of the Committee's operations) has been the careful individual counseling and persistent follow-up carried on by the State (Civil Rights) Commission staff (1 1/2 staff in the field and 1 full-time person on loan in the Urban League office). As a result, many of the clients who have been former renters, after careful credit check and counseling, have found that they are potential buyers. Also, immediate follow-up interviews have resulted in peaceful and satisfactory move-ins. Both (City and State) Commissions have cooperated to insure neighborhood tranquility where isolated incidents have occurred."[2] The difficult position in which the Urban League found itself is noted in the final sentence of its statement to the United Fund: "During the remainder of the (Fund fiscal) year a continuous evaluation will be made as to whether the League should continue this service or spin it off to a more appropriate agency."[3]

The life of the committee is tenuous. The state Civil Rights Commission or the governor could cause employees to be withdrawn from the committee. Motivation for such a move could be diverse. Private interests could make their influence felt; the real estate industry is no small lobby. Also the governor as an elected official is a political creature. The commission could decide that it should explore new avenues with its limited resources since it had demonstrated what the committee could do and now others could take over. Any day the Urban League could withdraw its support and allow a "more appropriate agency" to assume jurisdiction.

A free housing market will not be established in a year. It will take a considerable amount of time before blacks believe in and are willing to take advantage of the FHA acquired property program. What any committee must have *ab initio* is staying power, a willingness to see a project through. Progress comes slowly. Early target dates and firm assumptions are not desirable. If a committee is to succeed, flexibility is necessary.

The FHA acquired property program touches primarily the displaced in the inner city, many of whom have been renters. Each person must be treated individually and with sensitivity. On the one hand they have been dislodged by society, and on the other, they are being asked to consider acquiring a vested stake in that society through home-ownership. Properly and patiently treated, the displaced may serve as a group to free the housing market.

For the displaced a committee, working closely with FHA, seemed a useful device. Quite aside from a name intended to neutralize resentment, committee structure afforded a means for providing full service to applicants. The committee wanted full utilization of FHA acquired property. Those who had an interest in such property could be brought by one committee representative to the point of purchase. If their interests were elsewhere, they could, as a natural process, be taken over by the FHA counselor and channeled into to private market.

The use of a committee is no absolute for other communities that have strong community organizations willing to strike toward a free housing market. It should be noted, however, that both Fort Wayne and Gary, Indiana, have chosen both the structure and name Committee on Special Housing and the relocation authorities in these cities have chosen to cooperate.

As a beginning the committee has demonstrated that it is possible to design a conflict-free mechanism to achieve the right of an individual to buy a home of his choice at a fair price. The committee's approach is the element that may have value. It sought no instant solution. It left untouched the individual homeowner exercising his individual choice. The committee did find, however, a way to open a substantial number of homes to the benefit of buyers and sellers in their roles as buyers and sellers without regard to furthering integration as such. In exploiting the institutional sector of the real estate market the committee had hope that eventually individual homeowners would react in terms of their economic interests rather than personal prejudice.

Epilogue

This postscript is added to note the withering and death of the Indianapolis project not so much because of internal defects, though they surely were present, but rather because of action taken by the secretary of the Department of Housing and Urban Development. Government financing of FHA repossessions was withdrawn in January 1969.

The basis and effect of this action were explained in a letter dated September 3, 1969, from the acting head of FHA, William B. Ross: "Formerly the FHA financed the large majority of its sales through FNMA and subsequently GNMA. As a result of a decision by the Bureau of the Budget on January 24, 1969, the program was amended to provide that all sales would be financed by private lenders, thus obtaining a cash flow into the Treasury of some $350,000,000 annually. While no changes in this procedure are contemplated, a limited amount of mortgage funds are available through GNMA, and these funds are utilized where private financing cannot be obtained, particularly in sales located in inner city core areas. I don't believe that this change in the financing of sales has had an appreciable effect on the numbers of properties acquired by FHA. To some extent, however, it has become increasingly difficult in many areas to obtain private financing at a cost which FHA considers reasonable." The private mortgage market, as events have demonstrated, will demand and extract higher interest rates than government had made available. Higher interest rates compel stricter credit requirements, for in the final analysis more money is demanded of the prospective purchaser. The group most likely to be denied financing is that most in need the marginal, low-middle income residents of the inner city.

The federal government through the Bureau of the Budget evidently did not order HUD to eliminate federal financing of FHA acquired property. Money, substantial sums amounting to $280 million in 1969 alone, was appropriated to FHA for that purpose. In a letter dated November 6, 1969, Mark W. Alger, deputy director of the bureau's Human Resources Programs Division, contradicted the claim made by Ross. In pertinent part Alger wrote: "We are unable to find any record of a Bureau of the Budget decision on January 24, 1969, relating to the level of GNMA financing of sales of FHA property. On that date, however, Secretary Romney announced an increase in the maximum interest rate on FHA-insured mortgages. The increase was announced in order to increase the amount of private financing available for FHA mortgages. It was expected that one result would be an increased supply of private funds to finance sales of FHA property. On January 27, 1969, the Bureau of the Budget *increased* the apportionment (under the Anti-deficiency Act) for GNMA purchase of these mortgages to $280 million, to provide additional Government funds until the interest rate increase took effect."

There is an argument possessing constitutional and statutory roots that could compel the availability not only of FHA acquired homes, numbering more than 40,000 annually, but also those homes repossessed by the Veterans Administration totaling more than 20,000 each year. The argument that could make these homes available is brief and simplistic. Through urban renewal or highway construction it is government that displaces the inner-city residents. The same government by statute requires the displacing agency to provide an adequate relocation program. Those whose homes are to be destroyed must be afforded decent housing. Where government holds title to significant housing destined for public sale in a community subject to urban renewal or highway construction or any other governmental action then government should include its housing inventory in any relocation scheme.

The Constitution declares: "No State shall . . . deny to any person within its jurisdiction the equal protection of the laws."[1] Under the Housing Act of 1949 local agencies contracting with the federal government for urban renewal grants must provide dwellings and facilities that are not only decent, safe, and sanitary, but also no less desirable than those to be destroyed.[2] Applying the statute in the context of the equal protection proviso, the Second Circuit held: "Where the relocation standard set by Congress is met for those who have access to any housing in the community which they can afford, but not for those who, by reason of their race, are denied free access to housing they can afford and must pay more for what they can get, the state action affirms the discrimination in the housing market. This is not 'equal protection of the laws.' "[3]

The Second Circuit's ruling recognized the large measure of discretion that must be given urban planners; the court was not about to inject the judiciary into that decision making. As a court its role was to "evaluate agency efforts and success at relocation with a realistic awareness of the problems facing urban renewal programs."[4] In this context is it not a proper function for the judiciary to determine what might be included in the total housing inventory of any community in order to assess the efforts and success of any agency at relocation? For the purpose of ruling whether a state or any of its agencies might proceed with an urban renewal scheme can't a court require that all housing available for public sale be made a part of any relocation plan? Where the federal government itself is party to the urban renewal contract, where the federal government has set the criteria for relocation, is it not bound to make its own public offerings available to the dislocated?[5] If the federal government finds de facto housing segregation in a community where its public offerings of repossessions long have been sold on an open basis, isn't there cause for concluding that at least as to those dislocated, FHA housing is not available?[6] To make this housing available in a way where it can be used, it is possible to argue that government must afford a preference to the dislocated.

Congress has imposed the criteria of relocation. A court would only pass on FHA property in assessing the validity of a relocation program under the equal protection proviso. Any order from the court relating to property disposition would be conditional; FHA could follow its own sale patterns, but the court could impose a sanction that would forestall the government project. Finally, acceptance of a court directive would still leave it to the FHA to devise a plan that would make its property meaningfully available on a preferred basis for the dislocated. To illustrate, for those with limited resources who would have difficulty in financing a conventional mortgage, FHA on its own motion, without the need for recourse to the Government National Mortgage Association, could enter a contract sale.[7] That is, FHA could keep title and apply monthly rents to a fixed purchase price that would be amortized in the same way as a mortgage.

Even if equality through law should be ordered, even if the bureaucratic machinery would scrupulously follow the letter as well as the intent of the law, inequality would still result if different human and social factors were not understood and considered. The project discussed in this book, as well as many others in related areas, illustrates a profound difference between officially stated values and those experienced in everyday interactions. Where such a difference occurs, the credibility of legal doctrines and their expression in judicial as well as administrative processes suffers greatly. Promises and intentions that are logically attainable but do not consider psychological or sociological conditions increase either hostility or apathy, leading to unrest or withdrawal or both, alternately.

The project and its results could be viewed as a failure if one took the naive position that the creation of opportunities leads to their immediate acceptance. This often is the hope and expectation of innovators. The project, however, could also be viewed as a demonstration of the many levels of support that are necessary before actual social change takes place. In this light, the results of the committee were encouraging. There is good reason to believe that if our initial proposition were to be carried through carefully on a long-term basis, the results would improve.

Notes

Notes to Preface

1. "Curbs on Discrimination in Housing Prove Easy to Avoid in Most Areas," *The Wall Street Journal,* June 21, 1967.
2. Edith Evans Asbury, "Two Negro Sisters Thwarted Three Years in Efforts to Buy House," *The New York Times,* August 16, 1967, p. 28.
3. "Negro Pair Charge Bias on Housing," *The Cleveland Plain Dealer,* August 24, 1967.
4. Irving Spiegel, "Race Integration in Suburbs Urged," *The New York Times,* September 20, 1967, p. 31.
5. Editorial, "Enough of Playing Charades With the Open Housing Issue," *The Courier-Journal,* September 1, 1967.
6. *The Indianapolis News,* August 30, 1967. See also "The Mediation of Civil Rights Disputes: Open Housing in Milwaukee." *Wisconsin Law Review,* 4(1968):1127, note.
7. Gene Roberts, "Milwaukee Lifts March Ban," *The New York Times,* September 2, 1967, p. 13.
8. Homer Bigart, "Groppi Leads Largest March for Open Housing in Milwaukee," *The New York Times,* September 11, 1967, p. 44.
9. Donald Janson, "Milwaukee Priest Says Housing Protest Is Integrated and Urges Whites to Help," *The New York Times,* September 18, 1967, p. 34.
10. Donald Janson, "Milwaukee Council Gets A Bill Outlawing Bias in All Housing," *The New York Times,* September 20, 1967, p. 33.
11. Ibid.
12. William Borders, "Hartford March Ends in Violence," *The New York Times,* September 20, 1967, p. 33.
13. Clement E. Vose, *Caucasians Only: The Supreme Court, the NAACP, and the Restrictive Covenant Cases* (Berkeley and Los Angeles: University of California Press, 1967), p. 125.
14. Leslie W. Dunbar, *A Republic of Equals* (Ann Arbor: University of Michigan Press, 1966), p. 86.
15. National Committee Against Discrimination in Housing, Conference Report No. 8, April 13-14, 1967, p. 17.
16. Francis Fox Piven and Richard A. Cloward, "The Case Against Urban Desegregation," Social Work, 12(January 1967): 12.

17. Ibid., p. 18. The approach is that of the scientist of social behavior. It is not that of the law, and more particularly, the Constitution where values have been subscribed to for their own sake, even as a matter of faith, and, as such, have become national policy.

18. Ibid. The cited references are worth noting: "The Program for an Open City: Summary Report," New York Department of City Planning, May 1965 (mimeographed); David McEntire, *Residence and Race: Final and Comprehensive Report to the Commission on Race and Housing* (Berkeley: University of California Press, 1960), p. 41.

19. Piven and Cloward, p. 13.

20. Ibid., p. 14. Cited is Karl E. Tauber and Alma F. Tauber, *Negroes in Cities: Residential Segregation and Neighborhood Change* (Chicago: Aldine Publishing Co., 1965).

21. Ibid.

22. Ibid., p. 16.

23. Ibid.

24. Ibid., p. 20.

25. Clarence Funnye and Ronald Shiffman. "The Imperative of Deghettoization: An Answer to Piven and Cloward," *Social Work,* 12(April 1967). Shiffman was associate for design of Idea Plan and assistant director of the Pratt Center for Community Improvement, Department of City and Regional Planning, Pratt Institute, Brooklyn, New York.

26. Ibid., p. 7.

27. Whitney M. Young, Jr., "The Case for Urban Integration," *Social Work,* 12(July 1967):12.

28. Ibid., pp. 12, 13.

29. Ibid., p. 13.

30. Ibid.

31. The position was conveyed in a letter from Paget Alves, Jr., associate director of the National Urban League, to Tom A. Collins, research assistant to Daniel J. Baum, September 7, 1967.

32. Stokeley Carmichael and Charles V. Hamilton, *Black Power: The Politics of Liberation in America* (New York: Random House, 1967), p. 41.

33. "Declaration, Constitution Drafted—U.S. Black Nationalists Want a Nation," *The Louisville Courier-Journal & Times,* March 31, 1968.

34. Carmichael and Hamilton, p. 47.

35. See F. Shapiro, "The Successor to Floyd McKissick Might Not Be So Reasonable," *The New York Times Magazine,* October 1, 1967, p. 32; Earl Caldwell, "CORE Eliminates 'Multiracial' In Describing Its Membership," *The New York Times,* July 6, 1967, p. 1.

36. See "Black Power and Black Pride," *Time,* December 1, 1967, p. 20. See also Richard E. Mooney, "Harlem Negroes Seek Business," *The New York Times,* August 27, 1967, p. 1. It is estimated that Negroes own 25–30 percent of Harlem's businesses.

37. Carmichael and Hamilton, p. 45.

38. Ibid, p. 31.

39. Archibald Cox, "Direct Action, Civil Disobedience, and the Constitution," in *Civil Rights, the Constitution and the Courts* (Cambridge, Mass.: Harvard University Press, 1967), p. 21.

40. Edmond Cahn, "The Democratic Resolution" in *Confronting Injustice: The Edmond Cahn Reader* (Boston: Little, Brown & Company, 1966), pp. 402, 405.

41. *Report of the American Assembly* on "Law and the Changing Society," Center for Continuing Education, University of Chicago, March 14-17, 1968, p. 7.
42. The *Louisville Courier-Journal,* December 13, 1967. This constituted the central message of a quarter-page ad placed by the Louisville Board of Realtors.
43. Whyte, William H., Jr., *The Organization Man,* Anchor ed. (Garden City: Doubleday, 1957) pp. 303-307.
44. "The Negro Middle-Class is Right in the Middle," *Fortune,* November 1966, pp. 174, 231.

Notes to Chapter One

1. The lawyer lives in an area known as Highland-Kessler that constitutes a political precinct of homes priced from $19,000 to $60,000 and is adjacent to a middle-income black enclave called Grandview. About four years ago, the schools in Highland-Kessler (county not city) were integrated with a resulting racial ratio of 50-50. After a bitter battle a school redistricting followed and the white percentage in Highland-Kessler schools increased.

2. *Grillo v. Board of Realtors of the Plainfield Area,* cited in BNA Antitrust and Trade Regulation Reporter, May 24, 1966, A-1.

3. Peter Gall, "Government Plans Fight Against Bias in Housing Using Monopoly Laws," *The Wall Street Journal*, February 4, 1966.

4. They had suffered the pains of integration over a period of fifteen years. It began when whites complained over black use of the neighborhood library. By 1960 the turmoil had ceased; the neighborhood had become predominantly middle-income black. Of a greater Indianapolis population of about 750,000 in 1967, approximately 23,000 (mostly black) lived in the northwest or Golden Hill area. A community group said of their neighborhood, "This community was once a beautiful middle-class neighborhood, but due to the highway the beauty has been destroyed." *Holy Angels Church Report,* January 18, 1967 (mimeographed).

5. These people earned an average income of $5,500 annually. They lived in homes that had a market value of approximately $9,500. Those whose homes were taken by the highway were, in a sense, lucky. They received some compensation. Others were locked into homes that lost value because of noise, dead-end streets, and an elevated highway; their homes were not readily marketable. David Vinos, "The Interstate Highway in the Northwest Area," graduate paper, Indiana University, January 17, 1967.

6. Memorandum, "Conference with Governor Branigan regarding design of I-65," from Robert Treadwell, president of the Northwest Action Council, Inc., October 9, 1967 (mimeographed).

7. Forest Manor is an area of 189 blocks housing 3,761 families in which the price levels for homes ranged from $10,000 to $20,000 with a median of about $14,000 to $16,000 in 1967. By August of that year 61 blocks had no black residents; and, in all but 19 blocks white residents outnumbered black. Within two months the 61 blocks had been halved. This information was obtained from the files of Indiana Civil Rights Commission in November 1967.

8. The 1967 session of the General Assembly amended the existing statute to provide an exemption from possible sanction for "any person who has engaged in a discriminatory (housing) practice pursuant to a voluntary plan adopted to prevent or eliminate *de facto* segregation if such plan

established no fixed numbers or percent for any race, religion or nationality and is found by the *Commission* to be reasonably designed to prevent *de facto segregation* and consistently followed by persons privy to the plan." Indiana Annotated Statutes, 40-2312 (1) 1967 Supplement. The constitutionality of this proviso remains to be tested.

Sociologists also have opinions about a quota system: "The idea that a quota system should be used to limit Negroes to 10 percent of a white community is unacceptable to Negro leaders and rejected by the bulk of middle-class since it would subject the Negro to a permanent minority group status in his residential community." Bruno Bettleheim and Morris Janowitz, *Social Change and Prejudice,* 1964 ed. (Glencoe, Ill.: Free Press of Glencoe, 1950).

9. These figures were based upon an analysis of FHA sales in Marion County during 1967.
10. See Edmond Cahn, "The Lawyer, The Social Psychologist and the Truth," in *Confronting Injustice: The Edmond Cahn Reader* (Boston: Little, Brown & Company, 1966), p. 346.
11. Robert B. Semple, "FHA Asks Aides to Get Housing for Minorities," *The New York Times,* November 21, 1967, p. 30. Although delivered at a closed meeting, the speech found its way into the offices of several civil rights organizations.
12. Ibid.
13. Ibid.
14. Maurice Carroll, "Housing the Poor in Suburbs Urged," *The New York Times,* September 9, 1967, p. 1.
15. See Appendix A, FHA Property Disposition Letter Number 129.
16. Remarks of Carmen Pasquale, FHA assistant commissioner for Field Operations, before members of the Albuquerque Board of Realtors, Independent Real Estate Brokers, and Mortgage Lenders, Albuquerque, New Mexico, February 26, 1968 (mimeographed), p. 1.
17. FHA *Commissioner Letter No. 38 to Insuring Office Directors on Use of FHA Programs in Older, Inner City Neighborhoods,* November 8, 1965.
18. Martin Nolan, "A Belated Effort to Save Our Cities," *The Reporter,* December 28, 1967.
19. Leslie W. Dunbar, *A Republic of Equals* (Ann Arbor: University of Michigan Press, 1966), pp. 15-16.
20. Nolan, p. 17.
21. Ibid, p. 19.
22. Ibid.

Notes to Chapter Two

1. The personal links were even more intricate. When the committee tried to meet with Dr. Weaver, who had been scheduled to speak in Indianapolis, it was told at all levels that time permitted no interview. Oliver, however, telephoned "his friend" Dr. Weaver at home, and a brief interview was marked down on the itinerary.
2. *Trends in Housing* is a monthly publication that is offered to the general public for two dollars annually.
3. "NCDH Expands FHA Help Under New US Contract," *Trends,* October 1967. "Among the subjects which NCDH plans to survey and report to groups across the country are the impact of fair housing groups on segregated housing patterns, techniques and progress in integrating neighborhoods, the use of governmental housing programs in increasing equal housing

choice, and the participation of fair housing groups in community planning activities such as the new Federal Model Cities program."

4. "Coalition Pledges Fight on Urban Ills–Nation's Leaders Set Annual Goal: Million Jobs, Dwellings, Open to All," *Trends,* October 1967.

5. His view of the president's committee was not entirely favorable. It was educational, not an action-oriented organization. His question was how effective, even as an educational group, could the committee be until the president caused earlier executive orders to be enforced? For those in the power structure called upon to change, to modify their own practices, wasn't any educational experience emanating from the president's committee negative—until the federal government demonstrated willingness to comply with its own mandates?

6. See *Trends,* October 1967, p. 2.

7. NCDH Conference Report No. 8, "Model Cities and Metropolitan Desegregation–A Program for Grass Roots Action," April 13-14, 1967, introduction.

8. Ibid., pp. 35-36.

9. Ibid., pp. 20-21.

10. Ibid., pp. 22-23.

11. Ibid., pp. 28-29; NCDH Conference Report No. 7, November 18-20, 1966, pp. 23-25.

12. See note 5.

13. NCDH gives some recognition to the impotence of current legislation as this statement sets the tone of the NCDH pamphlet publication, "How the Federal Government Builds Ghettoes," February 1967, p. 6.

14. Ibid.

15. NCDH Conference Report No. 8, April 13-14, 1967, p. 17.

16. Other groups were interviewed by the committee. These include those who saw only committee or FHA listings; those who went through the regular FHA Counseling Service as a means for finding a home; and those who purchased FHA acquired property. It should be pointed out, however, that there may be a substantial difference in an applicant's decision in advance of seeing a home, and what he actually would do upon finding a home that he sincerely desires.

The committee found that its applicants were generally renters who desperately wanted homes. In the final analysis, some applicants would be willing to risk possible adverse reaction to take the homes of their choice. Others, nevertheless, felt strongly about living either in an all black or all white neighborhood.

17. One need only compare the early against the more recent history of the Student Non-Violent Coordinating Committee (SNCC). As to the group's early status see Howard Finn, *SNCC: The New Abolitionists* (Boston: Beacon Press, 1964), pp. 167-184.

18. See note 35 of Preface.

19. Ibid.

20. Stokeley Carmichael and Charles V. Hamilton, *Black Power: The Politics of Liberation in America* (New York: Random House, 1967), pp. 167-168.

21. James Farmer, *Freedom–When?* (New York: Random House, 1965), pp. 85-86.

22. Gene Roberts, "Dr. King Stresses Racial Pride in a Shift for His Rights Group," *The New York Times,* August 19, 1967, p. 12.

23. Lawrence E. Davies, "Urban League Set to Aid Militants," *The New York Times,* August 27, 1967, p. 72.

24. This is not to say that open housing has not played a major role in black civil rights organization work. It surely has, but times have changed. The direction of Black Power is not toward integration, not toward open housing, and, the force of Black Power had its effect, as noted above, even on Dr. King who marched so often for open housing laws, federal, state, and local. Nor do we say that some old-line groups such as the NAACP do not continue to press for open housing. We point out only a shift in emphasis, a change in mood that affects policy. Father Groppi, of course, identified with the NAACP.

25. Freemont Power, "Model City Ideas Cover Wide Range." *The Indianapolis News,* March 11, 1968.

26. Paul M. Doherty, "Independent Voter Turns Back on Ward Heelers," *The Indianapolis Star,* June 2, 1968.

27. Ibid.

28. Ibid., Power and Doherty have a reputation as incisive, accurate news evaluators.

29. The events were related to Baum by those who were in attendance.

30. Pat W. Stewart, "Plan Offers Repossessed FHA Homes to Displaced Persons," *The Indianapolis Recorder,* January 20, 1968.

31. Ibid.

32. From a militant black, Mrs. Gustafson received a card making her an honorary Negro, which, she will point out, is not quite the same as a black or Afro-American.

33. The congregation had moved to the enclave ghetto of Grandview. Near that area, but in the all white developments of Eagledale and Gateway West, the FHA had more than twenty acquired homes in inventory. The properties had a median price of about $13,000 to $14,000, which fit nicely into the congregation's economic bracket.

34. There seemed to be fear of Ku Klux Klan influence in the police department. The special unit had been screened for work of the sort indicated by Crump.

35. "Calling an area dangerous does not make it so," a realtor said: "A real estate agent, if he knows his neighborhood, can smooth the way far better than any civil rights group. The agent can talk and be accepted by people as one of them. A government employee has difficulty in this regard."

Notes to Chapter Three

1. Remarks of Carmen Pasquale, FHA assistant commissioner for Field Operations, before members of the Albuquerque Board of Realtors, Independent Real Estate Brokers and Mortgage Lenders, Albuquerque, New Mexico, February 26, 1968.

2. See Appendix B., FHA Counseling Service Interview, prepared by Dr. James Hawkins, Indiana University research sociologist, and Professor Baum. Results of the interviews were discussed by Karen Orloff Kaplan, chief social work consultant to the committee.

3. Interview between Mrs. Tate, Dr. Hawkins, and Professor Baum, December 7, 1967.

4. Three were later placed by the committee when the FHA acquired property program went into effect.

5. See note 1.

6. Ibid.

7. Proceedings of the Common Council of Indianapolis, General Ordinance No. 15, 1926, p. 53.

8. *Stephenson* v. *State,* 205 Ind. 141, 179 N.E. 633 (1932).

9. Proceedings of the Common Council, p. 53.
10. Ibid., p. 81.
11. These questions are from the interview forms, appendices B and C. The results were compiled and evaluated under the direction of Karen Orloff Kaplan, chief social work consultant to the committee.
12. See Appendix G, table 1.
13. See Appendix G, table 2.

Notes to Chapter Four

1. *Indiana Acts* 1961, ch. 208. Section 42, p. 500.
2. Ibid.
3. *Indiana Acts* 1961, ch. 208. Sections 6(c), 6(d), 6(f), 6(g), 9, and 11, pp. 502-505.
4. Information obtained in discussions between Tom Collins and Alan Goldstein, research assistants to Professor Baum, and Harold Hatcher, executive director, Indiana Civil Rights Commission, during 1967-1968.
5. 1962 Opinions of the Attorney General, Official Opinion No. 38. p. 197.
6. Interview between Governor Welsh and Professor Baum, June 11, 1968, Indianapolis, Indiana.
7. The new commission was empowered to:

> ... state its findings of facts after a hearing and, if the Commission finds a person has engaged in an unlawful discriminatory practice, it may cause to be served on such person an order requiring such person to take such further action as will effectuate the purposes of this act. Judicial review of such cease and desist order may be obtained in accordance with the provisions of [IND. ANN. STAT. sections 63-3001-63-3030], ... If no proceeding to obtain judicial review is instituted within thirty days from receipt of notice by a person that such order has been made by the Commission, the Commission, if it determines that the person upon whom the cease and desist order has been served is not complying or is making no effort to comply, may obtain a decree of a court for the enforcement of such order in a circuit or superior court upon showing that such person is subject to the Commission's jurisdiction and resides or transacts business within the county in which the petition for enforcement is brought, Indiana Annotated Statutes, section 40-2312 (1) 1965.

8. The governor appoints the five commissioners, no more than three of whom may be members of the same political party. They are appointed to four-year terms, which correspond to that of the governor. They may be removed for cause. The commissioners are paid twenty-five dollars plus necessary travel allowances for the monthly meetings they attend. Indiana Annotated Statutes section 40-2310 (1965).

9.
> It is the public policy of the State of Indiana to provide all of its citizens equal opportunity for education, employment, access to public conveniences and accommodations and *acquisition* through *purchase or rental of real property including, but not limited to, housing.*
>
> Provided, however, that no cease and desist orders shall be issued against an owner-occupant with respect to a residential building containing less than four housing units. Indiana Annotated Statutes, sections 40-2308, 40-2312(1) (1965).

10. The 1967 session of the General Assembly further amended the Act by defining the term "owner-occupant" and exempting from cease and desist orders

> any person who has engaged in a discriminatory practice pursuant to a voluntary plan adopted to prevent or eliminate *de facto* segregation if such plan established no fixed numbers or percent for any race, religion or nationality and is found by the Commission to be reasonably designed to prevent *de facto* segregation and consistently followed by persons privy to the plan. Indiana Annotated Statutes, section 40-2312(1) 1967 Supplement.

11. Indiana Civil Rights Commission, Budget Summary, June 30, 1967 (mimeographed).
12. See Appendix G, table 3.
13. See Appendix G, table 4.
14. See Indiana Annotated Statutes, section 40-2312(f)(1)(n) 1967 Supplement.
15. Of these commissions, at least six have one or more full-time employees: East Chicago, Evansville, Fort Wayne, Gary, Indianapolis, and South Bend. The state commission has entered into "agency agreements" with city commissions that have full-time staff members. It has also established machinery for its staff members to keep in personal contact with all city commissions on a regular basis. (Discussions between Tom Collins and Alan Goldstein, and the executive and deputy directors of the Indiana Civil Rights Commission–1967-1968). See also Indiana Civil Rights Commission, 1967 Progress Reports, pp. 13-14.
16. Among the groups represented on the Housing Advisory Committee are: Indiana Jewish Community Relations Council; Indiana Council of United Church Women; Indiana Real Estate Association; Catholic Interracial Council; Indiana AFL-CIO; Indiana Council of Urban League Directors; Indiana Real Estate Commission; Indiana Mortgage Bankers, Incorporated; Indiana State Chamber of Commerce; Savings and Loan League of Indiana; Veterans Administration; Apartment Owners Association; Urban League; Federal Housing Administration; NAACP; and the Indiana Council of Churches.
17. 1967 Report of the Indiana Civil Rights Commission, p. 6.
18. Interviews between Alan Goldstein and the deputy director of the Indiana Civil Rights Commission, March 19, 1968.
19. Prepared by the Indiana Civil Rights Commission, it sets forth 1967 racial density areas based upon independent survey and precinct analyses.
20. Although the secretary's address had been printed, it was not made generally available to the public. On request a copy of his remarks and the survey referred to in the text were forwarded. Letter from John G. Kester, attorney-adviser, Department of the Army, to Baum, August 2, 1967. "Remarks by Secretary of the Army, The Honorable Stanley R. Resor, at Fort Benjamin Harrison, Indiana, July 25, 1967," mimeographed, p. 6.
21. Ibid., p. 10.
22. Ibid., p. 9.
23. Secretary of Defense McNamara was quoted by Secretary Resor as saying: "The Deputy Secretary of Defense and I are dedicated as a matter of urgent priority to eliminate this discrimination [housing] against those who serve our country. There can and will be no compromise with this gross injustice. We are hopeful that the Department of Defense will have

constructive and responsive assistance from citizens throughout our country." (Ibid., p. 12.)

24. John H. Averill, "LBJ Appeals to House to Pass Civil Rights Bill," *The Courier-Journal,* March 28, 1968.

25. Ibid.

26. The information relating to enrollment in Lawrence Township schools did not come easily. It was not given voluntarily to the Committee on Special Housing, but was disclosed through channels that must remain confidential. The commandant's statement was made in a January 1965 conference with Baum.

27. On December 12, 1966, state Senator Patrick J. Chavis wrote the following letter to John Waggaman, the director of research for the Legislative Advisory Council:

Re: Civil Rights and Open Housing

Dear Mr. Waggaman:

New legislation concerning open housing may be introduced in the coming legislative session. So that I may react properly I ask that the following information be gathered by your office and forwarded to me as soon as possible. Needless to say, in-depth data is needed:

1. Supply a complete statistical breakdown on a monthly basis of open housing complaints forwarded to the Civil Rights Commission.
   a. In this regard, please set forth the information elicited from the complainant.
   b. Who accepts complaints for the Commission?
   c. What is the frequency of complaints from relevant geographic areas?
   d. State how the complaints submitted were disposed of.
   e. Set forth the time consumed between the filing of complaints and disposition.
2. Has the Civil Rights Commission conducted any investigation of discriminatory practices in housing markets where *de facto* segregation exists? If so, please describe the nature and results of such investigations fully.
3. Describe the relationship between the Civil Rights Commission and the Indiana Real Estate Commission.
   a. Has the Civil Rights Commission attempted to obtain the support of the Real Estate Commission in furthering open housing? If so, please set forth such efforts in detail.
   b. Has the Civil Rights Commission forwarded any housing complaints to the Real Estate Commission?
4. Has the Civil Rights Commission considered *de facto* segregation among real estate agencies in their hiring practices? If so, describe in detail the results of any such investigation, and any action taken by the Civil Rights Commission in this regard.
5. Has the Real Estate Commission taken any action in relation to its licensees to insure compliance with the open housing proviso of the Civil Rights Act?
   a. Describe these procedures established by the Real Estate Commission designed to insure compliance.

     b. Have licensees been informed of such procedures? If so, describe in detail what they have been told.

  6. Has the Real Estate Commission received any complaints directed against its licensees for violation of open housing proviso of the Civil Rights Act?

     a. If so, please give a complete statistical breakdown on a yearly, monthly and geographic basis.

     b. Describe how the complaints were handled in detail.

     c. In this regard (b) state the period of time between receipt and disposition.

The questions posed are without doubt lengthy. Answering them, however, should allow those of us in the legislature to act on a more informed basis in this critical area. I add this final thought: Please exercise whatever discretion you deem necessary to obtain a full reply. My questions were not intended to be rigid, to be the only inquiries made.

Your prompt reply will be appreciated; there is not a great deal of time before the General Assembly meets.

28. Memorandum from Civil Rights Commission to John S. Waggaman, director of research, Legislative Advisory Commission, January 11, 1967, pp. 2-3.
29. See Indiana Annotated Statutes, section 63-2401-23 (1965). Much of the information that follows through note 31 was taken from the unpublished response of T. C. Dickson, executive secretary, Indiana Real Estate Commission, to a questionnaire disseminated by the Legislative Advisory Commission in its study of administrative agencies. The response was returned on April 15, 1966.
30. Ibid., p. 3.
31. Ibid., at p. 9; see also Executive Order No. 4-63, Part 2, Section 2.
32. Joseph Phillips, "Owner v. Broker–Who is Villain In Open Housing Bout? " *The Indianapolis News,* June 11, 1968.
33. Neither the mayor of Lawrence nor the mayor of Indianapolis, both present at the meeting, endorsed the message of Secretary Resor. Only when Griffen Crump, executive director of the Indianapolis Human Rights Commission, stood to comment did the mayor of Indianapolis have something to say . . . "the executive director's jurisdiction was limited to the city of Indianapolis."
34. "F.H.A. Outlines New Home Buying Policy," *The Harrison Post,* January 26, 1968. "First Soldier Qualifies for New F.H.A. Benefit," *The Harrison Post,* February 2, 1968.
35. All comments of clients served by the Committee on Special Housing that appear in this book were noted and recorded by professional members or trained volunteers of the committee who were under the direction of Mrs. Karen Orloff Kaplan. The names of the applicants have been changed to protect their privacy.
36. The need to correct this condition was seen by the newly elected, thirty-five-year-old Republican mayor of Indianapolis, Richard Lugar. For the summer of 1968 Lugar accepted for the city the services of seven law student interns whose salaries were paid by major law firms. The interns were assigned to receive and act upon complaints. On Saturday, June 15, two children were seen splattering eggs on the home of a black couple recently moved to an all white area. The incident was minor. Only increased police patrol was desired for the neighbors had welcomed the couple. The Human Rights Commission could not be reached, and for a

variety of reasons regular police contact was not desired.

A law student intern immediately called the Internal Security Division of the Police Department. Within twenty minutes of his call to the mayor, a black police lieutenant called Baum, "Don't worry, we'll take care of it right away."

(Individual staff members of the state Civil Rights Commission do work during the weekend, despite the fact that the state has an absolute rule against granting mileage allowance for travel on Sunday. Evidently, even a harassed or discontented citizenry must recognize Sunday as a day of rest.)

37. *Help yourself,* a publication of the Indianapolis Human Rights Commission, undated but still disseminated in 1967-1968.

38. Interview between Alan Goldstein and Griffen Crump, executive director, Indianapolis Human Rights Commission, June 3, 1968. (See also Proceedings of the Common Council of Indianapolis, General Ordinance No. 56, 1964, as amended.)

39. General Ordinance No. 56, 1964, as amended, section 6(d).

40. Ibid. (g).

41. Ibid., Section 7. (The executive director is firm in his determination to have the ordinance strengthened. See Goldstein interview, note 38.)

42. Interview between Baum and Griffen Crump, June 14, 1968.

43. Ibid.

44. Ibid.

45. The money was to be used to advertise an open house sponsored by the Committee on Special Housing at FHA. Rather than advertise, however, the committee obtained a front page story in the black newspaper, The *Indianapolis Recorder.*

46. Memorandum from Civil Rights Commission to John S. Waggaman, director of research, Legislative Advisory Commission, January 11, 1967, p. 3.

47. See Appendix G, table 5.

48. In March 1967 the Legislative Advisory Council forwarded the following memorandum to Senator Patrick J. Chavis. It stated in pertinent part the following:

The Civil Rights Commission has issued two cease and desist orders, only one of which dealt with housing. Neither has had any effect in itself to date. However, according to Mr. Hatcher, both probably had an effect by bringing publicity to bear on the situation. . . .

Mr. Hatcher emphasized conciliation as the policy of the commission. He pointed to the lack of success in open housing legislation in many states. He particularly pointed to Gary city ordinance, which has been bogged in litigation for a year and a half, as being strong in wording but ineffectual. He felt with such a result, the militant drive for integration was paradoxical especially when compared with result of the state's efforts. He also noted that when conflict over housing arose the commission felt that if the Negro complainant found housing in another Caucasian or integrated neighborhood the solution was satisfactory, and that the commission encouraged such alternate solutions. He also noted, that the time lag when litigation was required hampered enforcement. In this regard, the lack of effective remedies also arose. In the Indianapolis and South Bend cases no means was available to provide satisfactory integrated housing in a short time. He

commented favorably and optimistically on the beginnings of efforts and the use of new provisions of the law permitting neighborhood agreement on racial balance.
49. Memorandum from Mrs. Howard F. Gustafson, Indianapolis Urban League, February 9, 1968.

Notes to Chapter Five

1. In March 1968 the first of several papers were produced as a part of a comprehensive housing study of Metropolitan Indianapolis (Marion County). Prepared by Hammer, Greene, Siler Associates, Washington, D.C., and ordered by the Metropolitan Planning Commission, the study sets forth, *inter alia,* preliminary projections of total need for additional housing units in the metropolitan area from 1967-1985. Much of the information that follows is based on that study, "Metropolitan Indianapolis Housing Study," *Technical Work Paper No. 1, Preliminary Projections of Housing Needs, 1967-1985.* (Hereafter referred to as "Metropolitan Indianapolis Study.") See pp. 3-4.
2. Ibid., p. iii.
3. Ibid., at p. 5.
4. Ibid.
5. Ibid., pp. 6, 7.
6. Ibid., p. 5.
7. Ibid., pp. 11-12.
8. Freemont Power, "Plan to Aid Displaced Is Going Well," *The Indianapolis News,* June 17, 1968.
9. "Metropolitan Indianapolis Study," p. 14.
10. Ibid., pp. 24-28.
11. Ibid., p. 15.
12. Ibid., p. 16.
13. Ibid.
14. Ibid., p. 18.
15. Ibid.
16. Ibid.
17. 1967 Labor Relations Yearbook (Washington, D.C.: Bureau of National Affairs, 1968), p. 550 (source: Bureau of Labor Statistics).
18. Harrison J. Ullmann and Lynn Dunson, "State is Agent of Slum Landlords," *The Indianapolis Star,* September 25, 1966.
19. Ibid. Through confidential random checks the conclusions reached by Ullmann and Dunson were validated.
20. Harrison J. Ullmann and Lynn Dunson, "Eviction Notices Sent to Renters— Inner Loop Owners Get 'Fair' Price," *The Indianapolis Star,* September 28, 1966. "The families who prefer 'outhouses' to 'decent, safe and sanitary' housing are admirably served by the rental listings kept at the department's five relocation offices in the Inner Loop project areas." This is a rather bold statement to be printed in a newspaper known for its conservative bent.
21. Ibid.
22. Alan Goldstein made random samplings of the cost for a two-bedroom inner-city apartment. The monthly rentals ranged from $70 to $90. This conclusion was substantiated by interviews conducted by Baum during 1967 with real estate agents and with an inner-city landlord holding 150 rental units.

23. Indianapolis Redevelopment Commission monthly report, April 1968, p. 2.
24. Freemont Power, "Plan to Aid Displaced is Going Well," *The Indianapolis News,* June 17, 1968. "Elwood W. Holder, relocation director, reported the bulk of the commission's work in this area is still to go, about 2,168 families over the seven year projection, compared to the 696 families and 220 individuals it has relocated in the last year and a half."
25. See Indianapolis Redevelopment Commission monthly reports, April, May 1968, pp. 4-5. Change, however, may be on its way. "The Redevelopment Commission took the lead in forming an interdepartmental committee on citizen participation in the planning of governmental projects. The committee, which has come to be known as 'Task II', is comprised of three members of the Redevelopment staff . . . a member from the Metropolitan Planning Department . . . and one from the mayor's Human Rights Commission . . . Purpose of this committee is to determine specific areas where decisions could be made by the citizens. This includes means of two-way communications between the citizens and the various agencies of government " (May report, p. 5). It should be noted that three of the five members of Task II are actively and individually involved in the work of the Committee on Special Housing.
26. Conference between Otis Bryant, Professor Baum, and Tom Collins, September. 15, 1967.
27, Harrison J. Ullmann and Lynn Dunson, "State Is Agent of Slum Landlords," *The Indianapolis Star,* September 25, 1966. The assertion was based on an unpublished "extensive survey of a 32-block area near the planned-northeast interchange of the Inner Loop. . . . " The survey was conducted by Community Action Against Poverty of Greater Indianapolis, Incorporated.
28. Indianapolis Redevelopment Commission monthly report, April 1968, p. 4.
29. See Minutes of April 3, 1968, mayor's Task Force on Housing and Relocation, item 2(d), p. 1 (mimeographed).
30. Ibid., item 4, p. 2.
31. Ibid., item 2(d), p. 1.
32. Graham Le Stourgeon, "Real Estate Report—Firm Assured Inner City Mortgages," *The Indianapolis Star,* May 12, 1968.
33. Ibid. The homes were advertised for $500 down, including closing costs, 30-year, FHA-insured mortgage at 6 and 3/4 percent, resulting in monthly mortgage payments of $89 to $95.
34. See letter from Rex Cox, general manager, Mobile Research Corporation of the Midwest, to Baum, May 24, 1968. The meeting described took place on June 6, 1968; see also *Value Line,* April 19, 1968, p. 48.
35. February 1, 1968, WFBM editorial broadcast.
36. Letter from Mayor Richard Lugar to Baum, March 19, 1968.
37. Only a few large Realtor firms have had the attraction in obtaining corporate listings. Some of these same firms are engaged in commercial as well as residential transactions. And some widely advertise their willingness to assist in transactions beyond the borders of Indiana.
38. Remarks of Carmen Pasquale, FHA assistant commissioner for Field Operations, before members of the Albuquerque Board of Realtors, Independent Real Estate Brokers and Mortgage Lenders, Albuquerque, New Mexico, February 26, 1968.
39. Ibid., p. 4.
40. Ibid. "As we have said in our press announcements, the housing counseling

service is free, and it is open to all. We know from experience that the persons who take advantage of this service are largely low-income families who may need some budget or credit counseling, before they would be in a position to become home buyers.

We appreciate that the real estate fraternity in New Mexico has an excellent reputation for civic mindedness as well as good business, but we also realize that you cannot devote the time that many low-income families might need for assistance in credit or budget counseling."

41. Ibid.
42. Ibid., p. 2.
43. Substantial reconsideration was given to this suggestion. See text referred to in note 38.
44. An early highly informal relationship was established between certain officials in the office of the secretary at HUD and the committee. The purpose of this relationship initially was merely to exchange information, to insure the dissemination of knowledge of the committee's work.
45. The legal role of the committee is delineated in chapter six.
46. "Open Housing Drive Planned April 27-28," *The Indianapolis News,* April 17, 1968.
47. The contractors present were largely inner-city developers of low-priced housing ($10,500 to $14,000). In Indianapolis, and in many other cities, two professional trade associations representing real estate sales firms and individuals have emerged. Both exist not only to protect the interests of their members but to establish and enforce codes of conduct for them in their relationship with the public and each other. Standards are accordingly established for admission to each association. Until very recently the Realtors of Indianapolis had no black members. Now the association has a few. The Realtists, however, coming into existence after the Realtors, consist almost entirely of blacks.
48. See Appendix C, *Open House Follow-Up Interview.* This interview is an amended, modified version of the *FHA Counseling Service Interview.* The Open House Interview was prepared by Karen Orloff Kaplan. The results discussed in the text are based upon her analysis of interview responses.
49. See note 40.

Notes to Chapter Six

1. Newspapers, radio, and television urged people to telephone the committee from 9 A.M. to 5 P.M., Monday through Friday, but also added that if the callers would leave their names and telephone numbers, they would be contacted at their convenience. Mrs. Deer, the committee's administrative assistant on loan from the Indiana Civil Rights Commission, took the telephone calls. Her concern and sincerity assured that the applicant's first committee contact would not be like a call to an answering service.
2. Professors James Gillespie, James White, and Ronald Polston were those who joined the committee.
3. Property Disposition Letter No. 129 states: "If two or more purchase offers are received for the same property during the ten-day waiting period, all such offers received shall be considered on a first come, first served basis. Back-up offers may be retained with the consent of the persons submitting such offers. Any priority system must be established and administered by the displacing agency."
4. Allen Dale was consistent and firm in this position. Quite early in the

committee program, questions arose as to whether the rehabilitation problem and the difficulty many of the applicants seemed to have in gathering the necessary down payment could be resolved through "sweat equity." That is, let the potential buyer, as a condition to being sold the home, do his own painting, at his expense. If it would meet FHA inspection standards the work done would constitute the down payment. Dale and the committee social workers firmly resisted the proposal. Homes should be put in sound repair, including painting, before any move took place. People should have pride in ownership. Neighbors should see a home in good condition; it would reflect on the buyer.

5. This was freely admitted to Baum by a major FHA rehabilitation contractor. At a cocktail party in February 1968, another FHA contractor bragged before his "kind of people" that he was giving the federal government "a taste of its own medicine." He said that in 1967 he "got $30,000 for doing nothing," for making repairs that never were made.

6. Smith could afford private counsel. He employed a widely known black lawyer who consulted with the committee before entering an appearance on Smith's behalf. The attorney sought assistance in challenging "the whole system of ejectment" in land contract matters.

7. In four cases of extreme hardship, buyers were permitted to move into their homes before closing. The permission was extended by drafting and executing a short-term lease; it was done reluctantly, only after all other avenues were closed.

8. This statement was based on one of a series of interviews conducted by Ronald Gottschalk, research assistant to Baum, with officials of six life insurance companies in Indianapolis. The companies ranged in size from Prudential Life Insurance Company to Wabash Life Insurance Company, from large to medium-small.

9. It would be foolish to term this anything more than hope. Corporate practices, like those of agencies, do not change quickly even when the corporations desire to change.

10. The oportunity to compel was present. A substantial proportion of Redevelopment Commission funds came from the federal government, and, more particularly, the Department of Housing and Urban Development. The Redevelopment Commission had placed itself in a delicate position. On March 25, 1965, it joined the city of Indianapolis in submitting a "Workable Program" to HUD. This detailed submission, necessary to a continuation of federal housing grants, contained an in-depth questionnaire on "Housing For Displaced Families." Item C (2), p. 19, raised the following questions: "What specific actions have been taken or are proposed by those responsible for seeing that additional housing is provided to meet any relocation deficit . . . such as securing the active participation of local builders and lenders to build or rehabilitate housing for families of moderate and low income . . . ; to use the special Federal financing aids, where needed; to make sites available at reasonable prices; and to eliminate discriminatory practices that limit the housing opportunity of minority families? " The response detailed the work of the Committee on Special Housing, describing it as a useful resource for the Relocation Commission (22a, 22b).

11. Evidently, for a period of two months he forgot. In its monthly reports for April and May of 1968 the commission detailed those private groups aiding the dislocated in finding adequate housing. The Committee on Special Housing was not mentioned.

12. In April 1968, Baum, in consultation with Dale and Mrs. Kaplan among

others, prepared a manual for the committee. The manual set forth, step by step, the approach to applicants: the facts to be presented and the tone or manner of presentation. Of utmost importance was the caution "The applicant is not forgotten after the first interview. The committee representative who spoke with the applicant stays with him until the housing problem is resolved. There is no shifting of responsibility."

13. Mrs. Gustafson attempted to draw on the offers made. For the committee's third open house on July 6, 1968, the following letter was sent to the twenty-two families, black and white, who had moved into FHA acquired homes under the dislocated program:

Committee on Special Housing
445 North Pennsylvania Street
Suite 501
Indianapolis, Indiana 46204
317:637-0320

June 27, 1968

Dear New Homeowner:

The Committee on Special Housing is pleased that you are now in your new home, and we hope that you are enjoying it.

It was a pleasure to work with you. We trust that our services were satisfactory.

If you have friends, or relatives or former neighbors who are living in crowded quarters or who are being displaced by the highways, parks or code enforcement, they may be interested in our program. We would appreciate your telling our telephone number (637-0320) and our location on the 5th floor at 445 North Pennsylvania Street, Suite 501 and suggesting that they talk with us.

We still have a number of nice homes available throughout the county. Remember, there are many who now rent who may qualify as buyers.

We are sponsoring another Open House on Saturday, July 6, at the FHA Offices, 333 North Pennsylvania Street, from 11:00 A.M. until 4:00 P.M. Please invite anyone who may be interested. Qualified people will be on hand to help them.

Sincerely,

Orville Gardner
Julia Fangmeier
Field Representatives
Committee on Special Housing
OG/JF:ss

14. More were scheduled to move into their already selected homes. The eight families, nearly half of the original total of black buyers, referred fifteen other families to the committee. By July 15, 1968, six of the fifteen had been served to their satisfaction. Five had selected FHA homes, and one obtained, through committee help, an inner-city mortgage loan to rehabilitate his property.

Notes to Chapter Seven

1. Mrs. Ruth Deer, committee administrative assistant, prepared the statistics. From January 4 to July 15, 1968 the committee had contact with 220

persons. For January and February there were 69 applicants; March, 26; April, 52; May, 14; June, 20; July 1-15, 39. The months in which committee open houses were held reflect an increased number of contacts. The committee could not sit quietly and wait for the applicants.

2. A total of 65 homes had been set aside by applicants, but for a variety of reasons 20 applicants chose to release their designated set aside property. Of the 20, a total of seven dropped from the committee's program. They are included in the 67 discussed later in the chapter.

3. The increase Gardner anticipated would spring from two sources: the July open house and the effort of a new field worker under his supervision.

4. The family seeking the $25,000 home purchased in the integrated "open" area of Butler-Tarkington.

5. These were white families and there was no delay in obtaining public housing. The city was desperately trying to maintain a condition of integration. White families were at a premium.

6. On June 28, 1968, FHA requested specific recommendations from the committee concerning changes in Property Disposition Letter No. 129 and the operation of the Counseling Service. The recommendations were submitted in a letter from the committee to the Indiana FHA director. See appendix F.

7. Sherwood Hill, B.S., Indiana University, 1966, FHA administrator and counselor in financing and housing.

8. John Kite, B.S., Indiana University, 1962, a social caseworker for four years.

9. Jerome Sobel, administrator and value analyst with a major national home products corporation.

10. See Appendix D. The statistical tables described in the text as follows. They include: (1) Average Age; (2) Heads of Household; (3) Dependents in Household; (4) Marital Status; (5) Working Females; (6) Average Net Income; (7) Years on Job; (8) Average Number Open Accounts Per Family; (9) Type of Open Accounts Per Sample Group; (10) Pay Pattern on Open Accounts; (11) Pay Pattern Over All Accounts; (12) Total Debt; (13) Assets Available for Closing; (14) Housing Expense; (15) Housing Payments Per Month; (16) Average Purchase Price; (17) Average Mortgage Amount; (18) Average Amount Amortized; (19) Employment – Male; (20) Employment - Female.

11. See Appendix E. Follow-Up Interview For Families Placed Through The Auspices of the Committee on Special Housing.

12. For the first twenty who moved, the committee found the written interview helpful in terms of providing essential documentation and material for ongoing program evaluation, and for creating an open channel of communication between these homeowners and the committee to be used at the homeowners' discretion. Strong recommendations have been made to the committee (letter from Mrs. Kaplan, to Mrs. Howard Gustafson, August, 1968) urging the continuation of initial follow-up interviews as well as the introduction of further follow-up contact at specified times in the future.

13. "Realty License Becomes Issue," *The Indianapolis News,* July 20, 1968.

Notes to Chapter Eight

1. Indiana Annotated Statutes, section 63-2409 (1949). This provides the answer to the legal challenge of the black brokers.

2. "Proposal for Augmenting Fair Housing Service and Pilot Project," Urban League (mimeographed), p. 2.

3. Ibid., p. 5.

Notes to Epilogue

1. U.S. Constitution, amendment 24, section 1.
2. Housing Act of 1949, section 105(c), 42 United States Code, section 1455(c) 1965. See "Judicial Review of Displacee Relocation in Urban Renewal," *Yale Law Journal*, 77(1968):966, 968 note 13. Congress has never weakened section 105(c), which concerns itself with adequate housing for the dislocated. "The 1964 amendments broadened the coverage to individuals as well as families and required that each community establish a special relocation assistance program to minimize the hardships of displacement. . . . In 1965, the requirements of careful planning and coordination with other federal programs were further elaborated, and Subsection 105(c) (2) was added to require the federal agency to extract, as a condition of further assistance, reassurances from localities carrying out projects that relocation housing is available. . . . The public housing statute contains a provision similar to section 105(c), and the new Demonstration Cities Act incorporates 105(c) by reference."
3. Norwalk CORE v. *Norwalk Redevelopment Agency*, 395 *Federal Reporter*, Second Series, 920, 931 (Second Circuit, 1968). The Second Circuit distinguished the the issues raised before it and those disposed of by the Seventh Circuit in *Green Street Association* v *Daley*, 373 *Federal Reporter*, Second Series, 1 (Seventh Circuit), cert. denied, 387 United States Supreme Court Reports, 932 (1967), and *Harrison-Halsted Community Group, Inc.* v. *Housing and Home Finance Agency*, 310 *Federal Reporter*, Second Series, 99 (Seventh Circuit, 1962), cert. denied, 373 United States Supreme Court Reports, 914 (1963). See 395 *Federal Reporter*, Second Series, 926-932. Those cases, however, dealt with the threshold questions of standing and justiciability, not the underlying substantive matter of equal protection. Further, it is not enough to say that urban planning demands the exercise of discretion. In a broader context Professor Kenneth Culp Davis wrote:

> The central inquiry . . . is what can be done to assure that where law ends tyranny will not begin. More precisely, the central inquiry is what can be done that is not now done to minimize injustice from exercise of discretionary power. The answer is, in broad terms that we should eliminate much unnecessary discretionary power and that we should do much more than we have been doing to confine, to structure, and to check necessary discretionary power. The goal is not the maximum degree of confining, structuring and checking; the goal is to find the optimum degree of each power in each set of circumstances. Kenneth Culp Davis, *Discretionary Justice: A Preliminary Inquiry* (Baton Rouge: Louisiana State Universy Press, 1969), pp. 3-4.

4. 395 *Federal Reporter*, Second Series, 937.
5. At its root, the argument rests upon equality in the administration of law. Government, through urban renewal, displaces; government, through law, commands fair and effective relocation; government, through its own housing inventory, has the means, at least in part, for achieving the statutory end.

   There is another, related side to equal protection of the laws. In the Housing Act of 1949 the state made an affirmative commitment to "the realization as soon as feasible of the goal of a decent home and a suitable living environment for every American family. . . . " (Housing Act of 1949, section 2, 42 United States Code, section 1441, 1964). On a broader scale adequate housing is but one of the universal human rights subscribed to by the United States in Article 25 (2) of the Universal Declaration of Human Rights adopted by the United Nations General Assembly. Those who are displaced may have an "inalienable right," quite apart from the statutory grant of relocation assistance, to adequate shelter. See "Development in the Law–Equal Protection," *Harvard Law Review,* 82(1969):1065, 1191-1192.

6. In housing, as in education, community-wide discrimination often can be demonstrated. See *Gautreaux* v. *The Chicago Housing Authority,* 296 Federal Supplement, 907 (Northern District of Illinois, 1969).

7. As to acquired FHA property the law seems clear. 12 United States Code, section 1710 (g) 1965, allows the secretary of HUD "to deal with, complete, rent, renovate, modernize, insure, or sell for cash or credit, in his discretion, any properties conveyed to him in exchange for debentures and certificates of claim. . . . "

Appendices

Appendix A

FHA Property Disposition Letter Number 129

DEPARTMENT OF HOUSING AND URBAN DEVELOPMENT FEDERAL HOUSING ADMINISTRATION	Series and Series No. PROPERTY DISPOSITION LETTER No. 129	
To: ALL INSURING OFFICE DIRECTORS	Control No. F-1323	Date Jan. 4, 1968

Subject: PROCEDURE TO MAKE FHA ACQUIRED HOME PROPERTIES AVAILABLE TO DISPLACED PERSONS PRIOR TO MARKET EXPOSURE

Families displaced as a result of governmental actions, such as urban renewal activities, highway construction, code enforcement, airport expansion, or as the result of a major disaster are often confronted with extreme difficulties in obtaining adequate housing. To aid in alleviating those difficulties, FHA acquired properties are to be made available for direct sale to such displacees prior to public offering. This letter provides a procedure for its accomplishment.

Legal occupants residing in any property which is being or will be taken through government action, tenants who are being forced to vacate a building because a recognized government body has declared that building unfit for continued residential occupancy for reasons of health or safety, tenants of public housing who are forced to vacate such housing because their income exceeds established limitations, and persons displaced by a major disaster shall all be deemed displaced persons for the purposes of this letter. Displaced persons shall retain that status notwithstanding the fact that they have established a temporary residence following displacement.

In order for a displacee to qualify for the purchase of an FHA acquired property, it will be necessary for such person except in case of disaster to obtain a written statement similar to FHA Form 3476, from an authorized representative of the acquiring agency involved, certifying that such person is or will become a displaced person and the cause of his displacement.

The director shall maintain a continuing surveillance of agency programs in his jurisdiction likely to result in the displacement of persons. The director shall inform each such agency or governmental body in his jurisdiction that he is prepared to furnish information concerning available acquired properties, so that they can relay such information to displacees.

In order to avoid any undue delay in the ultimate sale of acquired properties, displaced persons are to be furnished information as to the location and price range of acquired properties at an early date. Concurrent with the establishment of the 2060 disposition program, but in no event later than 15 days following acquisition or a determination to offer for sale properties previously held off the market, the director will provide each interested agency or governmental body in his jurisdiction, a preliminary list of properties which will soon be publicly offered for sale.

This list will include address, approximate price range, and room count of properties. Recipients will be expected to make this information available to displacees to enable them to take a preliminary look at the property. Such preliminary viewing of property must be external only and no one will be permitted entry at this time.

As soon as possible after completion of programmed repairs, the director will furnish interested agencies or governmental bodies within his jurisdiction, a second listing setting forth the identity, location, price, required down payment and maximum allowable mortgage term of properties then ready to be made available for sale to displaced persons.

In the ten day period following this second listing the local FHA office will receive purchase offers directly from displaced persons through the local displacing agency. Offers to purchase will be made on FHA Form 2384, Standard Retail Sales Contract, and must be accompanied by a minimum earnest money deposit of $50 in the form required along with an acceptable certification that the prospective purchaser is a displaced person. If FHA insured financing is requested, a completed FHA Form 2900 must also accompany the purchase offer.

During the ten day period for receipt of purchase offers from displacees, the properties which have been made available for sale shall be open for inspection by any displacee interested in purchasing a property. Such inspection shall be made only in the presence of an authorized representative of the agency or governmental body effecting the displacement. To enable the properties to be shown, the director will provide an adequate supply of lock-box keys to the agencies and governmental bodies involved. Those furnished keys are to be cautioned that keys are not to be given to prospective purchasers to inspect properties unaccompanied; that they are not to admit any person to an FHA acquired property other than during the ten day period; and, that they should exercise care to safeguard properties.

The director, at the request of displacing agencies and governmental bodies, will give such agencies and governmental bodies suitable instructions to enable them to assist displacees in the preparation and submission of purchase offers, and in obtaining necessary credit reports and verifications. In addition, the director will render such direct assistance and advice as is needed and may be available for aiding displacees in preparing and submitting their purchase offers, and in obtaining necessary related credit reports and verifications.

If two or more purchase offers are received for the same property during the ten day waiting period, all such offers received shall be considered on a first come, first served basis. Back-up offers may be retained with the consent of the persons submitting such offers. Any priority system must be established and administered by the displacing agency.

Credit reports must be ordered from FHA approved credit reporting sources for direct delivery to the local FHA office. Prospective purchasers will be responsible for all expenses involved in establishing credit. FHA will reimburse the amount so expended only in the event a sale to such person is actually closed. The displacing agencies assisting prospective purchasers should be encouraged to obtain promptly all necessary credit information and verifications.

Only fully repaired properties upon which FHA insured financing is available will be offered under the program. Purchase offers will be accepted only from those displacees who will be owner-occupants.

Properties for which no purchase offers are received during the ten day period, or properties for which all purchase offers received, including back-up offers, are either rejected or subsequently withdrawn, shall thereafter be placed on the PIR and made available to the general public in the usual manner.

No sales commissions will be paid on these sales.

The number of purchase offers received from displacees and the number of properties sold in this manner shall be reported on the reverse side of the Form 472. A negative report will be required.

Appendix B

FHA Counseling Service Interview

1. What was your age at your last birthday? (Check one)

____	0.	Under 20	____	5.	40 - 44
____	1.	20 - 24	____	6.	45 - 49
____	2.	25 - 29	____	7.	50 - 54
____	3.	30 - 34	____	8.	55 - 60
____	4.	35 - 39	____	9.	61 or over

2. How many children living here with you now are in grade school? (Check one)

____	0.	____	5.	
____	1.	____	6.	
____	2.	____	7.	
____	3.	____	8.	
____	4.	____	9.	or more

3. At the time that you first went to the FHA counselor's office, were you renting or buying?

    ____ 1.   renting
    ____ 2.   buying

4. After you talked with the counselor, did you decide to look mainly for a house to buy or mainly for a house to rent?

    ____ 1.   buy primarily   (Go to: 7 if conventional
                                              (62 if repossessed
    ____ 2.   rent primarily - Go to 5

5. Did the FHA counselor work with you to help find a rental?

    ____ 1.   Yes
    ____ 2.   No - Please explain: _____

    _____

6. Did the FHA counselor work with you to help you find a house to buy even though you were not primarily interested in buying?

    ____ 1.   Yes - Ask Q's 7 and 8, then skip to 62
    ____ 2.   No - Ask Q's 7 and 8, then skip to 62

7. Why were you looking for another house at this time?

    ____ 1.   Public project displacement
    ____ 2.   Private project displacement
    ____ 3.   Evicted; forced to move (specify)

    _____

    ____ 4.   Wanted other housing for personal reasons - not forced to move.

8. Did you feel that you had to find another home quickly?

    ____ 1.   Yes (because of some forced deadline)
    ____ 2.   Yes (no forced deadline, but really want to move for some personal reason)
    ____ 3.   No

9. Did you have a particular home in mind when you went to see the FHA counselor?

    _____ 2. No - Go to 17
    _____ 1. Yes - 9a Did you mention that you were interested in that particular house to the FHA counselor?
    _____ 1. Yes
    _____ 2. No - Why not? _____

10. Why did you go to see the FHA counselor at this time?

    _____ 1. Financing
    _____ 2. Other (specify) _____

11. Did you obtain the (financing/or other specific) you sought?

    _____ 1. Yes
    _____ 2. No - Could you explain that to me? _____

12. Did you actually try to buy this house?

    _____ 1. Yes - Go to 13
    _____ 2. No - Go to 14

13. What was the outcome - Did you get it?

    _____ 1. Yes, bid or proposition accepted. - Go to 70
    _____ 2. No, proposition or bid turned down - Go to 14
    _____ 3. No, could not get financing - Go to 14
    _____ 4. Bid made, but outcome still uncertain. (Interviewer: terminate interview at this point. Make arrangements to call back when outcome will be known. Take up interview at Q. 13)
    _____ 5. No, but some other reason. (Get details) _____

14. Why didn't you try to buy the house? _____

15. Did you get any other assistance or advice from the FHA Counselor?

    _____ 2.   No
    _____ 1.   Yes - What did he say or do? _____

    _____

16. Did the FHA counselor point out any other homes that you might look at?

    _____ 1.   Yes - Go to 17
    _____ 2.   No - Go to 56

17. Did you want to stay in the same neighborhood, or did you want to move to another area?

    _____ 1.   No feeling one way or other - Go to 23
    _____ 2.   Wanted to move to another neighborhood - Go to 19
    _____ 3.   Wanted to stay in the same neighborhood - Go to 18

18. Why did you want to stay in the neighborhood?
    (Go to 20)_____

19. Why did you want to move out of the neighborhood?
    (Go to 22)_____

20. At this first meeting, did you mention that you wanted to stay in this particular neighborhood to the FHA counselor?

    _____ 1.   Yes
    _____ 2.   No - Why not? _____

21. Was he able to tell you about any homes for sale in that neighborhood?

    _____ 1.   Yes
    _____ 2.   No

22. Did he tell you about any homes for sale in some other neighborhood?

    _____ 1.   Yes
    _____ 2.   No

23. Now, think back to the first interview you had with the FHA counselor. In this first interview, did the FHA counselor tell you about any homes that were for sale?

    _____ 1.   Yes - Go to 24
    _____ 2.   No - Go to 26

24. Did you finally settle on just one house to go look at?

    > Interviewer: At this point, the respondent should have settled on one house, not necessarily one he was really interested in. Usually, an appointment with a broker will be made while the person is in the FHA office to see this one house.
    >
    > Since much of the rest of the questionnaire focuses on what happened with this one house, the one agent, and this first interview, be sure the respondent has this situation well in mind.

    _____ 1.   Yes - Go to 25
    _____ 2.   No - The counselor had no houses that the person wanted to go out to see - Go to 26
    _____ 3.   No - More than one house was settled on. (Get details of what happened.) - Go to 26 _____

    _____

25. How did you feel about being allowed to go out to see just the one house? Probe: Was there another house that you wanted to go to see also? _____

    _____

26.

> Interviewer: if you checked "3" on Question 24, have the respondent focus on the first house he went to see. Questions 26 through 55 refer to what happened regarding this first house.

Was an appointment made with a real estate agent to see a particular house that was for sale during this first interview?

    _____ 1.   Yes - Go to 27

    _____ 1.   No - but made later - Go to 27

    _____ 2.   No appointment made at all - (26a)   Did you get any other assistance or advice from the FHA counselor? (Specify and go to 56) _____

_____

27. Did you actually make contact with the real estate agent that the FHA counselor set up the appointment with?

    _____1.   Yes - Go to 29

    _____2.   No - Why not? - Go to 28

28. Did you get any other assistance or advice from the FHA counselor?

    _____ 2.   No - Go to 55

    _____ 1.   Yes - Please explain - Go to 56 _____

_____

29. Did you actually go through the house?

    _____ 1.   Yes - Go to 31

    _____ 2.   No - Why not? - Go to 30 _____

_____

30. Did you get any other assistance or advice from the FHA counselor?

    _____ 2.   No - Go to 56

    _____ 1.   Yes - Please explain - Go to 56 _____

_____

31. Was the agent on time for the appointment? (Not more than 5 minutes late?)

    _____ 1.   Yes, on time
    _____ 2.   No

32. Were you on time for the appointment? (Not more than 5 minutes late?)

    _____ 1.   Yes, on time
    _____ 2.   No

33. Where did you meet the agent?

    _____ 1.   Office
    _____ 2.   At the home which was for sale
    _____ 3.   At the respondent's home
    _____ 4.   Elsewhere (specify) _____

34. Who was there when you went through the home? (Probe and circle "yes" or "no" for each)

Yes	No	
1	2	agent
1	2	other possible buyers
1	2	The owner or his family
1	2	neighbors of the owner
1	2	a relative of respondent
1	2	a friend of respondent
1	2	anyone else (specify) _____

> Interviewer read: "Now I want to ask you some true-false questions about what the agent said and did when he showed you the house. I will read each statement and you tell me whether it is true or false. It may be a little difficult to remember, but just give me your answer as you remember it now.

	True	False	
35.	1	2	The agent said that the schools near this house are good.
36.	1	2	The agent said that the schools near this house are not too good.
37.	1	2	The agent told me we probably could <u>not</u> get financing on this particular house.
38.	1	2	Generally speaking, the agent advised me to try to buy the house.
39.	1	2	Generally speaking, the agent advised me <u>not</u> to try to buy the house.
40.	1	2	The agent said that the owner probably would <u>not</u> sell the house to us.
41.	1	2	The agent said the property values in the neighborhood were stable or going up.
42.	1	2	The agent said property values in the neighborhood were going down.
43.	1	2	The agent said he would try to help me get financing.
44.	1	2	The agent wanted to be helpful.
45.	1	2	The agent understood our situation very well.
46.	1	2	The agent was not very friendly.

47. Was the agent white or black?
    ____ 1   White
    ____ 2.   Black

48. Which of these two statements best describe how you felt about the house after you went through it?

    ____ 1.   We liked the house, and wanted to buy it.
    ____ 2.   We didn't like it. It wasn't what we wanted.

49. Did you actually try to buy this house?

    ____ 1.   Yes - Go to 50
    ____ 2.   No - Go to 57

50. What was the outcome? Did you get it?

    ____ 1.   Yes, bid or proposition accepted. Skip to 70.

    ____ 2.   No, proposition or bid turned down. Go to 56

    ____ 3.   No, could not get financing. Go to 56

    ____ 4.   Outcome still uncertain. (Interviewer: call back when subject will know. Resume interview at Q. 50.)

    ____ 5.   No, but some other reason. (Get details) _____

    _____

51. Why didn't you try to buy the house? _____

    _____

52. After you went through the first house, did that agent try to get you interested in any other houses?

    ____ 3.   Don't remember - Go to 56

    ____ 2.   No - Go to 56

    ____ 1.   Yes - Go to 53

53. Did he or another agent from the same agency actually show you through any other houses?

    ____ 2.   No - Skip to 56

    ____ 1.   Yes - What was the address of the first house?

54. Did you actually try to buy one of these houses?

    ____ 1.   Yes - Go to 55

    ____ 2.   No - Go to 56

55. What was the outcome? - Did you get it?

    ____ 1.   Yes, bid or proposition accepted. - Go to 70

    ____ 2.   No, proposition or bid turned down. - Go to 56

    ____ 3.   No, could not get financing. - Go to 56

    ____ 4.   Outcome still uncertain. (Interviewer: call back when subject will know and take up interview at 55.)

    ____ 5.   No, but some other reason. (Get details and go to 56)

    _____

56.

> Interviewer say: "Now let's see if I've got the situation straight." (Review the questionnaire to this point, skipping the true-false questions.) At this point in the process you had not yet bought a house. Right? " (Interviewer: if you got here from 16, 28, or 30, ask 57. If you got here from 53, 54, or 55, ask 57a.)

57a. Have you looked at any houses for sale since that first interview with the FHA counselor?

    ____ 1.   Yes - Go to 58
    ____ 2.   No - Go to 64

57b. Have you looked at any other houses for sale besides this one (these) since that first interview with the FHA counselor?

    ____ 1.   Yes - Go to 58 (
                        (Do not include any mentioned in 53 above
    ____ 2.   No - Go to 62 (

58. Where did you learn about these homes? (Probe and circle "Yes" or "No" for each)

Yes	No	
1	2	friend or relative
1	2	from same agent
1	2	some other real estate agent
1	2	on my own - driving around, etc.
1	2	from the FHA counselor

59. Did you get any other assistance or information from the FHA counselor regarding any of these homes? (Probe and circle "Yes" or "No" for each)

Yes	No	
1	2	financial information or advice
1	2	advice about purchase
1	2	other (Get details) _____

60. Did you actually try to buy one of these houses?

    ____ 2.   No - Go to 62
    ____ 1.   Yes - Go to 61

61. What was the outcome? - Did you get it?

    ____ 1.   Yes, bid or proposition accepted. - Go to 70
    ____ 2.   No, proposition or bid turned down. - Go to 62
    ____ 3.   No, could not get financing. - Go to 62
    ____ 4.   Outcome still uncertain. (Interviewer: call back when subject will know, and take up interview at 61).
    ____ 5.   No, but some other reason. (Get details and go to 62).

---

62. Then, to this point, you have not found a house to buy? Is that correct?

    ____ 1.   Has not found house to buy - Go to 63
    ____ 2.   Has found house to buy. Clarify the situation by returning to beginning of Questionnaire and tracing steps through to find error. If you cannot figure out what the problem is, check answer "2" for "62" and go to 70.

63. I take it that you also have not found a house to rent?

    ____ 1.   Has not found a house to rent. - Go to 64
    ____ 2.   Has found a house to rent. - Go to 70

> Interviewer read: "Here are some true - false questions about what you plan to do at this point."

	True	False	
64.	1	2	I plan to keep on looking for a house to buy.
65.	1	2	I plan to look for a place to rent.
66.	1	2	I've given up trying to find a house to buy.
67.	1	2	I'm fed up with the whole process of trying to buy a house.
68.	1	2	I plan to keep in touch with the FHA counselor to see if he has any other suggestions.
69.	1	2	I have already called the FHA counselor back to see if he had any suggestions. (Skip to 72).

70. What proportion of the houses on the block where this house is located are occupied by blacks? (If don't know, ask for best guess). (Read responses)

    ____ 1.   None   ____ 4.   About 1/4 to 3/4
    ____ 2.   About 1/4 or less   ____ 5.   About 3/4 or more
    ____ 3.   About 1/4 to 1/2   ____ 6.   All

71. Generally speaking, do you think you will be more satisfied or less satisfied with this new house than with the one you are moving from?

    ____ 1.   Much more satisfied
    ____ 2.   More satisfied
    ____ 3.   About the same
    ____ 4.   Less satisfied
    ____ 5.   Much less satisfied

Interviewer read: "Here are some true-false questions about the counseling service itself."

	True	False	
72.	1	2	The F.H.A. Counseling Service is a flop as far as I am concerned.
73.	1	2	The F.H.A. counselor understood our situation very well.
74.	1	2	The F.H.A. counselor told me the price range of housing that he thought we could afford.
75.	1	2	The F.H.A. counselor wanted to be helpful.
76.	1	2	The F.H.A. counselor was not very friendly.
77.	1	2	If I knew of persons like myself who wanted to buy a home, I would recommend the F.H.A. Counseling Service to them.
78.	1	2	I have already recommended someone to the F.H.A. Counseling Service.
79.	1	2	I have never tried to buy a house before.
80.	1	2	I have never owned or bought a home before.

81.   1   2   Most people would be better off if they bought a home rather than renting.

82.   1   2   When you rent, you're just pouring money down the drain and you end up with nothing to show for it.

83.   1   2   I would much rather own a home than rent one.

84.   1   2   When you are renting, you don't want to spend money fixing things up because you never know how long you are going to be there.

85.   1   2   Absolutely the one best thing about owning a home is that you don't have to put up with a landlord.

86.   1   2   One of the best things about renting is that the landlord usually takes care of keeping things fixed up.

87. There has been a lot of talk in the papers recently about "racial balance," that is, the proportions of blacks and whites in an area. If you had your choice, what kind of a neighborhood would you most like to live in? (Read responses).

     _____ 1.   A neighborhood that is all white or nearly all white.
     _____ 2.   A neighborhood that is about 1/4 black.
     _____ 3.   A neighborhood that is about half white and half black.
     _____ 4.   A neighborhood that is about 3/4 black.
     _____ 5.   A neighborhood that is all or nearly all black.

88. Suppose a black were to buy a house on an all white block. Do you think he would have to pay more, the same, or less than a white person buying the same house?

     _____ 1.   substantially more ⎤ Do not read this alternative.
     _____ 2.   more | Check it only if respondent
     _____ 3.   the same | indicates "much more," etc.
     _____ 4.   less ⎦

ASK BLACKS ONLY

89. Suppose that you were able to locate two houses to buy: Both houses were just what you wanted in a house, and both cost exactly the same amount of money. However, one house was in an

all black part of town, and the other was in an all white part of town. Which of these two houses would you probably buy?

_____ 1.   Black house
_____ 2.   White house
_____ 3.   Why? _____

ASK WHITES ONLY

90. Suppose that you were able to locate two houses to buy: Both houses were just what you wanted in a house, and both cost exactly the same amount of money. However, one house was in a part of town that was about 1/4 black, and the other house was in an all white part of town. Which of these two houses would you probably buy?

_____1.   Integrated house
_____2.   White house
_____ 3.   Why? _____

_____

91. Now, back to the FHA Counseling Service itself. In your opinion, how could the service be improved? _____

_____

92. Interviewer, fill in: _____ 1.   White
                                    _____ 2.   Black
                                    _____ 3.   Other nonwhite

Appendix C

Open House Follow-Up Interview

(For those not served entirely by the Committee on Special Housing)

1.   What was your age at your last birthday? (Check one)

_____ 0.	Under 20		_____ 5.	40 - 44
_____ 1.	20 - 24		_____ 6.	45 - 49
_____ 2.	25 - 29		_____ 7.	50 - 54
_____ 3.	30 - 34		_____ 8.	55 - 60
_____ 4.	35 - 39		_____ 9.	61 or over

2.   How many children living here with you now are in grade school? (Check one)

____ 0.	____ 5.
____ 1.	____ 6.
____ 2.	____ 7.
____ 3.	____ 8.
____ 4.	____ 9. or more

3.   At the time you came to the "open house," were you renting or buying?

____ 1.   renting
____ 2.   buying

3a.   How did you hear about the Committee on Special Housing? ____

4.   At the open house, with whom did you talk first?

____ 1.   FHA Counselor
____ 2.   Relocation officer
____ 3.   Real estate broker

5.   (4) After talking with the FHA Counselor, the relocation officer, the broker, did you decide to look mainly for a house to buy or mainly for a house to rent?

____ 1.   to buy: Why? _____
_____

____ 2.   to rent: Why? _____

6.   (7) Why were you looking for another house at this time?

____ 1.   Public project displacement
____ 2.   Private project displacement
____ 3.   Evicted (forced to move) Specify why _____
_____

____ 4.   Other _____

7.   (8) Did you feel you had to find another home quickly?

____ 1.   Yes (because of forced deadline)
____ 2.   Yes (no forced deadline, but really wanted to move for some personal reasons)
____ 3.   No

8. (17) Did you want to stay in the same neighborhood you lived in or did you want to move to another area?

    ———— 1. No feeling one way or another

    ———— 2. Wanted to move to another neighborhood: Why?

    _____

    3. Wanted to stay in the same neighborhood: Why?

    _____

9. (20) When you talked with the relocation officer and/or the broker (circle one or both) did you tell them where you wanted to live?

    ———— 1. told neither: Why? _____

    _____

    ———— 2. told relocation officer

    ———— 3. told broker

    ———— 4. told both broker and relocation officer

10. When you talked with the relocation officer and/or the broker (circle one or both) did you tell them what kind of home you were interested in?

    ———— 1. told neither: Why? _____

    _____

    ———— 2. told relocation officer

    ———— 3. told broker

    ———— 4. told both broker and relocation officer

10a. What was the name of broker(s) you saw? (Questions 11 - 45 deal with the client's experience with broker — Ask all of those interviewed). _____

11. (21) Did the broker tell you of any homes for sale in the area you wanted to live in?

    ———— 1. Yes

    ———— 2. No

12. (22) Did the broker tell you of any homes for sale in other areas?

    ———— 1. Yes

    ———— 2. No

13. (26) Did you make an appointment with a broker to see (circle one) 1-2-3-more homes during this first interview?

    _____ 1.   Yes - Go to 14

    _____ 2.   No - but appointment made later - Go to 14

    _____ 3.   No appointment made at all: Why? _____
              Go to 13(a) _____

13a. What was the plan at the end of this first interview - (If the client has seen no homes, go to 38). (If the client has seen homes, continue). _____

14. Has this appointment(s) been kept?

    _____ 1.   Yes (Go to 15)

    _____ 2.   No: Why? _____

_____

              Then how do things stand currently? _____

_____

              (Go to 38)

15. Was the agent on time for the appointment? (Not more than 5 minutes late).

    _____ 1.   Yes, on time

    _____ 2.   No

16. Were you on time for the appointment? (Not more than 5 minutes late).

    _____ 1.   Yes, on time

    _____ 2.   No

17. Where did you meet the agent?

    _____ 1.   Office

    _____ 2.   At the home which was for sale

    _____ 3.   At the respondent's home

    _____ 4.   Elsewhere (specify) _____

18. Who was there when you went through the home? (Probe and circle "yes" or "no" for each).

Yes	No	
1	2	agent
1	2	other possible buyers
1	2	the owner or his family
1	2	neighbors of the owner
1	2	a relative of respondent
1	2	a friend of respondent
1	2	anyone else (specify) _____

Interviewer read: "Now I want to ask you some true - false questions about what the agent did when he showed you the house. I will read each statement and you tell me whether it is true or false. It may be a little difficult to remember, but just give me your answer as you remember it now."

	True	False	
19.	1	2	The agent said that the schools near this house are good.
20.	1	2	The agent said that the schools near this house are not too good.
21.	1	2	The agent told me we probably could <u>not</u> get financing on this particular house.
22.	1	2	Generally speaking, the agent advised me to try to buy the house.
23.	1	2	Generally speaking, the agent advised me <u>not</u> to try to buy the house.
24.	1	2	The agent said that the owner probably would <u>not</u> sell the house to us.
25.	1	2	The agent said the property values in the neighborhood were stable or going up.
26.	1	2	The agent said property values in the neighborhood were going down.
27.	1	2	The agent said he would try to help me get financing.
28.	1	2	The agent wanted to be helpful.
29.	1	2	The agent understood our situation very well.
30.	1	2	The agent was not very friendly.

31. Was the agent white or black?

    —— 1.   White
    —— 2.   Black

32. Where are the home(s) you have been shown? And what are the prices?

  Addresses 1. _____
  &   2. _____
  Prices   3. _____

32a. Is this (are these) home(s) in a neighborhood where you want to live?

    ——1.   Yes
    ——2.   No

33. (48) Which of these two statements best describe how you felt about the home(s) you have seen?

    ——1.   We like at least one and want to buy it. Go to 34
    ——2.   We did not like any home we saw. It (they) was not (were not) what we wanted. Why? _____
           Go to 36 _____

34. (49) Did you actually try to buy this house?

    ——1.   Yes - Go to 35
    ——2.   No - Why? _____
           Go to 36 _____

35. (50) What was the outcome? Did you get it?

    —— 1.   Yes, bid or proposition accepted - Go to 46
    —— 2.   No, bid or proposition turned down - Go to 36
    —— 3.   No, could not get financing needed - Go to 36
    —— 4.   Outcome still uncertain - Go to 36
        5.   No - (other reasons than above - ask for specifics)

    _____

    (Go to 36) _____

36. (52) If you did not purchase the home(s) you saw, did the agent try to get you interested in any other houses?

    —— 1.   Yes - Go to 37
    —— 2.   No - Go to 38

37. (54) Did you try to purchase any of these homes?

     ____ Yes - outcome
     ____ 1.   Bid or proposition accepted - Go to 46
     ____ 2.   Bid or proposition turned down - Go to 38
     ____ 3.   No, could not get financing - Go to 38
     ____ 4.   Outcome still uncertain - Go to 38
     ____ 5.   No - (other reasons - specify) _____

     Go to 38

Interviewer read: "Here are some true - false questions about what you plan to do at this point."

	True	False	
38.	1	2	I plan to keep on looking for a house to <u>buy</u>.
39.	1	2	I plan to look for a place to <u>rent</u>.
40.	1	2	I've given up trying to find a house to <u>buy</u>.
41.	1	2	I'm fed up with the whole process of trying to buy a house.
42.	1	2	I plan to keep in touch with the broker to see if he has any other suggestions.
43.	1	2	I have already called the broker to see if he had any suggestions.
44.	1	2	I plan to get in touch with the Committee on Special Housing to see if they have any other suggestions.
45.	1	2	I have already called the Committee to see if they have any other suggestions.

If yes, to 45 - <u>Ask 46 then go to 48</u>
If no, to 45 - <u>Ask 46 then go to 50</u>

(If individual discussed homes with relocation officer, <u>ask 46, then skip to 48</u> and continue interview)

(If individual saw no one else but broker, <u>ask 46 then skip to 52</u> and continue interview)

46. (70) What proportion of the houses on the block where this

house is located are occupied by blacks? (if don't know — ask for best guess). Read responses:

_____ 1. None _____ 4. About 1/4 to 3/4
_____ 2. About 1/4 or less _____ 5. About 3/4 or more
_____ 3. About 1/4 to 1/2 _____ 6. All

47. Generally speaking, do you think you will be more satisfied or less satisfied with this new house than with the one you are moving from?

_____ 1. Much more satisfied
_____ 2. More satisfied
_____ 3. About the same - Go to 51
_____ 4. Less satisfied
_____ 5. Much less satisfied

48. The homes which the Committee told me about:

_____ 1. Suited my needs - Go to 49
_____ 2. Did not suit my needs - Go to 50

49. I have seen these homes and chosen one.

_____ 1. Yes - Go to 51
_____ 2. No - Go to 50

50. The current situation is:

_____ 1. I will keep in touch with the Committee.
_____ 2. I will continue to look on my own.
_____ 3. I will seek further help from a broker (name if person has one picked).
_____ 4. Other (specify) _____

51. What are the main differences you can think of between your experience with the broker and your experience with the Committee? (Probe and get specifics) _____

_____

	True	False	
52.	1	2	I have never tried to buy a house before.
53.	1	2	I have never owned or bought a home before.

54.	1	2	Most people would be better off if they bought a home rather than renting one.
55.	1	2	When you rent, you're just pouring money down the drain and you end up with nothing to show for it.
56.	1	2	I would much rather own a home than rent one.
57.	1	2	When you are renting, you don't want to spend money fixing things up because you never know how long you are going to be there.
58.	1	2	Absolutely the <u>one best thing</u> about owning a home is that you don't have to put up with a landlord.
59.	1	2	One of the best things about renting is that the landlord usually takes care of keeping things fixed up.

60. There has been a lot of talk in the papers recently about "racial balance," that is, the proportion of blacks and whites in an area. If you had your choice, what kind of a neighborhood would you most like to live in? (Read responses).

_____ 1.   A neighborhood that is all white or nearly all white.
_____ 2.   A neighborhood that is about 1/4 black.
_____ 3.   A neighborhood that is about half white and half black.
_____ 4.   A neighborhood that is about 3/4 black.
_____ 5.   A neighborhood that is all or nearly black.

61. Suppose a black were to buy a house on an all white block. Do you think he would have to pay more, the same, or less than a white person buying the same house?

_____ 1.   Substantially more ⎤ Do not read this alternative.
_____ 2.   More   ⎟ Check it only if respondent
_____ 3.   The same   ⎟ indicates "much more," etc.
_____ 4.   Less

ASK BLACKS ONLY

62. Suppose that you were able to locate two houses to buy: Both houses were just what you wanted in a house, and both cost

exactly the same amount of money. However, one house was in an all black part of town, and the other was in an all white part of town. Which of these two houses would you probably buy?

____ 1.   Black house
____ 2.   White house
____ 3.   Why_____

ASK WHITES ONLY

63. Suppose that you were able to locate two houses to buy: Both houses were just what you wanted in a house, and both cost exactly the same amount of money. However, one house was in a part of town that was about 1/4 black, and the other house was in an all white part of town. Which of these two houses would you probably buy?

_____ 1.   Integrated house
_____ 2.   White house
_____ 3.   Why? _____

64. Now, back to the Committee on Special Housing. Do you feel the Committee has been of any service to you?

_____ 1.   Yes - How? _____
_____

_____ 2.   No - Why?_____

65. How, in your opinion, can the service of the Committee on Special Housing be improved? _____
_____

66. In general, do you feel the broker showed you the kind of home you wanted, in the area you wanted?

_____ 1.   Yes
_____ 2.   No - What was not satisfactory? _____
_____

67. Is there anything else you would like to tell me? _____
_____

68. Interviewer - Please write a brief summary of interview, giving your impressions & including anything not covered by the questions. _____

Appendix D

Tables Comparing Committee Applicants to other FHA Buyers

Table 1. Average Age (Years)

	CSG	FHAG
W1 (Male Wage Earner)	38.4	31.3
W2 (Female Wage Earner)	35.4	29.2
Head of Household	37.7	31.3

Table 2. Heads of Household (Year %)

	CSG	FHAG
Youngest Head of Household	21 yrs.	18 yrs.
Oldest Head of Household	57 yrs.	53 yrs.
Head of Household (Male)	81%	100 %
Head of Household (Female)	18.5 %	0 %

Table 3. Dependents in Household

	CSG	FHAG
Average Number in Household	2.4	1.7
% 1 Dependent in Household	25.9	40.7
% 2 Dependents in Household	14.8	37
% 3 Dependents in Household	18.5	3.7
% 4 Dependents in Household	14.8	3.7
% 5 Dependents in Household	0	7.4
% 6 Dependents in Household	7.4	0
% 10 Dependents in Household	3.7	0
% No Dependents in Household	14.8	7.4

Table 4. Marital Status (%)

	CSG	FHAG
Married	77.8	100
Divorced	11.1	0
Separated	3.7	0
Single	3.7	0
Widowed	3.7	0

Table 5. Types and Results of Complaint Investigations By Indiana Civil Rights Commission

	CSG	FHAG
Working Females	36.4	14
Working Female and Working Wife	36.4	14
Working Females % Whose Income was Effected	92.3	25

Table 6. Average Net Income (Monthly)

	CSG	FHAG
Male Wage Earner	621	597
Female Wage Earner	359	195
Male and Female Combined	854	760
Family Income (Effected* Only)	746	620
Family with Only One Wage Earner		
Average Income	625	593

* That income which under FHA regulations is considered applicable toward supporting a loan.

Table 7. Years on Job

	CSG	FHAG
Male Wage Earners	8.6	4.9
Female Wage Earners	4.4	1

Table 8. Average Number Open Accounts per Family

			CSG - 3.29		FHAG - 2.9	

	Number of Accounts				% Having Number of Accounts	
CSG	FHAG				CSG	FHAG
1	2	Family had 0 accts.			3.7	7.4
1	7	Family had 1 acct.			3.7	25.9
6	2	Family had 2 accts.			22.2	7.4
	5	Family had 3 accts.			33.3	18.5
4	4	Family had 4 accts.			14.8	14.8
3	4	Family had 5 accts.			11.1	14.8
3	2	Family had 6 accts.			11.1	7.4
0	1	Family had 7 accts.			0	3.7

There were 3 cases of bankruptcy in the Committee Group, or in 11% of cases. There were no bankruptcy cases in the FHA sample.

Table 9. Type* of Open Accounts per Sample Group

Type of Acct.	Frequency of Acct.		% Frequency		Ratio
	CSG	FHAG	CSG	FHAG	
A	5	5	5.6	6.2	1:1
B	9	16	10	20	1.7:1
C	4	1	4.4	1.2	1:4
D	15	27	16.6	33.7	1.8:1
F	40	25	44.4	31.2	1.6:1
G	2	1	2.2	1.2	1:2
H	5	2	5.6	2.5	2.5:1
J	5	2	5.6	2.5	2.5:1
K	.1	0	1.1		
M	2	0	2.2		
O	1	1	1.1	1.2	1:1
U	1	0	1.1		

* CODE (TYPE OF ACCOUNT)

A	Automotive	H	Home Furnishing
B	Bank	J	Jewelry
C	Clothing	K	Lumber, Hardware
D	Department Store	M	Medical & Related Health
F	Finance	O	Oil & National Credit Card Companies
G	Grocery	U	Utilities & Fuel

Table 10. Pay Pattern* on Open Accounts

Type of Acct.	1 CSG %	1 FHAG %	2 CSG %	2 FHAG %	3 CSG %	3 FHAG %	4 CSG %	4 FHAG %	9 CSG %	9 FHAG %
A	100	100								
B	67	100			11		11		11	
C	75			100	25					
D	67	92	7	7	27					
F	80	70	5	5	5	5	5	15	5	5
G		100							100	
H	60	100					20		20	
J	60	50	50						40	
K	100									
M	50								50	
O	100	100								
U	100									

* Code (pay pattern)

1	Pays as agreed
2	Pays between 30 & 60 days or 1 payment past due
3	Pays between 60 & 90 days or 2 payments past due
4	Pays between 90 & 120 days or 3 payments past due
9	Bad debt, in collection, suit, or judgment

Table 11. Pay Pattern * Over All Accounts (in %)

	1	2	3	4	9
FHA	92.4	6.3	0	1.3	0
Committee	73.3	4.4	7.7	4.4	10

* See Table 10 for Code (pay pattern)

Table 12. Total Debt

Range ($)	Frequency		% Families	
	CSG	FHAG	CSG	FHAG
0-500	10	10	37	37
501-1,000	7	2	25.9	7.4
1,001-2,000	2	7	7.4	25.9
2,001-3,000	5	2	18.5	7.4
3,001-4,000	2	1	7.4	3.7
4,001-5,000	1	1	3.7	3.7
5,001-7,000		1		3.7
7,001-10,000		1		3.7
10,001-12,000		2		7.4

Average Total Debt
Committee $1,333
FHA 2,696

Table 13. Assets Available for Closing (% of Group)

Range	CSG	FHAG
0-500	14.8	0
501-1,000	40.7	0
1,001-2,000	25.9	0
2,001-3,000	7.4	3.7
3,001-4,000	3.7	7.4
4,001-5,000	3.7	14.8
5,001-up	3.7	74

Average Available Assets

Committee $1,613
FHA 8,545

Ratio 5.29 to 1

Table 14. Housing Expense

Range ($)	CURRENT				PROPOSED			
	Frequency		% of Group		Frequency		% of Group	
	CSG	FHAG	CSG	FHAG	CSG	FHAG	CSG	FHAG
0-75	1	6	3.7	22.2	2	0	7.4	0
76-100	12	4	44.4	14.8	2	1	7.4	3.7
101-125	6	11	22.2	40.7	12	7	44.4	25.9
126-150	7	2	25.9	7.4	11	4	40.7	14.8
151-175	1	2	3.7	7.4	0	8	0	29.6
176-200	0	2	0	7.4	0	7	0	25.9

	Frequency		% of Group	
	CSG	FHAG	CSG	FHAG
Frequency Increase	15	23	55.5	85.1
Frequency Decrease	8	4	29.6	14.8
Frequency No Change	4	0	14.8	0

Average Change ($)

	CSG	FHAG
Increase	30.73	49.65
Decrease	25.37	10.75

Average Proposed Housing Expense

Committee	$119.48
FHA	156.81

Table 15. Housing Payments per Month

Range ($)	Frequency		% Families	
	CSG	FHAG	CSG	FHAG
0-25	7	8	25.9	29.6
26-50	7	2	25.9	7.4
51-75	3	4	11.1	14.8
76-100	3	2	11.1	7.4
101-125	1	4	3.7	14.8
126-150	3	4	11.1	14.8
151-175	1	2	3.7	7.4
176-200	1	0	3.7	0
201-225	1	1	3.7	3.7

Average Total Monthly Payments

Committee	$72.74
FHA	78.11

Table 16. Average Purchase Price

FHAG	$15,044	24.6% higher
CSG	12,070	

Table 17. Average Mortgage Amount

FHAG	$14,331	23.4% higher
CSG	11,607	

Table 18. Average Amount Amortized

FHAG	95.26%
CSG	96.1 %

Table 19. Employment* - Male Wage Earners

Type	Frequency		% of Group	
Job	FHAG	CSG	FHAG	CSG
1	5	2	18.5	9.09
2	12	6	44.4	27.27
3	1	5	3.7	22.72
4	9	9	33.3	40.90

Table 20. Employment* - Female Wage Earners

Type	Frequency		% of Group	
Job	FHAG	CSG	FHAG	CSG
1	3	7	75	38.88
2	0	2	0	11.11
3	1	4	25	22.22
4	0	5	0	27.77

* Code (Employment)

1	White Collar	3	Unskilled
2	Skilled	4	Semiskilled

Appendix E

Follow-Up Interview for Committee Applicants Who Bought Homes

FOLLOW-UP INTERVIEW FOR FAMILIES PLACED THROUGH THE
AUSPICES OF THE COMMITTEE ON SPECIAL HOUSING

Date of interview: _____

Place of interview: _____

Persons present at interview: _____

Interviewer: _____

Length of interview: _____

PRELIMINARY CONTACT: (By phone: I'm representing the Committee on Special Housing. We are interested in finding out how your move into your new home went and how you and your family are doing now. May I make an appointment to visit with you (and spouse's name . . . if there is one). Thank you.

PART I   (General introduction to put family at ease and to tell them again about the purpose of your visit. It is important to maintain a pleasant but <u>neutral</u> attitude so that the family does not feel that you are looking for a certain kind of answer . . . for instance, that you either want to hear that everything is fine or that you want to hear that everything is terrible.)

1. NOTE condition of home. Please check One:

____ Seems completely settled
____ Seems relatively settled
____ Looks as if there is quite a bit of settling to do
____ Looks completely unsettled

2. To the person or persons you are interviewing SAY (don't read) the following - or something close to it . . .

Thank you for letting me come to talk to you today. I am here because the Committee on Special Housing is interested not only in helping people like yourselves locate suitable homes, but also in discovering if your new home is turning out to be what you expected it to be like. I would like to ask you some questions about how things have been going. If you think of something you want to tell that I'm not asking, please feel free to add anything that comes to mind. (Note any spontaneous <u>relevant</u> comments in margin next to question which seems to have prompted the comment.)

PART II (Discussions of the move itself)

1. How did the move into your new home go? (Verbatim if possible) _____

2. What date did you and your family move into this house? (include day of week) _____

3. About what time of day did you move in? _____

4. How did you move all of your things in? (Read and check any mentioned)

   ____ movers
   ____ friends with a truck
   ____ friends with cars
   ____ by yourself

5. About how long did it take to get completely moved in?

   _____

6. Did any of your new neighbors help you move in?

   ____ NO
   ____ YES (ask for specific detail as to how they helped)

   _____

7. How did your neighbors react to your moving in?

   _____

8. Are you pretty well moved in and settled now?

   ____ Yes
   ____ No - In what way are you not settled? _____

PART III (The house & family's reaction to it)

1. How are you finding this house? _____

   _____

2. Is living in this house like you expected it would be?

   ____ Yes - In what way? _____

   ____ No - In what way? _____

3. How does the rest of your family find this house? _____

    _____

4. Do you like this house better than the house/apartment (circle one) from which you just moved?

    _____ Yes - Why? _____

    _____ No - Why? _____

5. Are you satisfied with the condition in which you found:

    _____ the house
    _____ the yard
    _____ Yes
    _____ No - Why? (be specific) _____

    If answer to 5 is NO - include 5a.

5a. With whom have you discussed this and what was the outcome of the discussion? _____

    _____

6. Are you planning to make any changes in the house or the yard?

    _____ No
    _____ Yes - What changes? _____

7. How do you think your home compares with the other ones in the neighborhood? _____

PART IV (Neighborhood)

1. What do you think about this neighborhood?

    _____

    a. What does your family think about this neighborhood?

    _____

    b. What do your friends think about your new home and neighborhood? _____

2. Have you met any of your neighbors?

_____ No - Why not? _____

_____ Yes - Who? _____

How did you meet? _____

How often do you see them? _____

3. Do you think you will be getting to know more of your neighbors?

_____ Yes
_____ No - Why not? _____

4. So far, do you think your neighbors have been friendly?

_____ Yes - In what way? _____

_____ No - Why not? _____

How have they been unfriendly?_____

5. Do you like this neighborhood better than the one from which you just moved?

_____ Yes - Why? _____

_____ No - Why?_____

PART V   (Children-School) (Asked only to families with pre-school or school-age children. Questions 1-8 for school-age children and 9-12 for pre-school-age children)

1. Where do your children go to school? _____

2. How far from this house is the school? _____

3. How do your children get to school? _____

4. How do your children like this school?_____

_____

5. How does this school compare to the school they went to before you moved? (Ask for specifics - verbatim if possible)

    _____

6. Are there children your children's ages in this neighborhood?

    ____ Yes - (go to question 7)
    ____ No - (go to question 8)
    ____ Don't know - Why is that? _____

7. Do your children play with these other children?

    ____ Yes - How do they get along?
    ____ No - Why not? _____

8. With whom do your children play? _____

9. Do you have any preschool age children?

    ____ No - (go on to PART VI)
    ____ Yes - (go on to question 10)

10. Are there any other children about the same age in this neighborhood?

    ____ Yes - (go on to question 11)
    ____ No - (go on to question 12)
    Don't know - why is that? _____

11. Do your children play with these other children?

    ____ Yes
    ____ No - why not?

12. With whom do your children play? _____

PART VI (Neighborhood Resources)

1. Do you do your shopping in this neighborhood?
    ____ Yes - How did you locate these stores? _____

    How do these stores compare with the ones in your old neighborhood? _____

    ____ No - Why not? _____

2.   Do you belong to a church?

_____ Yes - (go on to question 3)
_____ No - (go on to question 4)

3.   Did you belong to this church when you moved here?

_____ Yes - Do you plan to change to a church near here?
     _____ Yes - Why? _____
     _____ No - Why? _____

_____ No - When did you join this church? _____
          Why did you join this church? _____
          How did you find this church? _____
          How does this church compare with your other
          church (if there was previous membership)?
          _____

4.   Do you plan to join a church?

_____ No
_____ Yes - Why? _____

          In this neighborhood? _____ If not,
          why not? _____

5.   Are there any formal or informal social groups in this neigh-
     borhood?

_____ No
_____ Yes - Which ones? _____

          _____ Do you belong?   _____ Yes - (go to 6 & 7)
                                     _____ No - (go to 8 & 9)

6.   How do you like them?   _____

7.   Have you belonged to ones like this (these) before?

_____ Yes - the same ones? _____
_____ No

8.   Why don't you belong to this (these) group(s)? _____
     _____

9. Do you plan to join these groups?

____ Yes - the same ones? _____

____ No - Why not? _____

PART VII (General)

1. Have you run across any difficulties in this neighborhood?

____ No.

____ Yes - (GET DETAILS - Verbatim, if possible)
What kind? _____
What do you think might solve this (these) problem(s)?

_____

2. What changes or or improvements would you like to see occur in this neighborhood? (GET DETAILS - Verbatim, if possible) _____

3. Do you think this neighborhood is balanced well from a racial point of view?

____ Yes

____ No - what is wrong and what changes would you like to see? _____

4. Do you anticipate having any difficulties in this neighborhood? _____

____ No - Why? _____

____ Yes - Specify _____

5. What do you think about the COMMITTEE ON SPECIAL HOUSING? (Explain that this group was responsible for helping them, if they seem unfamiliar with the title) Verbatim, if possible _____

_____

6. How do you think the Committee's services could be improved? Verbatim, if possible _____

_____

7.   Is there anything else you would like to tell me that we
     have not already talked about? _____

8.   Thank you. If any difficulties do arise, perhaps you would
     like to contact the Committee at 637-0320. That number
     again is 637-0320. They may be able to help out.

                                        (Note if they make effort to
                                         note the name and number)

Additional Observations or Comments: _____

_____

___ Black
___ White

Appendix F

Committee Suggestions to FHA

(Proposals Submitted by The Committee on Special Housing
for Change in Property Disposition Letter 129)

Following are some suggestions for change in your Housing Counseling Service.

It ought to be divided into two parts. The Committee had suggested earlier to officials in HUD that Property Disposition Letter
No. 129 be revised as it relates to brokers. That suggestion was made
before sufficient experience had been acquired. As a result of the experience that has been acquired, the Committee does not recommend
any change in the Property Disposition Letter as it has been interpreted in Indianapolis. Specifically, the Committee urges that brokers
not be permitted to sell FHA acquired property in the sense of
obtaining a commission on the sale of such property under the terms
of Property Disposition Letter No. 129. The rationale is much like
that that has been given by Mr. Pasquale in his address before realtors
in Albuquerque, New Mexico on March 7, 1968. Specifically, Mr. Pasquale indicated that the brokers simply do not have the time to give
low income housing applicants the service needed. It has been the experience of the Committee on Special Housing that the overwhelming

number of those coming before the Committee can be characterized as being within the range of low to low middle income. If there is any change to be made in the Property Disposition Letter, it should be two-fold.

a. FHA acquired property should be made available to any within the inner-city on a preferential basis. There are many in the inner-city in desperate need of housing who do not qualify as dislocated under the terms of PD Letter No. 129, yet, if they were able to move to the suburbs, the filter process would open more property in the inner-city. The Committee on Special Housing has been forced to turn away a substantial number of individuals because they do not qualify as dislocated.

b. FHA acquired property should be made available for a considerably longer period of time than ten days following date of repair. The Committee is aware of at least fifteen pieces of property that it could have sold if it had a month following the date of repair to effect sales.

Counseling Service - The experience of the Committee on Special Housing in its analysis of the Counseling Service is that certain changes could be effected to make that service more meaningful. Those changes are as follows:

a. The Counseling Service should be funded.

b. It should be staffed by at least two full-time employees skilled and sensitive to the problems of the inner-city, dedicated to the proposition of a free housing market, and expert on mortgage credit matters. In this regard, it is the suggestion of the Committee that the grade level for FHA counselors of the type indicated be at a minimum Grade 12 and 11.

c. The Committee has discovered that brokers frequently are using the Counseling Service to further existing patterns of racial discrimination in the sale of properties. It is the view of the Committee that cooperation with brokers should be sought, however, it is also the view of the Committee that where private listings are submitted, they should be accepted by the counseling service for the purpose of finding cooperative realtors or realtists willing to sell such properties on a non-discriminatory basis. There ought not be any absolute rule against acceptance of private listings.

d. The Counseling Service should be encouraged to take affirmative action beyond merely referring to other agencies those individuals in need of budget counseling and, more particularly, debt consolidation. By way of example, there were occasions in which the FHA counselors in Indianapolis would take the initiative in calling a local bank and speaking with a key official of that bank in helping to effect debt consolidation after the applicant had earlier been refused a loan. It should be noted that the reaction of the bank official was "If FHA is willing to help in selling this person a home, we will do our job. Send him directly to my office." Credit problems constitute one of the major obstacles to home purchase to those who have come before the Committee. It must be added that those who have come before the Committee constitute the overwhelming number of those placed by the Counseling Service from January through July, 1968. Further, a very clear line must be drawn between credit problems and earning capacity. Most of those coming before the the Committee were upward moving; they had the capacity to earn, they lacked the knowledge and were bound by past deeds in terms of patterns of consumption.

e. The Counseling Service should not simply accept a person's statement as to where he wants to live; rather, the Counseling Service should assume the obligation of affirmatively demonstrating that individuals can live wherever they want to the extent that their income capacity allows. In this regard, should the acquired property policy be changed, an excellent vehicle is afforded the counselor. He can take specific properties, show pictures, and let the person make his own judgment as to where he wants to live.

f. The FHA counselor should be encouraged to work closely and cooperate fully with organizations such as the Committee on Special Housing. The result of such cooperation in Indianapolis has meant the effective placement of individuals who never would have owned a home before. More than 90 % of those placed under the acquired property program were renters, inner-city dwellers and more particularly, Negroes.

The above constitute only some of the suggestions of the Committee on Special Housing. It is urged that a fuller statement could be made following in-depth observation in the field by FHA and HUD officials of the Committee's work.

Appendix G

Table 1. Preference of Black Applicants Regarding Racial Composition of Neighborhood

Composition of Area	Number of Applicants	Percentage of Total Interviewed
All white	6	14
1/4 black	6	14
1/2 white - 1/2 black	16	37
3/4 black	2	5
All black	3	7
No preference	10	23

Table 2. Black Applicants' Opinions Regarding Cost of Home in White Area for Black Purchaser

	Number of Applicants	Percentage of Total Interviewed
Substantially More Costly	1	22
More Costly	27	64
The Same	10	23
No Opinion or "Depends" on Circumstances	4	9

Table 3. Budgets of Neighboring Civil Rights Commissions*

Place	Total Population 1960	Current Budget
Michigan	7,824,964	634,441.00
Illinois	10,081,158	261,373.00
Ohio	10,266,204	211,750,00
Kentucky	3,038,156	157,000.00
Missouri	4,266,204	164,812.00
Tennessee	3,567,089	50,000.00

* Indiana Civil Rights Commission, "Background information on Civil Rights Budgets," 1967, mimeographed.

Table 4. Executive Director Salaries*
(Offered for comparison)

State	Salary
Alaska	15,504.00
Arizona	11,600.00
California	19,518.00
Colorado	9,624.00-$12,276.00
Connecticut	12,400.00-$15,800.00
Illinois	15,000.00
Kansas	7,800.00-$ 9,500.00
Kentucky	10,344.00
Maryland	10,500.00
Michigan	19,000.00
Minnesota	10,500.00
Missouri	14,000.00
New Jersey	18,000.00
New York	16,655.00-$19,500.00
Oregon	7,500.00-$ 9,300.00
Pennsylvania	12,075.00-$16,170.00
Rhode Island	10,387.00-$12,025.00
Tennessee	9,480.00
Utah	9,600.00
Washington	13,500.00
Wisconsin	12,684.00

* Indiana Civil Rights Commission, "Salaries of Professionals in Civil Rights Agencies," 1967, mimeographed.

Table 5. Types and Results of Complaint Investigations
by Indiana Civil Rights Commission

	Employment		Housing		Accommodations		Other *		Total	
	1961-66	1966	1961-66	1966	1961-66	1966	1961-66	1966	1961-66	1966
Total complaints	546	122	86	41	176	16	48	13	856	192
Lack of Jurisdiction	32	13	0	0	13	1	7	3	52	17
Complainant did not proceed	71	24	15	5	11	1	1	1	98	31
Charge Not Established	305	53	36	15	27	2	23	6	391	76
Conciliated or Adjusted	119	13	32	18	125	12	16	2	292	45
Pending further action	19	19	3	3	0	0	1	1	23	23

* Education, law enforcement, police brutality, etc.

Two housing complaints were scheduled for formal hearings in 1966. One was withdrawn afterwards by the complainant and in the other a cease and desist order was subsequently issued. (1967 Progress Reports, Indiana Civil Rights Commission, p. 15.)

Index